STATESMAN
AND
SCHEMER

STATESMAN
AND
SCHEMER

William, First Lord Paget
Tudor Minister

SAMUEL RHEA GAMMON

ARCHON BOOKS : Hamden, Connecticut

This edition first published in 1973 in
Great Britain by David & Charles
(Holdings) Limited, Newton Abbot,
Devon and in the United States under
the Archon imprint by The Shoe String
Press, Inc., Hamden, Connecticut 06514

ISBN 0 208 01405 5

Set in 11/13pt Baskerville
and printed in Great Britain
by W J Holman Limited Dawlish

CONTENTS

ILLUSTRATIONS

PREFACE

THE active career of William, first Lord Paget of Beaudesert, covered the middle of the sixteenth century. Statesman and schemer, more a willow than an oak, greedy for land with the insatiable acquisitiveness of a new noble, scornful of the common people from whose ranks his family was emerging, he followed the then increasingly familiar path of Roman law study and government service to wealth and power. He was a favourite servant of Henry VIII's last years, principal adviser to Lord Protector Somerset, and one of Mary Tudor's chief ministers. During the twelve years of Edward VI and Mary, English prestige abroad and prosperity at home were at an ebb, and the Tudor system of government was functioning least successfully. Perhaps the confusion and low repute of governments during those years of wars, rebellions and plots are responsible for the obscurity into which Paget's reputation has fallen.

Though Paget was not a first minister of the crown of the eminence of Wolsey, Cromwell, or Cecil, he equals in importance such leading statesmen as Sir Francis Walsingham or Stephen Gardiner, and it is remarkable that he has not previously attracted a biographer. Perhaps a lack of enduring success for his policies has shadowed his reputation without giving it either the satanic brilliance or tragic gleam of those notable failures Northumberland and Essex.

Many reasons make Paget's career worthy of a special study. First of all, he claims attention by the fact of his survival in troubled times as a leading figure in successive regimes. At the same time, he was a typical product of his era. His chosen field of specialisation was diplomacy, though most of his diplomatic efforts were concerned with the pursuit of unattainable goals. Henry VIII's fixation on continental power and the retention of his newly won city of Boulogne saddled Paget's diplomacy with an impossible burden.

Chief strategist of his friend Somerset's rise to power as lord protector to the young Edward VI, Paget saw his sage advice on foreign and domestic policy ignored by the impractical and idealistic duke, while a remorseless succession of events justified his direst forecasts. Paget saw the indispensable need in the Tudor system of government for a strong ruler, and he sought to provide one by urging on Queen Mary as the husband of her choice a powerful and experienced prince, Philip of Spain.

In religion, Paget's pragmatic moderation was ignored by his sovereigns and earned him the distrust of both Catholic and Protestant zealots. Ironically, when there succeeded to the throne a ruler whose religious views were similar to his, Paget was too tarred by his service to the intolerant Mary Tudor and by his sponsorship of the unsuccessful Spanish match to retain place and power under her *politique* sister Elizabeth.

Yet with all of the failures in which he participated, Paget's skill in negotiations and his sagacity as a prophet won him the frequent tributes of contemporaries and brought him from obscurity to wealth and nobility. Like the Russells and the Herberts, the Paget family also rose to prominence in the sixteenth century to remain part of 'the establishment' for generations. Thus this statesman and schemer, who stands out as a major figure in the political eclipse marking the reigns of the lesser Tudors, deserves to be rescued from historical obscurity.

In the preparation of this biography, I am deeply indebted to the following individuals and organisations for their encouragement and assistance. To the Rotary International Foundation I am indebted for the grant which made possible the research on which it is based. I am deeply grateful to the late Professor E. Harris Harbison of Princeton University, who initially directed my interest towards Paget, and to Sir John Neale of University College, London, whose encouragement to an American student was both generous and stimulating.

I am also grateful to the officials of the British Museum and the Public Record Office, and to the secretaries of the Historical Manuscripts Commission, the Institute of Historical Research of the University of London, and the Northampton Record Society for their patient understanding and assistance in locating many manuscripts. To the Marquess of Anglesey I also extend my thanks for allowing me to examine the Paget family papers.

Washington, DC   Samuel R. Gammon
1972

CHAPTER ONE

ANCESTRY AND EDUCATION

SELF-MADE Englishmen of the sixteenth century, who had risen by their wits from lowly birth to positions of honour and wealth, were more inclined to conceal their humble origins than were their successors in the late nineteenth and early twentieth centuries. William, first Baron Paget of Beaudesert, was no exception to this rule. Even his father's identity has never been surely determined.[1] Information about any remoter ancestry is largely a matter of genealogical guesswork.

There are, however, a few scanty facts which shed light on Paget's background. For example, the heraldic visitation of Staffordshire in 1583,[2] during the lifetime of William Paget's widow, mentions his father as '— Paget de London, mediocris fortunae vir', but later investigators, who were more rash, have assigned this parent such widely varying given names as Thomas, Henry, William, and John.[3] However, his father's name can be correctly identified as John Pachet of London by the following evidence.

The desperate young Earl of Surrey at his trial in January 1547, denouncing men of low birth who served the crown, scornfully addressed Paget, then secretary, as 'Catchpoll'[4] referring, the chronicler explains, to his father's post as a constable or bailiff. Dugdale clarifies this by stating that the elder Paget was sergeant-at-mace to the Sheriff of London.[5] Further, among the papers of the Marquess of Anglesey,

present head of the Paget family, in a group of six bonds and
releases, is an acquittance dated July 1511 which refers to
John Pachet, shearman, of London, as 'alias John Paget,
sergeant, of London'. Other evidence indicates that this John
Pachet not only served the law but was something of a jack-
of-all-trades.

In 1502 he was described as 'barber' as also in 1515, but
in 1530 he was 'clothworker' to his creditors.[6] The absence
of any records in the Clothworkers' Company of London—
which included shearmen in its membership—prior to 1537
and a similar lack in the Barbers' Company makes it difficult
to determine exactly John Pachet's relation to the two companies.

Information about his financial activities enables us to
learn a little more about William Paget's father. Once he
addressed to Archbishop Warham, lord chancellor from 1504
to 1515, a petition, the mutilated original of which exists in
the Public Record Office.[7] In it John Pachet, shearman, pro-
tested against an award of 26s 8d damages against him to a
fellow citizen, one Hamnes, by an arbitral board for damages
which Pachet inflicted on a house of Hamnes in Colman
Street in which the former apparently lived. The fact that
Pachet was bound in a recognisance of £20 to stand to the
arbitration suggests that he was of moderate means at this
time. The bonds and acquittance in the possession of his
descendants, which have been referred to above, show that
on several occasions John Pachet had lent sums of money of
20s to 40s to residents in Worcestershire and Staffordshire.
For example, in 1515 he made a 40s loan to Thomas Benet
of Kyngswinford, Staffordshire; in 1522 George Gregory, a
yeoman of Stourbridge, Worcestershire, empowered him to
collect a debt owing him in London, and in 1524 and 1530
loans of 40s and 20s were made to Nicholas Chawnce, yeoman, and Katharine Bodok, widow, of Bromsgrove, Worcestershire.[8]

This connection with Worcestershire and particularly with

Bromsgrove lends substance to an early tradition cited by Dugdale[9] that the elder Pachet was born in Wednesbury, Staffordshire. There was certainly a Pachet family in Staffordshire as early as 1313.[10] In the neighbouring county of Worcestershire a prosperous Worcester attorney and gentleman, Thomas Pachett, died in 1465 leaving a minor son, John, who was to be apprenticed as a mercer in London, as well as a brother, John Pachett, and a first cousin John Pachett.[11] One of these numerous John Pachetts or his heir, most probably the minor son himself, was a suitor in Chancery (1515–18) for lands in Bromsgrove parish to which he had a claim, and for which his grandson was still vainly suing forty years later.[12] The fact that William Paget's father John was lending money to Bromsgrove residents during this period makes it plausible that he was related to the Worcestershire Pachetts, who so proliferated in sons named John. However, he was settled in London, and it was there that his son was born.

William Paget, the son of this obscure London artisan and city employee, was born in 1505 or 1506,[13] the eldest of three sons in a family of four children. He may well have been born in the house in Colman Street near the Guildhall from which his father had 'taken away a piece of timber'.

The visitation of Staffordshire in 1583 indicates that William Paget had two younger brothers, John and Robert, and a sister, Anne, but in his will he refers to her as Agnes and leaves a bequest also to another sister, Margaret.[14] Though the evidence is admittedly somewhat scanty, the family seems not to have been particularly close knit. These two small bequests are the only references to his sisters in the surviving personal papers of William Paget. His brother John who 'died without issue' may have done so at an early age, but the abrupt demise of the other brother at a rope's end as the penalty of treason in 1549 had little influence at that time on William's actions and opinions.

A fifty-eight line Latin poem addressed to Paget by his

schoolmate and boyhood friend, the antiquary John Leland, between 1543 and 1547 is the most ample source of information on his early life and education.[15] Leland, Paget, and their fellow Londoner, Thomas Wriothesley, later lord chancellor and Earl of Southampton, all attended St Paul's School and studied under the brilliant grammarian and humanist William Lilly, high master 1512–22. Both Paget and Leland were on intimate terms with him. Paget once took up the literary cudgels in defence of Lilly against William Gonell, a friend of Erasmus and More, in a now forgotten controversy. Friendships which the young Paget established with fellow pupils at St Paul's, such as Edward North, Anthony Denny, and Wriothesley, were to continue through his life, since these three men also rose to high place in the service of the crown.

At the conclusion of his schooling at St Paul's, Paget continued his education in Trinity Hall, Cambridge, a college specialising in the study of the civil law. Strype[16] alleges that Paget, like Heath, future archbishop of York, and Thirlby, successively bishop of Westminster, Norwich and Ely, and also a Trinity Hall man, was one of the deserving scholars maintained at the university by the father of Anne Boleyn. Strype is also the sole source for a story that at Trinity Hall Paget was inclined to the Protestant doctrine. He is said to have presented 'one Reynold West' with Luther's books and similar heretical German writings, to have read Melancthon openly, to have supported Dr Barnes and other young religious radicals at Cambridge, and to have 'helped many religious persons out of their cowls'. Although the worthy and indefatigable Strype must always be used cautiously, there may be some foundation for these tales. It has recently been shown that such activities by young men of the 'new learning' were tolerated to an amazing degree by the orthodox Master of Trinity Hall, Stephen Gardiner, and his master Cardinal Wolsey.[17] It was not unprecedented, even then, for a young man to be radical in his views.

In any case, William Paget attracted the attention of the master of Trinity Hall. In the course of his college training the two men formed a fast friendship which enabled Paget to set his feet on the ladder to success. It aided him in rising well towards the top before the younger man shattered this friendship conclusively by betraying Gardiner, his friend and former master.

A comparison of the careers of these two servants of the crown illustrates graphically the difference which the Henrician Reformation was to make in the lives of civil servants. Gardiner at the time he met Paget was a retainer of Cardinal Wolsey and chaplain and almoner to the king.[18] In his later career this doctor of civil law was employed as a chief adviser by his sovereigns, and was early rewarded with the post of Bishop of Winchester. Paget, a younger man whose rise as principal adviser to the crown occurred after the break with Rome, was likewise trained in the civil law. He remained a layman, however, whose rewards came in the form of land and titles and who owed allegiance to no other master than the state. The day of the churchman in government was passing already when Henry VIII first began to consider seriously the black tresses and vivacious eyes of Anne Boleyn.

Undoubtedly the years which Paget spent at Trinity Hall as a friend and intimate of the master were pleasant ones. In later years Gardiner was to comment in an amusing letter to Paget on how different the tangled skein of European diplomacy was from the life at Cambridge. Yet, Gardiner noted, the roles they were then filling were similar to those they had played in a college performance of Plautus's *Miles Gloriosus* in which Wriothesley, Paget and he had starred. Gardiner had been Periplectomenus, the wealthy, suave, agreeable old bachelor; Paget had the role of Meliphidippa, a clever maid, and Wriothesley played Palestrio, a facile scheming and evasive servant. How much more difficult to solve, commented Gardiner, were the problems involved in diplomacy than those of the stage.[19]

By modern standards, Paget must have been a very youthful collegian. In an age when many entering Cantabrigians were only fourteen, he probably began his studies about 1520. This is verified in the Grace Books of Cambridge for the year 1525–6 by a decree that Master Pachett had completed two years' study in philosophy and four in civil law, which sufficed for his acceptance as a bachelor in civil law. To this grace was added a notation in another and later hand identifying this Pachett as the lord privy seal of Queen Mary's time.[20]

According to Leland's poem, Paget left Cambridge and studied for a time in the University of Paris, perfecting his knowledge of languages, and then hurried back to England to continue his studies in civil law under Gardiner.[21] These Parisian studies must, therefore, have been undertaken sometime between the spring of 1526 and June 1528, a date when it is known certainly that he was in England in the royal service.

CHAPTER TWO

THE SERVICE OF THE KING

PATRONAGE was all-important if one was to be promoted in Tudor England. In the lower ranks, appointments depended on powerful sponsors. This state of affairs was thoroughly accepted by even the ablest men as normal and proper. Except for the few fortunate enough to catch the king's eye directly, most servants of the crown began their careers by being recommended to some small post by a powerful sponsor. From thence their rise to positions of greater power was the result of efficient service and continuing favour of the sponsor.

Paget embarked on his public career by this means under the sponsorship of Gardiner, whose household he had entered on returning to England from Paris.[1] It is possible that he may have travelled with Gardiner in September 1527 en route from Paris. Gardiner was the secretary and chief confidant of Cardinal Wolsey in negotiating a perpetual peace with the French king, designed to free King Henry's attention for the 'great matter' of his divorce.[2] Paget could not have returned to the continent with his master Gardiner the following spring, however, as by that time he had been appointed clerk of the signet.

Paget was first mentioned in this position on 18 October 1531 in a grant to him of the keepership of the castle of Maxstoke, Warwickshire,[3] a small sinecure of the sort often awarded minor officials for efficient and loyal service. But in June 1523, the French ambassador Du Bellay, writing to the constable of France about the ravages of the sweating sickness in the English court, mentioned that Paget and others of the chamber had been attacked.[4] Since in the organisation of the English royal household, the signet office was attached to that large section classed as 'the chamber',[5] Paget must already have held his appointment as clerk long enough to become familiar in that capacity to the ambassador. It seems plausible to assume also that the French government knew him during his stay in Paris, perhaps as a familiar of Gardiner's, or Du Bellay would hardly have troubled to mention such a minor official in his letter. In any case, with the appointment on 29 July 1529 of his patron Dr Gardiner to the office of principal secretary,[6] custodial officer of the signet, and chief of the signet office, Paget might have been sure that his good service would be amply recognised and rewarded.

It might be interesting to consider the functions of the signet office into which Paget was appointed. It had evolved in performing the work of the king's secretary as custodian of the royal signet. The regular staff consisted of four clerks, who received a small fee from the crown but took their main salary in fees extracted from suitors for signet letters.[7] With the tremendous growth of the secretary's sphere of action, culminating under Cromwell, the signet office had developed into the clerical headquarters for the executive branch of the government. Since the routine work of the office consisted of little but the writing of stereotyped warrants to the Privy Seal Office authorising it to issue further instructions to the financial departments or to the Chancery, while the secretary's executive work had grown by leaps and bounds, it was natural for a secretary to employ his four signet clerks' free time for his own pressing affairs.

In July 1534 a new secretary, Thomas Cromwell, reorganised his signet office so that he might take full advantage of this free time. He set up a duty roster of one half of the clerks who should perform the routine duties of the office. The other two staff members were left free for the secretary's use. Fees received for each document written for a suitor were to be kept by one of the clerks for equal division at the end of the month among them all, regardless of whether they had been engaged in the remunerative routine work or in the more important but unpaid work of the secretary on the royal correspondence, and the business of the Privy Council and Parliament.[8] The two duty clerks were required to inspect signet bills and sign the finished products before dispatching them to the Privy Seal Office.

An examination of the papers of the latter office reveals that this division of labour prevailed among the signet clerks during most months for which records exist.[9] Since each clerk of the signet had one or more assistants whom he paid himself out of his own receipts, the secretary had an imposing clerical staff at his disposal.

In the year 1540–2, for which a secretary's signet register exists,[10] the four clerks of the signet were receiving handsome incomes. A signet bill starting the machinery for a royal payment cost a suitor 6s 8d from which each clerk received a fifth. A grant of land or pension in perpetuity required from the suitor £3 to grease the cumbersome machinery which produced his patent under the great seal, and of this sum each clerk got 5s. Thus a large number of land and annuity grants in any month would materially enlarge the signet clerk's profits. During the period of 1540–2, when land sales were on the increase, each clerk averaged nearly £7 a month, a truly munificent income for that day.

As an added attraction, a clerk of the signet was a trusted aide to the crown's principal executive agent and thus in an excellent position to gain valuable experience and demonstrated his ability in important missions for the king, which might lead to his promotion. In this lucrative office William Paget was to remain until 1542.[11]

Paget alone of numerous clerks of the signet who held office

during the decade of the 1530s was destined to specialise in
diplomatic missions, which kept him away from much of the
desk-work of the office. His schoolmate and fellow clerk,
Thomas Wriothesley, became an expert in administration,
but other clerks remained undistinguished civil servants who
never rose above their office.

Circumstances at the time of Paget's clerkship were indeed
favourable for a rising young diplomat to make his mark.
King Henry had given up a brilliant but expensive policy of
continental conquests and Weltpolitik. Instead, he concentrated on divorcing Catharine of Aragon and on effecting an
ecclesiastical revolution in spite of the opposition of Catholic
Europe and Emperor Charles V. This decade was rich in
opportunity for diplomatic move and counter-move.

Henry changed his tactics after failing in his first attempts
to secure an annulment of his marriage. In early August 1529
Gardiner and the royal almoner, Edward Foxe, told him of
a suggestion made by a Cambridge scholar and theologian,
Thomas Cranmer. It was advised that he appeal to the divines
in the universities to unravel the problem of whether his
union with his brother's widow was a valid marriage.[12] By the
early part of the next year Henry had begun to carry out the
suggestion. Not only the English universities but all the
centres of Christian learning were to be approached. During
1530 the battle of the universities raged. Neither Henry nor
Charles hesitated to use every inducement possible in order
to sway the learned men of Europe.

Naturally this opinion poll of the scholars involved a great
deal of leg work for many diplomats and agents. And what
could be more logical for secretary Gardiner than to employ
his star pupil and friend, Paget, in such pursuits?

Paget plunged into the field of diplomatic skullduggery
as an aide to Edward Foxe, Reginald Pole, and Sir Francis
Brian, who were hovering around the University of Paris
in June 1530.[13] In the spring of the next year he earned com-
mendation for his skill and dexterity in getting a document

from Orleans University condemning the papal summons for Henry VIII to appear in Rome. This opinion Paget carried in triumph to Henry about the end of June.[14] Strype alleges that Paget was also sent to the University of Toulouse for a similar verdict from that institution. Such a project was certainly under consideration by the king at about that time.[15] However, Henry had plans for a more important mission for this able agent.

Paget's task grew out of the first of Henry's several diplomatic flirtations with the German Protestant princes. The king invariably turned in their direction whenever he suspected that a desertion of him by his nominal ally, Francis, was betraying him to the pope and the emperor. As soon as his fears were calmed, he let the overture to the Lutherans fade. In July 1531 Henry was planning with King Francis a joint diplomatic gesture to the Protestant princes to assure them of Anglo-French backing against Hapsburg aggrandisement, of which they took the recent election of Charles's brother, Ferdinand, as King of the Romans to be a sign.[16] This gambit would have weakened Charles by involving him deeply in Germany and might also have served Henry as a guarantee against a French-Papal marriage treaty.[17]

Thus, in September 1531 Paget appeared in Germany conferring with the Landgrave Philip of Hesse at Rothenburg, promising him English support with other Protestant princes against the emperor, and soliciting the opinion of his theologians in the matter of Henry's divorce.[18] The Landgrave duly wrote to Luther urging him for political reasons to give an opinion satisfactory to Henry. He also consulted his new University at Marburg, but neither source would comply with his request. During this German expedition, Paget communicated with his royal master by way of Brian and Foxe, the ambassadors with the French court.[19] It was vital for French and English policy to coincide as expressed through their agents in Germany, Dr Gervais and William Paget. This joint diplomatic effort succeeded almost too well to please

Henry, who by November had received the message through Paget from the German princes replying to his diplomatic gambit. It told him that Philip of Hesse and the other Protestant princes had made a confederation to defend their religion and restore one of their allies to the land from which the Hapsburgs had ousted him. The new confederation, while professing humble submission to the emperor, still asked financial aid of Henry, which they claimed he had promised them. This alarmed the English king, who had no wish to bind himself so far without more knowledge of the French intentions.[20]

After his agent had returned to England with a report of progress, and the German league's agent had followed to press for Henry's aid, that king resolved to send Paget back to Germany by way of the French court, where he should confer with the English ambassador, in order to co-ordinate English and French policy in Germany.[21] In December Gardiner, recently installed as Bishop of Winchester and still secretary to the king, had been sent to the French court to manage this delicate affair.[22] Paget was ordered to stop for a conference with him, to take Gardiner's advice on how best he might travel secretly in Germany, and to alter his instruction in accord with any agreement Gardiner might make with the French. Paget's principal mission was, on arriving in Germany, to make his way secretly to the Elector of Saxony and encourage him in his opposition to Charles V, instilling in him a deep-rooted and permanent distrust of any imperial promises of religious reform. To convince the Saxon that Francis and Henry were his only true friends, Paget might promise 10,000 crowns from each with more to follow in case of war. However, he was not to bind Henry to join the league openly. If the elector's Latin did not suffice for conversation, Paget was empowered to use his German escort, Christopher Mount, to interpret. Since Paget spoke no German, Mount was to supervise the collecting of intelligence and news of interest in Germany for him to send home to Henry.

The French king was sending William Du Bellay, Lord of Langey, to Germany to represent him. His real interest, however, lay in negotiating an understanding with the Duke of Bavaria. Though he generously urged Henry to give financial aid to the German Protestants, Henry noticed that Francis was frugal with his own resources. This made him fear that he would be driven into an open breach with Charles only to find then that the French would not support him, while the German Protestants would meekly give in to the emperor. Bishop Gardiner was instructed to keep a careful eye on the French in order to guard against this and was instructed to attempt to get Langey superseded by a minor official, who would not outrank Paget so greatly.[23]

Unfortunately for Henry's carefully designed plan to weaken the emperor through the Smalcald League, the Turks ruined it by overrunning Hungary and menacing Germany itself. This forced the emperor and the league to sink their differences and unite against the invader. A few religious concessions by Charles converted the Protestants into his zealous allies against the Turk.[24]

Nevertheless, Paget spent most of the year in Germany. According to the imperial ambassador in England, Eustace Chapuys, he was sent to confer with Melancthon and other Lutheran divines in order to persuade them to endorse Henry's religious policy, though when Chapuys charged Henry's ministers with this act they denied Paget had any authority to do such a thing.[25]

In spite of the fact that there were no concrete results, Paget's diplomatic experiences in Germany benefited him in two ways. The favourable impression Paget's superiors had of him was augmented, and the trip also gave him some knowledge of the tangled thread of German relations.

On his return, Paget found his first patron, Bishop Gardiner, in growing disfavour. The eighteen months from the summer of 1532 to February 1534 were critical ones in the perennial struggle for chief place among the king's advisers. These months brought the rise of Thomas Cromwell from one of the lesser councillors of Henry to a position of supremacy in the government unsurpassed even by Wolsey; they also marked the eclipse of Paget's friend and patron, who had been so prominent in the government for the past few years. In the battle of titans which preceded a change of influence in sixteenth-century government, the followers and friends of the chief contestants were often crushed in the struggle. How precarious political life was then—even for minor servants of the crown!

Paget must have been aware that Gardiner's decline began with his opposition to the king's attack on the powers of convocation to legislate for the church. This action placed Gardiner in temporary disfavour and probably cost him the archbishopric of Canterbury,[26] a post he might otherwise have expected when it had become vacant. While he retained the secretaryship, it was evident that about this time Thomas Cromwell had begun to manage almost all of the king's affairs.[27] In September 1533, Gardiner was ordered to retire from court to his see of Winchester.[28] He had tried the royal patience too far by continuing in Parliament to oppose the royal religious changes up to the very moment of their adoption. In spite of the fact that he had then accepted them loyally, he had forfeited completely the royal favour.[29]

Paget had stayed by his master and friend until the very last moment it was safe to do so. However, a trait which he was to reveal on several occasions in his life then exhibited itself: if the alternative were loss of position and possible confinement, his self-interest superseded his loyalty. In an age when promotion and wealth depended so much on this quality, he was of the same mould as his fellows. And so we have the earliest of Paget's preserved letters, a humble protest of duty written on 22 February 1534 to the new and all-powerful secretary Cromwell, into whose service Paget had discreetly elected to transfer:[30]

I have thought it my bounden duty to write unto you ...
most humbly to thank your mastership for the gentle and
loving kindness which once being some deal kindled in
you towards me, and after by my negligence well near
extinguished, your mastership of late, and in manner of
your own gentle instigation and humanity, did revive
and quicken again, reducing me into his favour and
grace, whose least displeasure towards me grieveth me
more than the most cruel death. In good faith, I speak
without dissimulation, I esteem myself more bounden
to your mastership *than to all other* [author's italics], the
King's Highness only excepted, for whereas indeed other
men had somewhat heretofore advanced and set me forward, and yet afterward being by my own folly retired
and cast back to the extremity, being in the King's displeasure, the rest of my friends not being able to set me
afoot, ye have friendly [sic] and naturally regendered me
and brought me *quasi jure postliminii ad pristinum
statum et antiquam apud regiam majestatem gratiam*,
for the which I protest before God ye have and shall have
my heart, prayer, and service next to the King's Highness above all men.

In December 1533, Henry contemplated a final break with
the papacy. Such a move would make his quarrel with the
emperor even more serious, and his council resolved to ap-
proach the German Protestants again, if the French could be
persuaded to renew a joint diplomatic offensive there.[31] Once
the resolution was taken, Cromwell quickly decided to divide
the mission among Nicholas Heath, Dr Thomas Lee, and
William Paget, who was to go to Prussia and Poland in this
quest for allies.

Each of the agents was given an initial allowance of £120.[32]
In almost identical terms the three were instructed to sound
out the princes to whom they were sent. Should it be found
that they were not favourers of the pope, the agents were ord-

ered to convince them that the king's divorce was just and to
point out how blatantly the pope had denied him justice.
It was to be further pointed out that Henry had already
contributed 50,000 crowns towards their defence and now
wished them to join him in striving to secure justice and a
true reformation of the church by a general council whenever it should meet. Henry would agree to follow a similar
course and would promise to aid them against all their
former and future enemies. Heath and Paget were told also
to deny that Henry was motivated in his divorce proceedings
by mere lust for Anne Boleyn, and they were instructed to
praise 'the purity of her life, her constant virginity, her
maidenly and womanly pudicity, her soberness, her chaste-
ness, her meekness ... [and] her aptness to the procreation of
children'.[33] Paget's selection as emissary to Lüneburg, Mecklenburg, Prussia, and Poland was the proof that Cromwell
had restored him to favour after his near eclipse with Gardiner. Paget thanked his new sponsor most obsequiously.

Paget's mission was complicated by a singular series of
miscalculations by which Henry allowed himself to become
involved with the revolutionary democratic government of
Lübeck. Henry was tempted by a promise of the vacant
throne of Denmark. He made an alliance with the city in
August 1534[34] in spite of an accurate forecast in February
from Paget that the most powerful Protestant princes were
supporting a Lutheran duke for the Danish crown.[35]

After he had written his unheeded warning, Paget set out
from Hamburg with a large escort of hired men-at-arms to
make the dangerous trip across unsettled Pomerania to Grif-
fenberg. From this Prussian city he besought Cromwell three
weeks later to pardon his long silence which was the result
of uncertain mails rather than negligence.[36] After Paget communicated his mission to the princes to whom he was sent, he
wrote home anxiously for further orders, while he awaited
their reply.[37] What policy, he asked, should he follow with
regard to Henry's Lutheran rival for the Danish crown,

unaware that at that very moment Henry was negotiating his alliance with their Lübeck opponents. Also, he inquired whether he should stay in Mecklenburg until recalled or return automatically when he had seen that prince and carried out his original instructions. And what, he asked cryptically, was he to do about Melancthon? He asked that the king's thanks be expressed to the Prince of Lüneburg and to the popular 'burgermaster George' (Wullenweber) of Lübeck for their gracious reception of him.

The reply to these queries on the part of Paget was an immediate recall, and in May he passed through Hamburg where his colleague Dr Lee was busily negotiating with the Hanse cities. Thus it is probable that he arrived in England early in June 1534.[38]

His mission had been fruitless. Henry's negotiation with the Prussians and Polish princes had temporarily served to allay their suspicions of him. However, Albert, Duke of Prussia, had formed such a high regard for Paget that he scarcely credited reports that Henry was aiding the Lübeckers against the new Danish king. Subsequently, Albert used his friendship with Paget as a channel of influence to the English court and as a route for diplomatic presents to the English king and his advisers.[39]

The two years following Paget's return to England are the most obscure of his career as there is little evidence of his whereabouts or activities. Probably he remained at court, absorbed in his much-neglected post as clerk of the signet. It was evidently during this cessation of his travels that he married. His bride, Anne Preston, was the sole daughter and heir of Henry Preston of Preston in Lancashire. The family, an old one, was founded by Sir John Preston, Anne's great-great-grandfather who had been one of Henry V's justices of the peace.[40] As no inquisition post-mortem has survived for Paget's father-in-law, it cannot be told how great a fortune his wife brought, but she must have been a substantial catch, even for a rising young royal servant with great expectations. In any case, the match, followed by the birth of a son and heir, Henry Paget, sometime in 1537[41] was to prove a most happy marriage for William Paget, justifying his friend Leland's lyric description of the event, *Quo tibi conjuncta est Presdunia tempore virgo, Qualis in aethereis Cynthia vecta rotis.*[42]

At some time in the first half of 1535 Paget made a trip across the Channel and back, but the nature of his mission remains a mystery because the only evidence of it is an allowance in the exchequer to a customs collector for advancing the money for such a trip to 'Mr Paget'.[43]

His reputation continued to be high in diplomatic circles. One of his former colleagues, Edward Foxe, later Bishop of Hereford, who was still in Germany, strongly advised that Paget be sent to help him. Foxe implied that Paget was persona grata to the Protestant princes and told Cromwell that there was 'no man more meet for that purpose' or one who 'could better serve in the good handling and conducting in the King's said purpose than the said Pachett'.[44]

However, 'the said Pachett' must have been of more value at court than in the mire of German negotiations. In May 1536, Queen Anne Boleyn was executed; Jane Seymour became queen; and Paget made the second step on the ladder of success by being selected as secretary to Queen Jane.[45] The duties of this office, which included custody of the queen's signet and direction of her correspondence, were more honourable than arduous. It was a handsome indication of official approval for the handling of that diplomacy that had engaged the attention of the thirty-year-old signet clerk for the past five years. Although this post lapsed with the death of the young queen in October 1537, it was re-created and restored to him for the brief tenure of Anne of Cleves as the next queen consort.[46] Perhaps his German experiences made him especially welcome to her. She spoke no other language than German and must have been a very lonely 'great Flanders mare' in this alien English stable. At any rate, she regarded him highly all her life and at her death left him a diamond ring in her will.[47]

Paget's principal duty as her secretary seems to have been that of discharging her retinue and returning her ladies to Cleves when Henry found that she was really his 'good sister' and not his wife after all.[48]

Another friend instrumental in advancing Paget's career was Thomas Wriothesley. While Paget had been busy on diplomatic missions, his schoolmate and colleague in the signet office had surpassed him in distinction as Cromwell's assistant in the sweeping reorganisation of the administrative structure of the government. Indeed, by the beginning of 1537 Wriothesley was referred to as 'principal clerk of the signet'. He was Cromwell's under-secretary in charge of the three branches of his clerical staff—the signet office clerks (including Paget), the Privy Seal Office clerks, and Cromwell's personal staff. Wriothesley assigned tasks to all the clerks, and his appointment in 1540 as secretary merely regularised his *de facto* position of the preceding four years.

Their long friendship gave Paget a favoured position. In December 1537, the under-secretary sent his friend to examine the recently surrendered abbey of Titchfield to see what its possibilities for development would be in the event that Wriothesley should acquire it for himself from the crown. Paget's account of the work of the surveyors there indicated chiefly that he was anxious to return to court for the Christmas holidays. He did hasten back to give the oral report of Titchfield's desirability,[49] which led Wriothesley to acquire it. Shortly after this episode, Paget was busy assisting him to secure the lease of a house belonging to the provost of King's College. His reward was Wriothesley's favour with the cofferer of the household.[50] In October 1537, Paget was named to the commission of the peace in Middlesex, a mark of trust reserved for substantial figures in government, society, or commerce, and one which was renewed to him regularly thereafter.[51] Paget was regarded as sufficiently dependable to be named on the grand jury which at that time indicted Sir Geoffrey Pole, Sir Edward Neville, and other 'conspirators' guilty of being relatives and friends of Henry's detested and feared cousin, Reginald, Cardinal Pole.[52]

In the last years of his tenure as signet clerk, Paget was being groomed for further advancement. He continued to demonstrate his competence away from the court on responsible missions, such as that to Ireland in the autumn of 1539 as bearer of £2,600 sterling and paymaster of a detachment of nearly a thousand soldiers. It was Paget's first experience as commander of troops, as Cromwell sent the force its instructions through Paget, who was also responsible for discipline, promotions, and the transportation of his army.[53] He must have enjoyed himself thoroughly, for in later years he repeatedly showed a civilian's yearning to play soldier. Travelling with his troops and a personal retinue of servants by way of Chester and Holyhead, Paget embarked with them on thirteen small vessels and arrived in Dublin on 5 November. After delivering his command and the remains of the treasure to the lord deputy and his treasurer, Paget returned to England bearing letters and reports on the state of Ireland to Cromwell.[54]

Beside talents as an emissary and agent, Cromwell and Wriothesley must have seen in Paget considerable ability as an administrator. In the closing months of Cromwell's career, Paget appeared as something more than merely a signet clerk. Even before Wriothesley's elevation to the secretaryship in April 1540, important state papers were being drafted in Paget's hand.[55] Not yet an originator of policy, Paget had entered the intermediate stage between mere stenographer and policy-maker.

Although he had left Cambridge without an advanced degree, Paget remained in close contact with his university, which regularly took care to encourage the friendship of men of eminence or alumni in the royal service who might be in a position to favour the university. A presentation of gloves to a Master Pachet and his wife in 1533 is probably not to William Paget,[56] but in 1538 he was active on behalf of the provost of King's in discovering and halting depredations on college lands near Westminster, after which he sent the provost the draft of a petition to the crown for redress, which he suggested should be forwarded to Cromwell through Wriothesley.[57] While he kept a benevolent eye on his alma mater, Paget contracted a liaison at about this time with a totally different type of institution—in 1537 he was admitted to Gray's Inn.[58] It cannot be determined on what status he was admitted or whether he contemplated a serious study of the common law, which he never had sufficient time to do. Probably he was admitted as an ancient, some of whom were distinguished and influential men not expected to live by the law but merely admitted to set a tone of manners and conduct in the society. If, indeed, this honorary status was his, Paget's reputation in the government was of a very high order to be so marked by the 'Noble Men of the Company' of Gray's Inn.

By 1540, William Paget had come a long distance from his humble origin as the son of a London shearman. For some time he had been William Paget, 'esquire', having accumulated sufficient means to support the state of a gentleman. As early as August 1534 he had secured from the Earl of Northumberland the twenty-one-year lease, at twenty marks a year, of a handsome house in Aldersgate. This town residence, known as Northumberland Place, was situated in two ample gardens and abutted on the city wall, extending from St Anne's parish High Street in the east to the Greyfriar's Convent garden.[59] Three years later, in June 1537, he became a country gentleman as the lessee of a manor in West Drayton, Middlesex, which he expanded in later years to a great estate. Paget's original acquisition was the remaining eighteen years of a thirty-year lease from Robert Hill, yeoman, for which he paid £30. Hill held it from the Dean and Chapter of St Paul's Cathedral, to whom Paget was to pay a rent of

B

£27 and thirty-two quarters of wheat a year.[60] To this property
he immediately added by the purchase or lease of Drayton,
West Drayton, and Colham Mills.[61] And, if his assiduous
quest for oak timber can be taken as an indication, he began
a modest building programme.[62]

The wealth of the many statesmen who made their fortunes
under the Tudors never consisted solely of land purchased
from or granted by the crown, or of their 'profits of office'
of legitimate fees and (to modern thinking) less legal pour-
boires. These sources did provide the majority of their
incomes, but a surprisingly large portion was derived from
the steady trickle of petty sinecures which dripped from the
crown into the perennially parched palms of favoured suitors. In the county of Staffordshire alone, the fees of half
a dozen keeperships and rangerships of royal properties
amounted to nearly £21 a year,[63] quite apart from the lands
held by the crown for its wards or the unlimited number of
import licences at its disposal for residents of that and other
counties. Even a clerk of the signet was not too lowly to
enjoy some of these sinecures; Paget, for example, in 1531
acquired the posts of keeper of the castle and park of Maxstoke, bailiff of the manor there, and constable and doorward
of Maxstoke Castle during the minority of the owner, a royal
ward. Three years later he was licensed to import 400 tuns
of Gascon wines at reduced customs, and in still another three
years the reversion of the lease of another house in Middlesex.[64] Thus, the financial advances of a servant of the crown,
partly the reward of honest toil, partly the favour of powerful
friends, and partly the fruit of canny investment of the profits
of office, kept pace with his increases in position in the government.

CHAPTER THREE

THE KING'S AMBASSADOR LIEGER IN FRANCE

ENGLAND'S court was rocking in the throes of a struggle between Thomas Cromwell and his enemies, Bishop Gardiner, the Duke of Norfolk, and other religious conservatives, during the late spring of 1540—a struggle which ended in Cromwell's arrest and execution in June. He had already divided his office of secretary into a dual post and given it to Ralph Sadler and Thomas Wriothesley. However, both these men made their peace with the successful faction, while the most prominent of the signet clerks, William Paget, had never lost the esteem of his former patron Gardiner in spite of the fact that he had left his service in 1534 for that of Cromwell.

Once its dominant minister was eliminated, the council's role became more evident in the royal government and some readjustment in the administrative machinery became necessary. One scholar even dates the real emergence of the Privy Council as such at the close of Cromwell's rule, because then it clearly satisfied for the first time, a number of criteria which distinguished it from the less regular King's Council of earlier years.[1] One such point was that the Privy Council then acquired a regular full-time clerk and a register kept by him. William Paget was the first clerk of the new Privy Council.

It is true that the earlier kings' councils had had a senior and a junior clerk, but the former had evolved into the clerk of the council in the Star Chamber, something entirely different from the clerk of the council, while from 1512 to 1533 there had been no junior clerk. In 1533, Thomas Derby was appointed by a privy seal writ as 'clerk of the Council attendant on our person', but he remained a clerk of the signet as well, and was principally concerned with the duties of the latter post, merely collecting the fee of £20 per annum from his council position. At the same time, Cromwell employed other members of his clerical staff to do the occasional work of the council. In 1539, Derby was transferred to the King's Council in the west and no immediate successor was appointed.[2] Thus, on 10 August 1540 the Privy Council register, which began then to be kept with scarcely a break to our times, commenced very properly with the appointment of William Paget, late the queen's secretary, as clerk attendant to write, enter, and register the council's decrees in a book.[3] His patent, which was not delivered to him until a few weeks later, increased his stipend over that of earlier clerks to £30.[4]

The disappearance of Henry's second and last 'prime minister' left the Privy Council a much heavier burden of work than any royal council had faced before, as it was forced to add to its earlier function of policy discussion many details of administration formerly left to the competent hands of Cromwell.[5] Part of its work could continue to be left under the joint supervision of the two principal secretaries, but much of it was deposited on the shoulders of its new clerk. Paget's main concern was the council register, the first volume of which survives today principally in his own hand. Judging from the neat format of the first few pages, he had large ideas about keeping the new register, but the press of business soon forced him to jot down the entries as rapidly as possible, some of them being scarcely legible. Apparently, the register was written out soon after the meetings of the council had adjourned and constituted a rough log of routine conciliar actions for the council's own information, and was no longer a complete list of matters discussed nor a permanent legal record. The clerk also kept a letter book for copies of Privy Council letters, though, in later years, other clerks abandoned this practice in favour of noting the contents of a letter in the register and referring to the draft copy 'in the Council chest'.[6]

The nature of Paget's clerical duties may be understood by examining the various types of fees which came to him from suitors. It must be kept in mind that in the sixteenth century every officer, great or small, took advantage of every service he rendered for a private suitor by extracting a fee. This was not bribery but, rather, a part of his salary. Whereas now the service charge which the state extracts for issuing a marriage licence or registering a deed goes into its treasury, and the fixed salary of the state official coming from that treasury is ample remuneration for his work, in Tudor days the clerk eliminated this double transfer of funds into and out of the treasury by keeping the fees as his perquisite to supplement a fixed and usually hopelessly small stipend established several generations before.

Paget, as clerk of the Privy Council, was entitled to charge fees ranging from 4d for a letter of appearance to 2s for a copy of a recognisance, and similar amounts for the taking of depositions, recording decrees, or entering appearances— provided these services were done for an individual and not at the council's order.[7] To judge from the frequent notes in the register of such services 'by me, clerk of the Council', his income from this source was substantial.[8] The amount of work that he did with his pen may be estimated by his quarterly consumption of fifty shillings' worth of paper, ink, and pens.[9] Within three years it was found necessary to appoint an under-clerk of the council and to increase the salaries of both individuals.[10] The clerk's right to double lodgings in the outer court of Hampton Court, when the king was in residence, amounted to a substantial sum also, and Paget may have installed his wife there.[11]

The clerk of the council was regarded as an immediate

assistant of the secretaries and might be entrusted with considerable responsibility in the implementing of conciliar
policy. When the secretary was engaged, the clerks were often
sent to bear official messages to the foreign ambassadors at
the court, missions important enough to require a responsible
representative. It seems also to have been a royal policy, when
on a progress with part of the council, to leave either one of
his two secretaries or the clerk of the Privy Council with that
portion remaining in London. Thus a competent administrator was always available there to write dispatches and oversee
the clerical organisation.[12]

On the other hand, Paget, although clerk of the council,
was not himself a councillor, and all high matters of state were
likely to find him excluded from the council chamber. Indeed,
it is possible that at some periods he was rarely admitted even
as a recorder of business, but was regularly told by the secretary what decisions should be recorded in the register. For
example, in an interesting letter to his friend Wriothesley in
June 1541, Paget gave his absent chief the news of the court,
including an eye-witness account of the trial of Lord Leonard
Grey and an 'ear-witness' account of a council meeting. Paget
had heard them discussing a possible pardon for young Lord
Dacre, who had been condemned as a murderer. He mentioned it as though it were a familiar circumstance to be
summoned to the council, but be excluded from the meeting chamber. Only the fact that the councillors debated so
hotly he heard them through two doors explained his knowledge of their topic. Indicative of the times and of people of
the sixteenth century was Paget's unemotional account of
Lord Leonard's condemnation for treason and his distress at
the fate of Lord Dacre, whose offence was the deliberate murder of a farmer.[13]

A further promotion came to Paget in the summer of 1541.
He was named clerk of the Parliaments at a fee of £40 a
year, plus, of course, the inevitable perquisites attached to
the post.[14] The duties of the office were negligible when

Parliament was not in session, but required the clerk's continuous presence in the House of Lords during sessions to maintain the journal and engross bills.[15] Since Parliament did not meet until after Paget had been sent abroad, he never performed his duties except by deputy.[16] In his council clerkship also was 'John Masyn...admitted and sworn clerk of the Privy Council during the absence of Mr William Paget'.[17]

As the summer of 1541 drew to a close, the King of England was in the process of launching a new policy which was to exhaust the resources of his country for nine more years. Having succeeded in altering his matrimonial status and the religion of his realm, as well as strengthening and maintaining his personal government, despite a constant fear of foreign intervention, he now turned in his last years to extending his power throughout the British Isles. He focused his attention especially on the task of bringing his nephew, the Scottish king, within the English orbit instead of that of the French.

With this in mind, he journeyd to York in the hope of meeting with James V, taking Paget, among others, with him. Henry was well aware that whether or not the Scots allied with him willingly or resisted him, the French would not view any change in their ancient ally's status with indifference. The king also knew that it behooved him to have an active and talented representative at the French court to advise him of their reactions. The fact that any English forward policy in Scotland depended on a renewed war between Francis I and Charles V, which was rumoured to be pending at that time, made it doubly valuable for Henry to have early and accurate intelligence from the French court. His ambassador resident, Lord William Howard, was both pro-French and indolent in the gathering and dispatch of news. Therefore, to the disgust of the French, the nobleman was recalled and replaced by a humble clerk of the Privy Council, William Paget, who was sent to reside at the French court in Lord William's place.[18]

The new ambassador's instructions were to ingratiate himself with the pro-English and anti-imperial faction at the French court. But he was primarily advised to 'travail by all the means he can devise' to learn the French king's policy and relations with all other states and to report his findings diligently.[19]

Paget fulfilled this ambassadorial role of accredited spy to Henry's satisfaction; only once was he urged by the king to be more alert and prompt in his reports. His letters from his sovereign frequently contained expressions approving of his zeal and dexterity, and, sometimes, a more concrete expression of royal approbation, the unsolicited grant of certain land rents.[20] An ambassador, however, was not always in his master's confidence. Henry VIII, firmly believing in the aphorism that an ambassador was sent to 'lie abroad' for his country, often felt that the ambassadorial lying was more effective if the envoy believed in it himself. Thus, Paget was apparently not told by Henry of his alliance with Charles V against France during his stay at the French court. Henry even denied it categorically in a letter to him.[21] In the face of such treatment, which he plainly suspected, Paget's consistent aim was to avoid making any statements to the French which would betray any information about Henry.[22] As he himself expressed it, in the absence of any specific instructions, his aim was 'to hold the balance so upright, as Your Majesty may put your foot in which side you will, not withstanding anything that I have said'.[23]

In undertaking this mission for his king, Paget's first care was to equip himself for the journey. An ambassador's equipment was usually furnished by the king, if it were beyond his own means. Therefore, Paget received from his predecessor a quantity of plate and 'a carriage mulet' to enable him to live within his salary as ambassador. That salary was fixed initially at £1 a day, but Paget found he could not afford to keep open house and a table befitting his master's representative, and the Privy Council persuaded the king to increase his allowance to 30s. The following year another 10s was added.[24] This stipend and a basic allowance of £14 each quarter for posting charges was usually sent at the beginning of each quarter and supplemented by large amounts at irregular intervals for special couriers.[25] This income permitted Paget to maintain an extensive menage, which, at its lowest point on his return journey eighteen months later, included no less than nine servants.[26]

On his way to Paris to take up his duties, the new envoy stopped briefly in the English Pale to examine and report on the new fortification near Calais. By the end of October, however, he had joined Lord William Howard in Paris, and they were preparing for the formal presentation of his credentials.[27] On 20 November at Fontainbleau Paget was presented to Francis I as his good brother Henry's new ambassador.[28]

In his very first audience, the new emissary had a delicate mission to perform. He had to describe the discovery and punishment of Queen Katharine Howard's 'naughtiness'. Francis received the news with appropriate gravity and sympathy and asked Paget if anyone else were implicated in the queen's misconduct.[29]

The instructions for Paget's conduct of his embassy were directed primarily at gathering for Henry information on French policy and plans. In order to carry out this requirement, he habitually made use of the factions which divided the French court. France in 1541 was on the verge of a renewed attempt to conquer the Duchy of Milan by making war on Charles V the following spring. Its court, however, was split into two parties. One, led by the heir to the throne, the Hapsburg queen, the constable, and most of the French cardinals, opposed a war with the emperor and favoured the papal attempts to mediate the dispute. They were consistently hostile to any alliance with schismatic England and would have preferred war with Henry to hostilities with Charles. The other party, then in the king's favour, sought an English alliance for a joint war on the Hapsburg ruler.

Its leaders were the king's mistress, Madame D'Estampes, his sister the Queen of Navarre, his son the Duke of Orleans, the admiral, newly restored to power as chief minister, and Cardinals Du Bellay and De Tournon.[30] Therefore, Paget's principal sources of information were his frequent contacts with the admiral and his courtesy calls on the Queen of Navarre. Only after it became apparent that England and France were drifting into war did those friendly sources cool towards him and cut off his information.[31]

It was also in the faction-ridden French court that Paget acquired his intimate knowledge of the art of intrigue or 'practising', which later earned for him the admiration of his friends and the title of 'Master of Practices' from an enemy.[32]

Much of his intelligence about the French came by means entirely legitimate for an ambassador in that century or any other. During military operations he was allowed to send the pursuivant attached to his staff to the French camp to view operations as a rudimentary military attaché. No one could prevent him gathering news of papal diplomacy from the friend of a friend of the church's emissary, from chatting with other ambassadors, from hanging about the court catching the latest gossip at that fruitful whispering gallery, or even forbid him to 'go abroad alone in my cape (I believe) unknown, and talk with him and him and hear the world' to sound public opinion.[33]

Paget's position was also advantageous as long as Henry was seen as a prospective ally. The French government could not prevent important people at court, who hoped to win English favour, telling Paget French diplomatic and military plans. One of these gentlemen, with an eye to the future, was the maître d'hôtel of the Duke of Orleans, who regularly revealed to the Englishman French proceedings in Flanders and with Cleves.[34] Many of the numerous Scots at the French court acted in the same manner until Henry made war on their country, after which Paget could occasionally win news from only one of them, the captain of the Scots Guard, by skilfully baiting him.[35]

Not all the intelligence came from such respectable sources. Then, as now, ambassadors were provided with secret funds for intelligence work. Though the English espionage net in France can never be clearly seen, tantalising hints crop up occasionally in Paget's correspondence. Once he mentioned a successful ruse by his clerk and pursuivant who passed themselves off as natives in order to become friendly with the servant of a French agent destined for Scotland.[36] On the other occasions, he referred to people in the French camp in his service, darkly hinted of unnamed sources in the court, or spoke of an agent in northern France disguised as a merchant.[37] Many years later one Thomas Barnabie was a suitor to secretary Cecil for employment in espionage work, and claimed to have lived in France serving several ambassadors, Paget among them.[38] In July 1542, Paget's information service was extended in scope by using a Scot named Melville, a former agent of Cromwell's, who lived in Rome and had contacts in the papal court and with Cardinal Pole. This agent was instructed to send regular information through his brother in the French king's guard, and also by way of a merchant in Lyons who was in Paget's pay. Melville was given a code to use and, by September of that year, had reached his post and begun his work of spying on Pole and the English exiles.[39]

An ambassador's work did not consist entirely of spying or preparing for war, or negotiating peace and great matrimonial alliances. Indeed, there were always a tremendous number of routine cases involving his own nationals and their interests in which it was necessary for him to intervene. This was especially true for William Paget in an age when the one emissary combined consular and diplomatic functions. A steady stream of cases dealing with trade came to him for assistance, often with letters from the English Privy Council on their behalf. He was even used, on occasion, as convoy control officer for the wine fleet at Bordeaux.[40]

Paget was unfortunate in the role of policeman arresting English fugitives. Having apprehended one named George Dudley en route to join Cardinal Pole, and having tried to hold him for extradition, he found that by the negligence of the 'beastly fool' his doorkeeper, the 'false traitorous boy Dudley' escaped from his house and clutches.[41]

However, the proposed marriage between Henry's eldest daughter, Mary, and the Duke of Orleans, second son of the French monarch, was the great negotiation which absorbed most of Paget's attention during his embassy. This project was a diplomatic manoeuvre in the great struggle, then at its peak, between Valois and Hapsburg. France had to secure English assistance, or at least benevolent neutrality, in order to wage successful war on the emperor, who in turn was seeking Henry's favour for the same reasons. This rivalry placed Henry in the enviable position of being able to offer his services to the highest bidder. If the bids were equal, however, ancient alliances and commercial ties inclined Henry to join the emperor against the traditional enemy across the Channel. In this competition of offers during 1542, Henry was being wooed in England by the imperial emissary, Eustace Chapuys, and in France through his ambassador Paget. The French desire was to attract Henry's aid and bind him firmly to them through a royal marriage between Valois and Tudor.

Thus, in the late spring of 1541, before Henry's northern progress, the French ambassador Marillac made an overture to the Duke of Norfolk for a marriage between Orleans and Mary. But the matter was delayed until the following winter, when Norfolk, the Earl of Southampton, Bishops Tunstal and Gardiner, and Secretary Wriothesley, were commissioned to negotiate with him. However, the negotiations were obstructed almost immediately by the English refusal to acknowledge Mary as legitimate. Although Marillac then (March 1542) felt that the English were insincere in the negotiations, the Admiral of France and the Queen of Navarre and their faction pressed forward eagerly. It was at this point that Paget was drawn into the negotiations.[42] When King Francis pressed him to agree that Mary should be declared legitimate, he shrewdly replied that the question might wait until the other conditions of the match were settled upon. Francis agreed to this, provided that her marriage portion increased in the event she were then held illegitimate. On that basis, the matter was taken up by the commissioners in England, only to bog down entirely over the thorny question as to the size of the marriage portion.[43] The French wanted Henry to give an acquittance with his daughter for the million crowns of debt and interest on the loan he had made them to be used in ransoming their king fifteen years earlier, as well as a resignation of his life and perpetual pensions from France, established by the treaties of Picquigny (1475) and Etaples (1492).

Notwithstanding the fact that the French obviously had small intentions of paying this debt, the English claimed that such a prodigious marriage portion was quadruple the size of the largest previous marriage settlement in their history and, therefore, unreasonable. The English commissioners added that Francis had never voiced any such enormous claim to Paget. Therefore, the matter was again suspended for a change of scene back to the French court, leaving Marillac by then hoping for a successful outcome.[44]

Francis quickly convinced Paget that if he had said anything contrary to the claim he certainly did not mean it and indicated that he was determined to insist on the elimination of the pensions and the debt, hinting that their validity was open to doubt because Henry had not fulfilled the terms of the treaties. However, at Paget's urging, he consented to send another fully empowered agent to join Marillac and bring about more acceptable terms. Paget replied somewhat bitterly to this. He said that he hoped that this time Henry would find 'his report whom you intend to send and my writings to agree'. Meanwhile Henry resolved to urge the French anti-imperial party to more zeal in the pursuit of the English alliance. He authorised Paget to suggest to the admiral that such a huge marriage portion as they demanded required more of a return on their side than merely the hand of the Duke of Orleans. In connection with this, Paget then reminded the admiral that an alliance with England was indispensable in undertaking the war with Charles V towards which he was urging his king. Therefore, Paget pointed out that it would behoove him to use more moderation in his demands on Henry, or not only would his policy fail but his pro-imperial rivals would surely oust him from office.[45]

This plan made Francis reduce his demands by a small amount, offering to let Henry retain the perpetual pension only. In turn, Henry rejected his offer and made a counter-proposal to Marillac that he would give 200,000 crowns with his daughter, saying that the debt and pension should stand unless the French offered some 'reciproque' for them. Marillac felt that the English resistance was due partly to their feeling that Mary's prospects of becoming a queen regnant of England compensated for her moderate dowry and partly to their conviction that the French must buy their favour at all costs in their plans against the emperor. To this shrewd analysis he added the gravely mistaken opinion that the English would never ally with the emperor, so the French might be slow to raise their bid.[46]

In France, the English ambassador, Paget, continued to press the admiral hard to moderate his demands or else offer a 'reciproque'. To the admiral's doleful sighs and remark that the million crown debt was nothing, he replied that if the admiral were that sort of an accountant, 'Par Notre Dame, you shall not be mine auditor!' The only result of his urging was the admiral's strange suggestion that England join France in attacking the emperor and recompense themselves from the spoils. Shortly afterwards, King Francis summoned Paget and made his final offer: let Henry cancel half of the debt and the life pension, and the remainder, with the perpetual pension, would be paid in instalments. Thereby, it would be made possible for Henry, with no cash outlay, to marry his daughter to France and recover some of the debt which the French otherwise would be unlikely to pay.[47] This same offer was also sent to Marillac to present to Henry. It was accompanied by the false assertion that Paget had suggested a joint war on the emperor. Henry refused the offer and his council indignantly denied the suggestion that the French were attempting to father on Paget.[48] Thus, by the middle of May, the negotiations had reached an impasse; their only tangible result had been to irritate each ambassador at his opposite number as well as infuriating Paget with the admiral and the French king for attempting, as he saw it, to discredit him with his sovereign.[49]

Why had these promising negotiations failed? Henry undoubtedly planned to sell his services to the highest bidder, and the French had not met his price. His coy requests for a 'reciproque' indicated his desire for some substantial profit from the marriage. The resolution he showed in striving to conquer continental lands the following year indicated that he desired a French land cession to increase his holdings at Calais. However, it was more likely that he really wanted the French to agree to abandon Scotland, with which he was rapidly becoming embroiled and with which he hoped to unite England. Moreover, only one French faction desired the alliance while the other fought it strenuously on religious grounds.[50] In any case, by 18 May 1542 the other bidder in the auction, the imperial ambassador, Chapuys, had progressed to the stage of secret negotiations with Henry, and, by the end of the month, their alliance was all but complete.[51]

Later in 1542, the French became suspicious of Chapuys's movements and attempted to revive the marriage project.[52] Henry, always open-minded about new offers, told Paget to suggest the county of Ardres 'with some other such corner or piece of ground as might be commodious for us' as a 'reciproque' for his friendship.[53] But it was too late. By then Henry was openly at war with Scotland. The French efforts, though they dragged on into February of 1543 and contributed to Henry's reluctance to sign his new alliance with the emperor, were in the end futile.[54] As Chapuys ably summarised the affair, Henry was using the overture to keep the French from interfering with his projects in Scotland, and, since the French would never leave the Scots to their fate, Henry was bound firmly to an imperial alliance.[55]

Following the collapse of Anglo-French marriage negotiations, the principal efforts of Paget, as English ambassador, were directed more than ever before to the securing of information on French plans. But he was then concerned with keeping the French suspicions of his master's hostile alliance with the emperor from becoming a certainty, or, failing that, convincing them that Henry intended no open hostilities. This was an impossible feat since the record of the next twelve months was marked with signs of continually mounting hostility between the two powers. Henry, to gain his objectives in the British Isles, was very obviously prepared to risk a war with France, if not actually planning to provoke one. The utmost that his ambassador, Paget, was able to achieve was to retard the hour when the French would realise a war with England was inevitable. He worked tirelessly in an atmosphere of growing suspicion towards this end.

At the very beginning of this year-long ambassadorial rearguard action, in July 1542, Paget skilfully extricated himself from an unpleasant incident which might have lost him the services of one of his retainers. He had sent his lackey to Ligny near the court to secure himself more accessible lodgings. The servant became involved in a quarrel with a servant of Horatio Farnese, the grandson of Pope Paul III, and wounded him mortally after sustaining a serious injury from the other's attack. Paget hurried to the admiral to see that his servant was cleared of the assault charge and followed up his advantage by securing a letter from Henry VIII to the admiral to request a pardon for the Englishman.[56] These steps, together with an appeal to King Francis, secured the

pardon and foiled a desire on the part of the friends of Farnese for revenge on Paget's man. This favour from King
Francis might not have been granted him a few months later,
when cross-Channel relations had deteriorated further.

As early as May 1542, the French suspected Henry's 'practice' with the imperials and that made the current stalemate
in their own negotiations with him seem highly significant.
Their emissary, Marillac, by reporting various favours being
shown the imperial ambassador, strengthened their doubts.
Paget noted this feeling and ascribed to it the fact that his
movements were under surveillance and his visitors were
being carefully observed.[57] In fact, the French precautions
were fully justified; Chapuys, after spending the last week
in May conferring with Henry's council over the terms of
a treaty of defensive alliance, made a flying trip to the
Low Countries for verification of its terms, and thereby
betrayed the secret of the negotiations to the already suspicious French.[58]

To counter these alarms, Paget assiduously courted the anti-
imperial party, hinting to them that unjustified suspicions of
a friend like King Henry might breach the strongest amity.
He 'let slip' that Chapuys's trip to Flanders had really been
only to settle commercial disputes. In England his efforts
were supported by Henry who similarly assured the French
of his faithfulness and promised he would never break his
friendship unless provoked. Marillac was so far persuaded by
the arts of the king that he informed his master that Henry
would at least not attack him during the current year, and
his king was inclined to accept this, reinforced as it was with
Paget's account of Henry's peaceful intentions—for the time
being.[59]

Early in July the French renewed their war with Charles
V, feeling fairly sure of Henry's neutrality. To explore his
sentiments more fully, they sent a special ambassador to
invite him to join their attack on the Hapsburgs.[60] French
continental wars, however, were England's opportunity, and

the English public was fully prepared to take advantage of
this new recurrence of their ancient enemy's war with the
emperor. The long habit of rivalry had been intensified by
the scandal felt in England when the French allied with the
Turks; the English people were again showing their anti-
French sentiments. Marillac noted late in August that their
'indignation is so great and increasing daily, that in the end
this boil must burst'.[61]

Thus, the French no sooner felt Henry to be harmless than
they were swept by a new wave of suspicion reaching its height
in September. Their own small success against the emperor
and Henry's open war with Scotland brought on the new
crisis,[62] which the then current detention of French shipping
in England on a charge of breach of neutrality did nothing
to allay. In a rage, the admiral challenged Paget's secretary,
saying that if England desired war they might have it. Paget
employed all his skill, swallowed his own wrath, and smoothed
the ruffled Gallic temper, while countering with tales of
wrongs done to English shipping.[63] The principal cause of the
steady deterioration in Anglo-French relations was the inevitable dispute over outrages to each other's shipping, which
always occurred in wartime, complicated at the same time
by the English attack on Scotland, the old ally of France.

In a stormy interview with Paget on 12 December, following the news of the utter rout of the Scots at Solway Moss,
King Francis went to the heart of the matter, declaring he
could not see his Scottish ally utterly broken by the English.
He offered to come to terms on a marriage contract on the
condition that Scotland be an equal member of their alliance.[64] This offer came too late; the death of James V of
Scotland two days later seemed to leave Henry's way clear in
Scotland—a week-old queen, a French woman regent, and
her chief adviser, discredited by the military defeat, alone
stood in his way. On 26 December, Henry's only reply to the
French offer was written by his council and sent to Paget
indicating that

... whereas his Majesty thinketh there may be devices set
forth there for the aid of the Scots upon this news of the
King's death, which King left behind him a daughter
lately born, which perchance the Frenchmen will be glad
to get into their hands. His Highness' pleasure is that
you shall now seek by all the ways and means to you possible to learn to know what hath hereupon come from
Scotland to France and what shall be determined in
France to send into Scotland. And if for the better attain-
ment of knowledge at this time you shall spend twenty
or forty pounds it shall be repaid unto you. And spare
not now to give often advertisement.[65]

Paget carried out his instructions. In January he was able
to warn Henry that the French were sending 2,000 German
troops to Scotland, that three warships would sail from
Dieppe before the end of the month, and that a great quantity of munitions were en route to the coast for shipment to
the Scots.[66]

Simultaneously with the growing hostility over Scotland,
the mutual grievances over injuries to trade reached a climax.
The French were permitting Scottish privateers to capture
English vessels within the very harbour of Le Havre and only
replied to Paget's spirited protest with grievances of their
own.[67] In spite of the heated dispute between Paget and the
French Council in which each freely belaboured the ministers of the other power, and in spite of Paget's asking the
recall of Marillac as persona non grata, the arrests of shipping
remained in effect. King Henry sent a virtual ultimatum
demanding either redress or 'we will take order for the
preservation and safeguard of our subjects and for the re-
quital of their injuries'.[68] This blunt hint did not move the
French, and Paget felt certain that they knew war was imminent and desired to detain the vessels until they became
lawful prize.

Matters having reached this pass, on 24 February Paget

presented his letter of recall. The French king, who saw this as the rupture of relations, was thoroughly aroused. Though the retiring ambassador assured him a successor would be sent, Francis in a blunt and accurate fashion summarised the folly of Henry's course: if he had allied with France, he might have remained neutral and still received money from the French, but, by joining the emperor, he must fight the French and forfeit his pensions while disbursing huge sums on war.[69] This Delphic pronouncement was completely in vain; on 2 April the imperial ambassador in England was able to write to his superiors that Henry was resolved to enter the war this year. The rearguard action was concluded.

His recall was most welcome to Paget. Three months before he had asked Secretary Wriothesley to press for it, since he had been promised in the beginning that he would only be kept abroad one year.[70] His homesickness was understandable since he seems to have left his wife and young children in England.[71] But the impatient husband and parent was to find that recall and return were not synonymous terms, as there raged around him a heated dispute in diplomatic protocol. In the current state of Anglo-French relations, the French dared not let Paget leave their country until their own emissary was out of England. Yet, to detain him by force was a violation of the immunity of an accredited agent. They tried vainly to get him to tarry until his successor arrived, and finally gave him an escort to the border, with every courtesy shown him en route. But when he arrived at the border town of Boulogne on 6 March he was detained by the local commander to await the coming either of his successor or Marillac.[72] The English retaliated by detaining Marillac until Paget should be released and a stalemate resulted during which Paget busily gathered and sent home what intelligence he could glean concerning the defences of Boulogne.[73] After three weeks of haggling, Marillac was sent as far as Calais to tarry there for Paget, but all Paget's toil to persuade the local French commander to release him first proved vain.[74] Finally, on 18 April, in company with one of his spies whom the French had uncovered but whose release he had secured, he was exchanged on the border for his detested opposite, Monsieur de Marillac.[75]

He returned to England with a cordial dislike of the French based on his unpleasant experiences as ambassador in a hostile land, which was to increase with his every subsequent contact with French diplomacy. This same dislike strengthened his conviction that the best alliance for England was with its traditional economic and political ally, the ruler of the Low Countries. His health had suffered during his eighteen months in France, and he complained both to Henry VIII and Francis I that he had suffered for three or four years from sciatica and, of late, from 'another disease not meet to be named, whereby I am in great pain whensoever I ride', which was probably piles.[76] While his derrière and disposition had suffered from his contacts with France, his reputation and fortune had been enhanced. The invaluable training of a regular embassy, added to his earlier experience in diplomacy, made him one of the chief figures in Henry's diplomatic service. This fact was duly acknowledged within three days after his return to England by his appointment as one of the two principal secretaries of state.

Since Paget had, during his absence, been granted only the small annual rent of lands he farmed from the crown and two licences for the export of wheat and the import of Gascon wine, his income did not increase materially over its earlier dimensions.[77] But his honourable condition as a gentleman was firmly established by his acquisition of a coat of arms.

On 4 June 1541, Clarencieulx King-of-Arms awarded him coat armour bearing a crest of a half tiger with a branch of a peach tree in his paws, a heraldic allusion to the common spelling of his name, Patchett.[78] This grant, however, was not to his taste, for three years later he exchanged it for a grant from Garter King-of-Arms of 'sables, a cross engrailed between four eaglets displayed silver; upon the cross five lionceulx passant of the field, armed and langued gules, tusked, fasshed, a coronell about the neck silver, set upon a wreath silver and sables, mantles sables lined silver, buttoned gold' and the motto *Per il suo contrario*.[79] These arms the Paget family still bears unchanged.

CHAPTER FOUR

PRINCIPAL SECRETARY
OF STATE : PART ONE

WILLIAM PAGET did not return to England from his embassy
for a rest. Only five days after he wrathfully shook the dust
of France off his riding boots at Calais he was in London and
in the thick of royal affairs. The register of the Privy Council
for 23 April 1543 records briefly that William Paget was that
day sworn as one of the two principal secretaries of state and
admitted to the council. On the same day John Mason and
William Honninges inherited Paget's former tasks as clerks
of the council.[1]

What sort of a post was the secretaryship in 1543? In
essence, the secretary was the chief administrative officer of
the crown and potentially the most powerful and influential
gentleman in the royal government. His office was of such
importance for two reasons. The steady baronial and parliamentary attrition on the other great offices of state and its own
recent evolution had left it one of the few offices with powers
as wide as the royal prerogative chose to make them. The
tremendous energy and administrative skill of Thomas Cromwell had made real the potential power of the office.

The lord chancellor's office had evolved from the initially
humble post of keeper of the Great Seal only to be hedged
around with all the checks of custom and baronial suspicion,
and the lord privy seal's office had risen from a clerkship of

the royal household to change in its turn to a department of state. Similarly, the principal secretary of state had his beginning in the late fourteenth century with the creation of new private seals in the king's household. The new secret seal or 'signetum' of the king was by the end of the century in the custody of a subordinate household officer, who was called the king's secretary. His seal was used both to authorise issues under the Privy Seal and Great Seal and to seal the kingly personal correspondence. In the sixteenth century he still retained his original intimate relation to his ruler. The sapling of the Great Seal had hardened and matured into a massive trunk of the tree of commonwealth. That later growth, the Privy Seal, had matured and grown from a slender twig to a rigid and ponderous branch of government. The sixteenth-century signet, however, was a flexible shoot, easily bent to a multitude of uses in the hands of a skilled craftsman.[2]

The greatest individual involved in changing the secretaryship from a small household office to a major government post was a craftsman indeed. Thomas Cromwell, trained under Cardinal Wolsey, was the first to perceive the possibilities of this office as a key to the royal administration. He used his growing influence with Henry VIII to oust Bishop Gardiner and secure the office for himself. It served as his pathway to increasing influence and control of all branches of the government.[3] Under earlier secretaries the office had secured a growing control of diplomatic business, but Cromwell added to it an equal control of domestic affairs, and from this came his power. Just before his fall from power, the secretaryship was divided between two co-equal secretaries, Thomas Wriothesley and Ralph Sadler.[4]

Although two men bore the title of secretary, the office remained a single whole, each man being privy to the other's actions and competent to act in his absence.[5] They were both recognised as great officers of state, ranking after the treasurer of the chamber, the comptroller, and the vice-chamberlain,

and ahead of all other privy councillors. When Sir Ralph
Sadler was dispatched on a lengthy diplomatic mission into
Scotland, William Paget was appointed to his place.

To analyse Paget's work as secretary, it is essential to consider the office in the light of the several types of work which
have been distinguished as typical of the Elizabethan and
Stuart secretaries.[6] After an analysis of the duties and preroga-
tives of the secretary as keeper of the signet, his role as a
channel of royal influence and of access to the royal person
will be discussed, followed by his relationship to the Privy
Council as an adviser to the crown. This chapter will conclude with the relatively minor role that parliamentary duties
played in Paget's years of office under Henry and with his
duties as home minister. His principal care and the chief
source of his influence—the conduct of foreign policy—will
be reserved for the following chapter. Similarly, his relationship to matters of religious policy will be treated in a later
chapter, since it concerned rather the statesman Paget than
the secretary.

The raison d'être of the secretary was his custody of the king's
signet. The signet office with its four clerks, which had grown
up around the function, was one with which Paget was very
familiar. Following Cromwell's example, he made it the central nucleus of his official staff. The nomination of the clerks
was at his disposal,[7] and their obligation to hire an assistant
apiece gave Paget a basic staff of eight clerks.

The signet office was also the source of his principal official
income. To supplement his annual salary of £100, paid in two
instalments,[8] he received half of the two secretaries' share of
the profits of the signet. Henry's last years of war and huge
land sales must have made these profits enormous. For each
warrant written at an individual's suit, the two secretaries
divided one-fifth of the half mark fee, but for land grants in
perpetuity they each received £1. In 1541, a relatively inactive
year for the signet, each secretary's share was over £200.[9] The

secretary was also entitled to 'bouche of court', which provided his lodgings and about £22 a year for fires, lights, and rations.[10]

Although the two secretaries were theoretically equals, in practice, seniority usually made one of them a dominant force. When Paget entered on his office in April 1543, his colleague Wriothesley had been secretary or acting secretary for six years. As the junior, Paget served as his old schoolmate's assistant, but in the autumn of the year Wriothesley's health broke down, and he was absent for over a month.[11] On his recovery, he was elevated to the peerage and became lord chancellor, being succeeded as secretary by Sir William Petre.[12] It was then Paget's turn to be the 'premier secretary' for the rest of his four years' tenure of that office and to instruct his new colleague in its weighty and manifold cares.

Paget's primacy was evident. It was noted by correspondents, who addressed him as 'chief secretary'. Petre himself, sixteen months after his appointment, on his first diplomatic mission, begged for a continuance of his advice and instruction.[13] Indeed, in describing the secretaries' clerical staff, it would not be far from accurate to describe Petre as the chief of staff.

Privy Council or royal letters of importance, which were drafted by Petre, were often corrected by his senior colleague prior to dispatch.[14] When Paget was absent from court, he felt free to write his orders to the other secretary. From the Low Countries in the spring of 1545 he directed to Petre instructions to secure a grant for the lord deputy at Calais and notify him of it 'with some little knock not to be hereafter so list to promise such things without knowledge first of his Majesty's pleasure' or, as he later phrased it, to 'beware another time to promise so large thongs of another man's leather'.[15]

The routine of the signet office has already been described, and it has been shown how Cromwell's reorganisation of the signet left most of the four clerks and four assistants free for other government business. Ordinarily these were joined by the clerks of the Privy Council, Paget's personal retinue, and often by the Latin and French secretaries. On one occasion

Paget complained bitterly to Petre from Calais about the meagreness and public nature of the office space for this large staff and deplored the fact that the king's business could not be written in a more secluded place and under his personal supervision.[16] The full staff was usually reduced when the government was divided between the king's personal following and that part of the Privy Council left in London. The scarcity of existing papers and drafts in Paget's or his clerks' hands during the months he travelled with the king in 1545 suggests this reduction in force had its effect on the efficiency of the filing system practised by his staff.[17]

Paget's personal clerks were headed by his secretary, a Fleming, Nicasius Yetsweirt, who often wrote the routine letters to outlying officials and ambassadors when Paget himself was too busy.[18] Yetsweirt was occasionally sent on a semi-official diplomatic mission and on one of these he was able to invoke the powerful aid of his influential master to procure himself a profitable marriage.[19] The same Nicasius was promoted by Paget to be a clerk of the signet and from that post was advanced to the even more prestigious one of French secretary.[20]

The clerk of the Privy Council, John Mason, served as a principal and trusted assistant to the secretary. He was also called on for such routine tasks as drafting letters. In Paget's temporary absence he took over even more of the correspondence, an event which once left him 'more troubled than my nature can well endure'.[21] The Latin secretary also was at the call of the principal secretary, who referred to him letters to foreign rulers for translation.[22]

Important royal letters or acts of state were examined and checked by Paget prior to royal approval if they had not actually been penned by his own hand. A late Elizabethan story quoted Henry VIII as telling Petre not to brood at his drafts being corrected by the king, 'for it is I, said he, that made both Crumwell, Wriotheslie, and Pagett good secretaries and so must I do to thee. The princes themselves know best their own meaning and there must be time and experience to acquaint them with their humours before a man can do any acceptable service.'[23] These humours Paget learned swiftly for few examples can be found of Henry's bold and sprawling handwriting correcting his drafts.

Many of the secretary's manifold duties and, indeed, much of his far-reaching power had their sources in his intimate relations with his sovereign. Even a complete cipher of a secretary could not fail to be a power in the court as the medium through which the royal will was made known. He was a private secretary to the king as well as a secretary of state. Paget, for example, wrote most of Henry's private instructions to his military commanders. Questions of tactics too secret in nature for conciliar debate were decided by the king and passed on to the commanders by Paget's hand under the seal in his custody.[24] Even Henry's holograph epistles to his royal contemporaries were often drafted in his secretary's hand before being penned in the kingly scrawl.[25]

In both his capacities as private secretary and officer of state, Paget had access to Henry's mail. Paget opened and sorted letters from subjects and officers before reading them aloud to the king.[26] Often a letter to Henry would be accompanied by a note from the writer to Paget asking him not to show the king his letter unless he considered it advisable.[27] Paget was even requested, on occasion, to correct and modify a letter as he thought advisable before showing it to his master. One instance of this occurred early in 1546 when Archbishop Cranmer solicited royal approval of a plan to modify the stringent ceremonial observation of Lent.[28] Indeed, it was a very common practice to include a separate letter to the secretary when writing the king. As the influence of Paget grew, matters intended for the royal ear would be written to Paget alone with a request that he show or read the pertinent portion to Henry.[29]

Thus, as the ageing king relaxed his hold on, if not his control of, government business, the state papers which em-

bodied that business underwent a transition from the letters
and papers of Henry VIII to the letters and papers of William
Paget.

Control of the royal correspondence carried as a natural
corollary the power to speak for the crown with authority by
letter and by word of mouth. It was a very common occur-
rence for Paget to write to a commander in the field, or an
ambassador or agent, that the king had seen his letters and
commended his zeal but desired that certain things be done.
Then would follow the royal commands as expressed in
Paget's words.[30]

These royal instructions were not always based on the king's
specific directions. In September 1544, on his own authority,
Paget refused the Lord Deputy of Calais permission to come
to England on leave, saying that the state of the world would
not permit the secretary honestly to solicit such a licence from
Henry.[31] This power to speak for the sovereign will be illus-
trated frequently in the course of the following chapter. Sym-
bolic of this role as spokesman for the king was the secretary's
ceremonial function at the creation of a peer. The new peer's
letter patent of creation was handed to the king, who delivered
it to his secretary to proclaim aloud.[32]

Paget could act for his ruler because he was close to him in
repeated daily contact and was acquainted with his slightest
wish. The dispatches of foreign ambassadors frequently tell
how the king called the secretary away from a meeting of the
Privy Council to attend him. The imperial ambassador once
wrote his master that the English king, when passing by in his
chair on his travels, sent Paget to give a greeting. It is evident
that from 1544 until his death, Henry never allowed his chief
secretary to stray far from his side.[33] Paget, for his part, was
assiduous in cultivating the royal awareness of his own indispensable talents. In 1546, the little Prince Edward, aged eight
and a half and the apple of his father's eye, mentioned to his
tutor that the chief secretary had given him a little sandbox.
Indeed, he even extended a helping hand to assist the prince

in getting along with his father. A few months later the tutor,
Dr Richard Cox, wrote his 'Gulielme, mihi longe charissime'
to thank him for a friendly warning about the king's dissatisfaction over some unnamed boyish deed of the prince and
promising a reformation on the part of the prince.[34]

Others were aware of the influence of the principal secretary with the king, and showed it by directing a tremendous
volume of mail to Paget soliciting his influence at court and
with the king. One of the earliest examples of this power of
patronage was dated in the late spring of 1544, when he had
been secretary a little over a year. At that time he wrote to his
friend Lord Cobham that he had that very day fulfilled his
promise and had Cobham's patent as Lord Deputy of Calais
passed under the Great Seal.[35] Not all requests from clients
were of such importance. Many of his peers on the Privy
Council would merely solicit his aid in securing a minor office
for a retainer, or acknowledge a royal permission to return to
court, which had been procured with his assistance.[36]

Typical of a missive from an important royal officer was a
letter from the lord deputy in Ireland, Sir Anthony St Leger,
written in the summer of 1545. Sir Anthony in his letter to
Paget was scrupulously careful to explain why he had not
written sooner, excusing himself on the grounds that he had
believed Paget was on the continent. He then explained the
nature of his two suits to the king and solicited aid, mention-
ing the gift of a goshawk on the way to Paget, and closed by
rejoicing that Paget's son was to be married to the daughter of
a kinsman of his.[37] Such friendly little presents from persons
who sought his favour were a pleasant increment to Paget's
other income for they were a constantly recurring event. It is
significant, for instance, that in the midst of a prolonged
correspondence between John Dudley, then Lord Lisle, and
Paget concerning the former's numerous suits to the king in
the winter of 1545–6, Lord Lisle sold Paget a dwelling house
at 'Kayo' (Kew) in Surrey for an unnamed sum. Unfortunately
the records do not reveal whether Paget was successful on

Lisle's behalf in getting the royal 'okay' in return for Kayo![38]

Not all of his favours were inspired or rewarded by presents, however. Paget had a genuine desire to see that his master was well served and that able men in his service were rewarded.[39] His own rapid rise by sheer ability may have strengthened this desire in him, and one of his letters substantiates this hypothesis. In June 1544, while he was in the Rhineland on a mission to the emperor, he wrote to his junior colleague, Petre, urging him to secure some advancement for Nicholas Wotton, the able English ambassador with the emperor. The same letter shows the keen eye with which he noted future vacancies likely to occur which would make offices available for the king's gift. Paget had observed the sickness of another English emissary 'whereby all the physicians of this country have determined that he cannot live' and suggested some of this man's offices for Wotton 'as I think he be already dead or will shortly die'.[40] Less than a month later Wotton was writing gratefully to his patron, having heard from a clerk of Paget's that he had been granted the deanery of York.[41]

In the closing years of Henry's reign when Paget's influence as secretary was at its height, he formed a close and friendly connection with Edward Seymour, brother of the late Queen Jane, who was then Earl of Hertford. This relationship was to be of inestimable profit to them both at Henry's death, but for the time being Paget was able to be of considerable help to the earl. During the war with France, Hertford was frequently away from court with the armies, and his heavy expenses in the service made him a regular suitor for royal financial aid. Paget served as his intermediary. First, he secured a licence for Hertford to import a thousand tuns of wine duty free and also persuaded the king to put pressure on the Bishop of Salisbury to facilitate a land exchange for Hertford. Later he was active in pushing a request for the grant of the college of Beverley in Yorkshire and the college of Leicester. When this request was refused by Henry, Paget substi-

tuted a request for the college of Glassney in Cornwall and
the remission of the royal tenth owed by the earl for his
monastic properties in Devon. The last letter in the long
series over these suits found Paget writing to Hertford ruefully that the king was opposed to the grant, but that he was
continuing to try for a favourable decision.[42]

The stature which his influence with the king gave him
may be summed up with a final example from the early part
of 1546. The University of Cambridge, fearing for its existence because of the new chantries act of Parliament, wrote
three letters to its most influential friends to ask exemption.
It wrote to the Lord Chancellor of England, the High Chancellor of the University, Bishop Gardiner, who was then the
leader of the conservative element in the council, and 'Mr
William Paget'.[43]

Second in importance only to his relationship to the king was
Secretary Paget's connection with the Privy Council. The
secretaries of state were regularly appointed to be councillors
by virtue of their office, which entailed many responsibilities
in the council. The secretary was, first of all, the chief of its
clerical staff. He drafted as letters its decisions, which as a
member he had helped make, and he was responsible for its
files. A strong individual could exploit the role of the secretary as messenger between the king and his council, who
informed each of the other's opinions. Paget, by virtue of his
own talents, also had a great amount of influence over the
council's order of business, and often served as its spokesman
in its meetings with petitioners. This influence, combined
with the steadily increasing sway he held over the ageing King
Henry, gradually brought Paget to a powerful position as the
council's only direct and regular means of contact with the
king—a position comparable to that held by Cromwell and
Wolsey. Paget, however, neither lost his head nor found his
monarch ungrateful for his services in the end.

Of the duties imposed on him by his membership in the

Page 65: William, first Lord Paget of Beaudesert.
Portrait by an unknown artist

Page 66: Edward VI, as Prince of Wales, c 1546-7
by an unknown artist

council, the first was attendance at its meetings. In this respect he was most faithful. For example, of the seventy-one meetings noted in the council register during May, June and July of 1545, Paget was present at sixty-eight. In the last critical months of 1546, just before the king's death, he was present at every meeting.[44] In these many sessions he was kept occupied for they were not concerned solely with the trivia of settling disputes between 'one Fylpott' and his adversary, which the register seems to indicate. It has already been pointed out that the clerk of the council was not admitted to secret conferences. In such cases the labour of keeping notes on council decisions fell to Paget, and no record was made in the clerk's register.[45]

Again, although the clerk of the council handled much of its paperwork, the secretary was charged with the custody of its important documents, of treaties with foreign powers, and diplomatic papers.[46] Less important council papers sometimes strayed into his own private files, for among the Paget papers of the Marquess of Anglesey are a few examples of letters addressed to the council, which he must have carried off.[47] With the supervision of its files, Paget joined a careful attention to the circulation of its incoming mail. He examined and sorted letters to the council before they were taken up by the assembly.[48] In addition he sent letters addressed to the council to absent members beseeching 'your good lordship to return to me both this letter and the other that I sent last being addressed to the Council'.[49]

The council's large volume of outgoing correspondence was also prepared under Paget's supervision. Sufficient examples of original letters or their drafts survive to show that Paget was responsible for many of them. The letters were either drafted in his own hand, or dictated to a clerk and corrected or altered by him to an approved form.[50] In some cases his corrections are intermingled with those of another councillor, but these instances are rare.[51] Apparently the drafting of the letters by the clerks and their review and correction on the

c

part of Paget were completed before the finished product was returned to the council for signature. The appearance from time to time of the words 'me the secretary' in the council's letters clearly indicates the composer.[52] The Privy Council, like all committees, was inclined to say 'let the secretary do it'.

These duties of supervising the clerical staff and the files, and of writing the council's letters, which Paget performed, were part of the routine of his office. These routine duties made him the executive agent of the council just as he was the king's. And this dual role of adviser and councillor of the king, as well as being executor of policy, placed a strong secretary head and shoulders above the other members of the council in knowledge, activity, and in power. Other facets of his relationship with the council depended on his ability to impress his own personality on that body. As he grew more secure in his intimacy with the king and more powerful in the council, it is interesting to note the diminution of the more routine duties performed by Paget. From 1545 only half as many council letters drafted and corrected by him survive as from 1544, and this trend continued in 1546. A doubling and redoubling of the volume of letters addressed to him from local officials and diplomatic agents also occurred during this period, which reflected his increased esteem in the eyes of his countrymen.

One of the ways by which Paget influenced the council was his control of its business agenda. A paper in his junior colleague's writing, probably penned soon after Petre's entry into office, illustrates this control. Of numerous items of customary procedure for a secretary, seven concerned his relationship to the conciliar agenda. On Sunday nights he was to show the king a list of business pending in the council and arrange with him the schedule for the week, the earlier part of the day being reserved for affairs of the realm and answering letters. If a council quorum of four members was not present on any day, it might still meet to open letters and bring them to the king. A group of four to six members might debate subjects but should not reach decisions. If the king desired to be present to hear the council discussion, the secretary would brief the council for the event. No private suits should be permitted on days reserved for affairs of state. If the council adjourned without action on a matter discussed, the secretary noted the progress made with the arguments of each side and read his notes at the next session. If letters of moment arrived or other urgent questions arose, the secretary was empowered to bring them to the attention of the council without regard to the normal agenda.[53] With this control of business it is not surprising that Paget could confidently direct Petre not to bother the king over a money matter but to let the council accomplish it by warrant.[54] It is also possible to understand the freedom with which Paget could schedule an interview with the council for a foreign ambassador.[55]

Once a matter had been brought before the council and discussed, it was usually Paget who referred the collective decision to the king for his approval. Petre's short guide to a secretary's duties mentions that on Friday evening he had to make a summary of the week's business in the council giving a summary of the reasons for its various actions. On Saturday morning it was shown to the king and his decision was sought concerning open questions or his approval secured for conciliar actions.[56] But on important points, the council usually sent some of its members to the king for an immediate decision, as on one occasion in 1544 when the chancellor and Paget were rushed out of the room by the council to consult Henry and return with an answer for the importunate imperial emissary.[57] Paget's increasingly firm hold on Henry's favour and confidence led him to assume this intermediary role to the near exclusion of the other members. It was not that the others had no access to the king. They saw him often enough until his last months of portly immobility and ill-health, but it was natural for them to refer questions for decision by the hand of one who was in constant and favoured daily contact. In December 1546 a foreign ambassador mentioned having seen the whole council except Paget who was with the king.[58] Usually when he returned from the king he was the bearer of instructions for the council. The council saw him serving thus as the royal mouthpiece in July 1546, when he brought the Earl of Arundel from the king to the council and made known the royal pleasure to the lord chancellor that Arundel be sworn as lord chamberlain and privy councillor.[59] Similarly, in January 1547 Thomas Seymour was admitted to the council after Paget had declared it to be the king's desire.[60]

This personal role as intermediary showed up especially clearly at times when the king was away from London and the council divided between his court and Westminster. At such times it was nearly always Secretary Paget who wrote the king's commands to the council in London, either in his own letters or as spokesman for the council with the king.[61] The council in London in return addressed a large proportion of its letters to Paget personally, or included special messages for him in letters to the King's Council.[62]

An illustration of this influential relationship between the royal court and the council in London may be found in a three week period during September 1546. On 6 September, Paget drafted a letter for the King's Council to the London Council giving certain instructions. In transit it crossed a letter to him from Wriothesley, the chief of the London councillors. Four days later three letters reached him, one to the council with the king from the London group, and two to him personally from the individual members in London telling him of their recent activities. On the thirteenth, he wrote to the Earl of Hertford, who had joined the London group, and gave him the king's instructions for a trip to the continent and several missions for the other councillors. On the seventeenth, his private secretary Nicasius, who was passing through London, sent him an account of the financial activities of the London Council fragment, which was followed the next day by a report of its diplomatic business.

Not until the twentieth did the group make its official report in a letter to the council with the king and request approval of several actions taken to supply the Calais garrison.[63] By such tireless and unceasing activity the king's principal secretary kept his finger on the pulse of the government's business.

One of the chief duties of a privy councillor in the sixteenth century was to represent the crown in Parliament. In this respect the secretary did not differ from the other councillors, except that he had duties in the House of Lords as well as in the House of Commons. In the statute of precedence in 1539, the secretary had been given a courtesy rank just below a baron 'at the uppermost part of the woolsacks in the middle of the house'.[64] They regularly received special writs of summons to the House of Lords as did the judges and other legal advisers of the crown. In 1540, it was decided that the two secretaries should divide their time between the two houses, sitting alternately, so that one might always be present in each house.[65] Paget, however, found his parliamentary duties light in Henry's reign. During much of the session of Parliament which met in the autumn of 1545, he was in the Low Countries on a diplomatic errand, though he regretted his absence when he read Petre's account 'of the most godly, wise and kingly oration' which Henry made to this Parliament. 'I wish myself bound to have eaten fish this twelve-month (as ill as it is for me) upon condition that I had heard [it] ... whereat I am sure mine eyes would largely have uttered the affections of mine heart, hearing it expressed *tam florida et viva voce* as I know His Majesty can, and I doubt not did, when that reading your recital but of a piece of it my heart doth yearn. Our Lord save him, good King, and make his subjects good.'[66] In spite of this florid and effusive expression of desire to attend Parliament, he had little opportunity for and showed no tendencies towards that manipulation of parliamentary business in which his predecessor Cromwell had surpassed.

In the sphere of domestic affairs, also, Paget was less influential or interested than Cromwell had been. The secretary's duties included a vague responsibility for the domestic tranquillity of the kingdom and ultimately for the safety of the king's person. This idea was a natural outgrowth of his work as the executive agent of the government and of his peculiar knowledge, through his intelligence system at home and abroad. Even the early Tudors had often made use of the secretary along with other councillors to examine suspects, and Paget was frequently concerned with this activity. All these domestic affairs might be classified together as that part of his duties over which the modern home secretary holds sway.[67]

Where Cromwell had maintained a close and constant alertness to every phase of these domestic concerns, Paget was only occasionally active. Although he was concerned for the royal safety at Boulogne in the summer of 1544, it was rather as one of several privy councillors than as a chief guardian of the king's person.[68] Only two examples can be found of his issuing instructions for the apprehension and custody of domestic prisoners,[69] and in both these instances he was acting at the behest of the king, rather than at his own initiative. Perhaps the best illustration of his duties in the treatment of domestic prisoners was his share as a councillor in the celebrated case of Anne Askew in the summer of 1545.

After the unfortunate lady had been sentenced to the stake for heresy, the council attempted with the rack and with other less concrete arguments to persuade her both to name her allies and to recant and save herself. After the others had tried and failed to move her, Paget had his turn. Following an introduction in which he insinuated that she could always withdraw her recantation once it had served its turn, he tried theological arguments and quoting scripture only to be overwhelmed with a flood of quotations by the prisoner on her side.[70] The episode illustrates the quality in Paget which made his colleagues regard him in later years with suspicion

—his practicality of views which subordinated religious doctrines to the immediate question. One can perhaps ascribe part of this view to a kindly streak in his nature which sought to avoid heedless cruelty. Paget revealed the same practical nature in the autumn of the same year when the council discussed dismissing a Spanish mercenary for having stated in the heat of an argument that the English were all heretics. Paget successfully urged the folly of weighing too heavily words spoken in passion and secured the mercenary's retention in the English service.[71]

In another celebrated state trial only a few months later he again played an important part as secretary and councillor. When the Earl of Surrey and his father, the Duke of Norfolk, were imprisoned by their enemies in December 1547, Paget was a key figure in bringing Surrey to trial and to the block. Several of the depositions of key witnesses were written down under his supervision—and, perhaps, dictation—and he was a member of the commission which sat in judgement at the trial. Paget was one of the two councillors who interrogated Norfolk in order to gather evidence against the duke and his son.[72] This complex role as privy councillor to the government which prosecuted the case, as secretary and head of the clerical staff which assembled the documents for the prosecution, and as a judge in the trial, was typical of the age and goes far to explain the usual verdict of guilty with which the state trials ended. Indictment could not fail to be tantamount to conviction when those responsible for law and order themselves tried offenders against their rules.

The one area of domestic business in which Paget did take a very active part was in the vital field of finance. By virtue of the royal confidence in his ability, he was associated with the chancellor, Lord Wriothesley, in a general supervision of the government revenue and its disbursement from the early summer of 1544 until the death of the king three years later. The pressing nature of this assignment became increasingly evident as the war with France dragged on, at a staggering cost to England. It was to this conflict that Wriothesley and Paget owed their initial appointment, for the lord treasurer, who would normally have carried out these duties, was the Duke of Norfolk. However, he was Henry's best general and was employed accordingly at the head of the army in France. Both men were, in fact, acting for the Privy Council and constituted an ex-officio committee on finance. They might write orders to the English financial agents as personal letters or in the form of Privy Council letters. Similarly, they received mail addressed to the council or to themselves as individuals.[73] Inevitably this led to overlapping of duties between the two men, but it caused surprisingly little confusion. Many of Wriothesley's letters to Paget of 1545 are preserved in the Public Record Office and bear witness to the care which they gave to the problem of keeping in constant touch.[74] Their principal subordinate, the English financial agent in Antwerp, Stephen Vaughan, often wrote duplicate letters to the two in order to further unify their operations.[75]

Before the war with France began, the king and his council had accumulated a substantial reserve of treasure from subsidies and forced loans. But Paget and Wriothesley had estimated the cost of the summer campaign of 1544 at £250,000 and it actually consumed £650,000.[76] The shortage was made up in a number of ways. Wriothesley supervised a royal squeezing of the Bishop of Bath and Wells, whose 'generosity' was imitated by other unhappy donors. Paget was involved in scouting the prospect of confiscating all debts due English merchants in the Low Countries.[77] Most of the funds were raised from three sources, however. The coinage was debased, a loan was secured in Antwerp, and large sales of monastic lands were made.[78]

Both Paget and Wriothesley participated in the land sales. In March 1544, the first great commission for such sales was issued to Wriothesley and three other councillors authorising them to sell crown lands and lead from monastic roofs. In

January 1545 Paget and Secretary Petre were added to the commission, and from that date Paget's name occurred with increasing frequency on the documents of sale.[79]

In carrying out the emergency measures of debasing the coinage and borrowing money abroad, the two financial directors effected a rough division of their duties. Wriothesley, bound by his duties as chancellor to the vicinity of Westminster, assumed direction of London transactions, including supervision of the mint and the coinage, of short-term loans from the mint, of the government's loans from English merchants, and of the mechanics of transferring coin from the Low Countries to England through those merchants.[80] He shared with Paget the general oversight of procuring military supplies from abroad,[81] and of furnishing funds for the English armies and garrisons. Paget remained with the king, except when he was sent abroad as a special ambassador or peace commissioner, to supervise the negotiations for foreign loans, the co-ordinating of fiscal policy and military disbursements, and the receipt and auditing of accounts.

In arranging foreign loans, Paget worked closely with Vaughan, the English agent in the Antwerp money market, and received regular reports from him.[82] On occasion, he negotiated directly with foreign lenders, but ordinarily Vaughan was his channel to the Fuggers and other continental bankers.[83] Vaughan rendered faithful service under trying conditions. Only once was he reprimanded by Paget for promising the king more than he could perform.[84] He requested and received many favours from Paget for his honest and burdensome efforts. They ranged from the apprehension of an immoral maidservant in the Vaughan household to the furthering of his matrimonial suit to an English widow and courtesies to her by Lady Paget.[85]

The provision of funds for the armies and garrisons on the Scottish border was a duty which fell to Paget. He received periodic accounts of their expenses and needs. Wriothesley ordinarily performed this service for English forces in France, but in 1546 Paget became more active in that area.[86] He was already deeply involved in the hiring of German mercenaries, who were even more expensive than Englishmen, since much of their pay came directly from Vaughan at Antwerp.[87] It was a most exasperating duty. Armies in the sixteenth century were, if possible, more insatiable financially than those of four centuries later, and the exasperated Paget often referred to his country's defenders as 'blood suppers [sic]'.[88] The expenditure of money was normally effected by a Privy Council warrant to the appropriate treasurer, but on at least one occasion Paget directed Vaughan to disburse money and only secured the warrant after the payment was made.[89]

It has been mentioned that Wriothesley shared with Paget an interest in the provision of military supplies from abroad. Paget's concern was from a fiscal point of view, as many of the payments were made from the agent in Antwerp.[90] His knowledge of supply problems was improved by his close friendship with Bishop Gardiner, who was acting as purveyor general of rations for the armies, and who regarded his former protégé with great affection. Paget's fiscal duties also involved him in supervising the auditing of accounts, which gave him control of the government's principal check on the honesty of its financial agents. He not infrequently included himself on these commissions.[91]

The careful and active supervision of matters financial by Wriothesley and Paget suffered from only one handicap. There was simply not enough money to finance the war effort. England had scraped through the campaign of 1544, which brought Henry his cherished Boulogne victory, but the treasury was exhausted. Late that year, Paget estimated that the first half of the next year would require an outlay of £104,000. The subsidy would bring in £100,000 of which £40,000 was owed in Flanders. Thus, he felt only £64,000 was lacking.[92] He believed it should be raised by a large-scale benevolence, since this was faster than relying on a parliamentary grant. Henry adopted the idea.[93] Unfortunately for Paget's optimism, the war cost more than he anticipated. A reverse in Scotland required a major effort there; Boulogne cost twice as much as expected, and the frantic preparation of three armies and a fleet to counter the French invasion threat completed the ruin of his estimates. The total cost for the year came to £560,000.

Desperate expedients were tried. Land sales were redoubled. Chantry and collegiate foundations were confiscated by the king in Parliament. The coinage was debased anew, and nearly £67,000 borrowed from the mint, which Wriothesley called 'our holy anchor'. Paget supervised negotiations for huge loans abroad, desperately offering to borrow at 10, 12, 14 or even 16 per cent. A large sum was raised, but part of it had to be accepted in jewels at an inflated valuation in order to secure the loans.[94] Vaughan also arranged, at Paget's instigation, to exchange English lead for alum from Spain, thus avoiding the obstacle of a cash transaction.[95] Every potential source of revenue was exploited or investigated. Paget even seriously considered the confiscation of silver from all the parish churches throughout the land.[96]

It was not surprising that this continued strain had its effect on dispositions. Poor Wriothesley became increasingly lugubrious in his letters, while Paget grew more and more testy. One cannot help sympathising with the former, who saw his painfully accumulated balances continually dissipated by royal orders, in Paget's hand, for enormous expenditures. In spite of his continuing plaints that the treasury was 'swept clean', and one that ended 'God help us; for, for mine own part, it maketh me weary of life', he continued to be called on.[97] Finally a letter of his denouncing Paget's blithe demands for money evoked an embittered and venomous retort from the secretary. Wriothesley in a handsome letter, however, apologised and enlisted Lady Paget on his side to restore harmony.[98]

But the worst of the financial crisis was over. By June of 1546 there was peace with France, and sufficient money was coming in from the parliamentary grants of 1545 to meet current expenses. The French payments for Boulogne further eased the situation later in the year.[99] It was time to survey the damage.

In April 1546 a special commission of Wriothesley, Paget, Petre, Gardiner, and several other councillors was appointed to examine the state of the revenue, the debts, and all accounts to ascertain the financial status of the realm. The commission found debts to foreign bankers amounted to nearly £150,000. About half of the debt was extended to a later date, while some of it was refinanced among English merchants. A substantial portion, almost a third of it, was repaid during the year.[100] Thus, Henry found himself at the end of the year with an empty treasury, a debased coinage, and with considerable debts abroad, but with his credit still fairly sound. As for Paget, he had realised painfully how vital to the government was a sound financial policy, and in this subject he maintained an intense interest thereafter.

In summarising these phases of Paget's secretaryship, it can be said that his work as custodian of the signet and chief of administration for the government maintained the wide influence which Cromwell's regime had established for the secretary in this field. As a channel of influence and of access to the king, Paget, through the increasing favour with which Henry regarded him, reached a position of power second only to those truly *prime* ministers, Cromwell and Wolsey. His position as the Privy Council's executive agent and as a royal favourite enabled him to exercise great influence in that body without arousing the hatred of the other councillors which an omnipotent minister always stirred up. In relation to Parliament neither opportunity nor inclination was present with which to manipulate that body, while in domestic affairs Paget confined his attention primarily to financial matters. But what of his field of paramount interest and activity, the foreign policy of his government?

CHAPTER FIVE

PRINCIPAL SECRETARY
OF STATE : PART TWO

THE most important field of a secretary's duties and the one on which Paget concentrated his abundant energy was the conduct of foreign policy. The principal secretary was the chief of his king's foreign service. In this capacity he had four major areas of duty. They were: the operation of a central government office for the foreign service, the control of the corps of English ambassadors abroad, the supervision of and liaison with the foreign diplomatic corps in England, and the operation of a far-flung espionage and intelligence system. In all of these fields Paget was deeply involved.

Maintaining an administrative headquarters for the foreign service involved many duties. The most essential of these was serving as a personal medium of communication between the king and council and the English emissaries abroad for the conveyance of news and dissemination of information and instructions. The liaison was a natural outgrowth of the secretary's membership and regular attendance at the Privy Council and his daily contact with the king.

Such matters as the reception of distinguished foreign visitors and ambassadors also came within his province. Details of such receptions were arranged by the great master of the household, but, once the dignitary had been received, it was the secretary who arranged his audience with the king, and who negotiated with him both as head of the foreign service and as a councillor. Lesser luminaries not entitled to full honours were received and entertained by the chief secretary.[1]

A closely related duty was dispatching and receiving letters of introduction and recommendation. Paget only occasionally commended someone to the hospitality of English officers abroad or suggested them for employment. But he was continually in receipt of letters of this sort himself. He was forced to write to the Lord Deputy of Calais, 'My lord, I beseech you send over no more strangers...' However, a continuous stream of foreign adventurers, mercenaries, artillerymen, mariners, and inventors continued to arrive equipped with introductions to the busy Paget.[2] The secretary had sufficient occupation with issuing passports for travel abroad as the council's administrative agent.[3] Other visitors were a great nuisance.

Paget's office was also responsible for supervising the government postal and courier system. The secretary was its most frequent user, and Paget held the title of master of the posts jointly with John Mason, the French secretary. His appointment to this office in November 1545 gave Paget an immediate as well as a general control over the posts.[4] The two men divided the fee of 100 marks of the office. They were empowered to appoint thirty regular posts to operate the relay stations on designated routes, and they controlled the two regular royal couriers.[5]

The postal system was the nucleus of Paget's communication system with English ambassadors and agents abroad. A courier might be sent as far as southern Germany with dispatches to an ambassador, travelling by relays of post horses to Dover, and from there financing his travel out of an advance allowance from the secretary. Ambassadors also had an allowance for such expenses with which to pay couriers' return passages.[6] For messages of major importance the secretary had the services of lesser officers of the college of arms available and could employ a herald or pursuivant to carry such items.[7]

To every ambassador at his distant post, Paget was a sponsor, adviser, and friend, as well as a chief to be constantly informed of developments. Before he left for his station, his instructions were very likely drafted in Paget's hand, embodying the king's policy for the new minister. Any changes in policy or added instructions were written in the same hand either as letters from Paget personally or from the king or the council. Even the ciphers in which secret matters were discussed were made and assigned by the secretary.[8]

All ambassadors were required to make frequent reports. As Paget informed one, the more he wrote the better the king liked it, for Henry became restless if many days passed without news. This requirement was generally fully carried out. Normally an emissary sent two letters together at each opportunity, an official report addressed to the king or his council, and a personal letter to Paget. On occasion the same mail might bring these letters, one to each address, but the secretary had initial access to both.[9] A vague but essential custom differentiated between the content of the different letters. A report to the king or council would contain a factual description of the principal negotiations conducted, with detail on ceremonies, compliments, and other sovereigns' appearances for the king, and any major news items from the court at which the writer served. Such matters were suitable for an official report.[10] A letter to Paget was another type. In it might be included the ambassador's advice or recommendations, his speculations on future events, routine news items, rumours or gossip current at his post, excuses for shortcomings, and requests for instructions on minor points of policy.[11] A letter to the king or one to Paget was more secret than one to the Privy Council, and it could be used to bypass that body. Indeed, on one occasion the king and Paget gave oral instructions to the commander at Boulogne contradicting a council letter and directing him to rase a French fortification by night.[12]

Every ambassador took pains to write to Paget even more frequently than to the king or the council. If by chance he missed a mail, he usually explained the omission in his next letter.[13] For an ambassador was dependent in his turn on the principal secretary for news from home. The king's emissaries in France, in the Low Countries, and with the emperor, his financial agents abroad, and any special agents were, like the military commanders, receivers of periodic news-letters from Paget or his personal secretary, which summarised the latest events in England. Any delay in these news-letters was usually the subject of immediate plaintive notes in the would-be recipient's next letter.[14]

Secretary Paget was also the principal source of aid in any of the numerous problems which beset an ambassador. Financial difficulties were numerous. Often a minister's salary would be long overdue when the government was short of cash. Paget was the first to hear of such a crisis and usually managed to speed the action of the disbursing authorities. When an ambassador's expenses for travel soared as he trailed an itinerant emperor, Paget secured him an increase in pay.[15] Expediting salaries was not the only help for which he was asked. Permission to export horses or provisions from England were eagerly sought by agents for their own use or profit. Stephen Vaughan's marital problems and the secretary's assistance have been mentioned, but, even earlier, he had successfully cried for help in an emergency. When Vaughan's first wife's illness was known to be fatal, he wrote Paget an urgent request for licence to return to her side, and the normally ponderous wheels of government were speeded to give him the desired permit within two weeks. A grant of office or a land purchase from the crown could often be furthered by a timely ambassadorial appeal to Paget, who frequently received such requests. The tremendous opportunities for the acquisition of land and offices open to an official near the king were available to an emissary only through his friend or superior on the scene.[16]

In return, Paget used the services of the king's officers abroad to do Lady Paget's and his own shopping for rare items of merchandise. This was particularly true of the financial agents and ambassadors in the Low Countries. The former were often merchants by profession on whose judgement of anything from horseflesh to crimson velvet or the best grain he could rely.[17] Ambassadors, on the other hand, being perhaps more learned and sophisticated, were employed as sources of fine wine, drugs, and fine plumes.[18] They were also better able to secure licences from the government to which they were accredited for export of restricted items. The Paget household, therefore, was well furnished with foreign products. Its master slept in an imported nightgown, while his lady was attired in sables and damask from abroad. The fireplace was furnished with imported latten and irons and tools and its chimney was tiled with tiles from Antwerp. His tables was graced with £250 value of silver service stamped with his arms, and on it could be found imported delicacies and vintages from his wine-cellar.[19]

The foreign diplomatic corps in England also had a special relationship to the secretary. It was clearly shown in their repeated contacts with him, indicating that they were aware of his activity as foreign secretary. At his arrival, a new emissary might be welcomed by the secretary and other councillors, but his formal audience with Henry was arranged through the secretary. At any occasion which arose subsequently necessitating an interview with the king, he must apply to Secretary Paget for his appointment. Or if Henry desired the ambassador, it was Paget who summoned him and escorted him to and from the king's presence.[20] He was able to advise the emissaries on the royal disposition and to warn them against bringing up dangerous subjects at an inopportune moment. He was normally present during the interview.[21] It was understood that minor points would not be the subject of a meeting with the king but could be discussed with Paget or the council. Paget used this custom to the maximum extent he was able in order to spare the king during his last months of increasing debility.[22]

All of the routine aspects of an emissary's relation to the court were handled by the secretary. If he had complaints about his lodgings at court, he aired them to the secretary, who could see that the court officials improved his lot. If the court was on a royal progress, the matter of lodgings became more important, as housing was then at a premium.[23] An emissary's use of the king's horses for travel also had to be secured through the ubiquitous Paget. A constant flow of selected news releases garnered from abroad was also forthcoming from Paget, in return for which the emissaries, too, would pass items of propaganda to the secretary.[24] Upon completion of an emissary's assignment, the secretary arranged for the royal permission to depart and the formal concluding interview. The king's customary present to the departing ambassador was likewise arranged and sometimes presented by Paget.[25]

Numerous instances might be cited concerning the role of Secretary Paget in negotiations conducted between his government and the representatives of foreign rulers in England. Suffice it to say that in any discussion between the Privy Council and the ambassador, he was present as a spokesman. If a few of the council were commissioned to confer apart with an emissary, he was almost invariably one of them. The multiplicity of private conferences between Paget and the various ambassadors testifies abundantly both to his grasp of his master's policy and to his control of the machinery by which it was put into effect.[26]

Continual and close relationship of this sort with Paget gave ambassadors an excellent chance to further their own sovereign's affairs. It also gave the secretary an equal chance to establish an influence over an ambassador who might serve Henry well. An unusual instance of this was his exploitation of the imperial ambassador, Francis Vanderdelft, who was accredited to the English king in December 1544.

Vanderdelft was a much less able man than his predecessor and in a few months had been completely charmed by Paget, with the result that he became progressively more inclined to accept Paget's version of events. For one thing, he spoke little or no English and thus was less able to judge events around him.[27] The secretary turned on his charm. He began to speak confidently and unofficially to Vanderdelft, giving him the 'inside story' on all events and assuring him continually of Henry's sincere and abiding passion for his alliance with the emperor.[28] The fascinated emissary believed that Paget was a staunch upholder of religious conservatism at a time when the secretary was already secretly allied to a radical element in the council.[29] In the midst of their negotiations on various items, Paget would laugh at Vanderdelft's wit or enjoy secret jokes with him about France's war potential.[30] The ambassador's reports to his sovereign simultaneously reflected his growing esteem for Paget and revealed his credulous nature. Even Vanderdelft admitted that his sole source of information on affairs diplomatic was the secretary. This caused him no alarm for he was convinced that Paget was the key man in the English government and was flattered by his friendship.[31] Such a situation was an immense advantage to the English government but, in the next reign, it became embarrassing to Paget, who was reproached by Vanderdelft for acts of state over which the naive emissary erroneously thought him still all-powerful!

The secretary's duty as chief of the national intelligence service is easy to establish but impossible to unravel. The network of information sources over which he presided may be likened to a ladder leading down into a murky pit. At the top of it were the king's several ambassadors abroad—in plain sight and serving as gatherers of information. Just a few rungs lower was the agent, whether one with a permanent station or a roving retainer, and he too was recognisable as the king's man, though less clearly. Farther down still and only occasionally recognisable as part of the chain was the pensioner, and behind him, in complete obscurity, the spy, professional or amateur.

The central headquarters and consolidation point for all items of intelligence was naturally the secretary's office. He saw all correspondence.[32] He had the regular reports of the king's ambassadors to give him a framework of information about other countries and the policies against which to evaluate the tit-bits which came in from the less reliable sources. The ambassadors were continually alert to pick up new sources and place them in contact with Paget, as well as to gather information. The English commanders of Calais and Boulogne also fitted into his intelligence system. They had funds for local military espionage in the parts of France near them, but took pains to advise the secretary of the gleanings.[33] Army commanders in Scotland followed the same practice.

In France during the war, only spies could furnish on-the-scene information, although neutral travellers might supply some news. One of these spies, an obscure man named Hance Garbrand of Lille, was ordered on a mission by the commander of Boulogne at the request of the English admiral, but his report of discoveries, significantly enough, was made to the secretary.[34] In Italy, Paget and his king could depend for information on pensioned agents of England, like the notorious Ludovico da l'Armi, who was in perpetual difficulties with the Venetian government. But any source which had or claimed to have access to papal secrets was welcomed with open arms.[35] With German information the situation was much the same. For nearly fifteen years Henry had retained the scholarly Dr Christopher Mount as a roving source of information on the affairs of the Protestant powers. Paget himself during his diplomatic apprenticeship had worked with him as a special agent to the Protestant princes. Other less savoury characters were employed in the area too. An Italian gentleman of fortune, Antonio de Musica, who initially entered Paget's pay at £75 as an expert on Italy, was a trial as well as an aid. His reports were regular, but he was a spendthrift and, when well primed with wine, would 'tell all, and more than is true'.[36]

Scotland was another hostile country in which the spy must be employed, but it differed from France in having a large group of nobles who by conviction or greed favoured Henry above their rulers. Paget's papers are full of news items reaching him through these dissidents.[37] One of the more interesting Scots traitors in Henry's pay was a John Drummond, a servant of the Earl of Angus, who from the Low Countries supplied a steady flow of intercepted mail between France, Rome and Scotland, including the very letters in which those governments indicate their distrust and suspicion of him.[38] Not all of the sources of intelligence from Scotland were venal, however. At least some of them were moved by religious zeal and anti-papal sentiments to join forces with the English.[39]

Secretary Paget was fully as concerned with foiling enemy espionage agents as he was with planting his own. His indefatigable scribe, Stephen Vaughan, in Antwerp, supplied him with many hair-raising spy scares from the neutral financial centre, which continually seethed with rumours. French agents were said to be scouting English harbours; the mercenaries garrisoning Calais were plotting its betrayal, or the magazines of Boulogne were being mined. Paget was sceptical of many of these 'plots', for he was aware that a number of the tipsters were interested in the fat rewards they could secure with imaginary plots. A careful background and identity check of one such informer revealed that he was a French agent.[40] Not all leads, however, were false. The lucky capture at sea of a Scottish priest and a tip from an imperial employee gave Paget the names of two French agents in England, who made their headquarters within a stone's throw of Old St Paul's.[41]

This system of haphazard counter-intelligence had its failures. One of the most outstanding was the case of a Frenchman, Jean de Fontenay, Sieur de Bertheville, who was employed by the English. He must have been an intriguing lad in his personality as well as in his habits, for Paget thought highly of him. Bertheville was technically a traitor to France, since his country was at war with England, but several of his family either joined him in England or supplied news from France. They were all put on the payroll. Bertheville received £150 a year and his brother £100. Bertheville's service was judged so worthy that he was granted the reversion of his brother's pension.[42] After the peace with France, however, Bertheville began to play both sides and to ingratiate himself secretly with the French ambassador, De Selve. He began to reveal the names of other traitors in France, who figured in possible future English planning. He promised to bribe one of Paget's clerks to betray secretarial confidences, and he began to communicate with the French government under a code name. Suggestively—and erroneously—he informed De Selve that he was receiving 1,400 crowns a year from Henry and implied that Francis could do no less. Nevertheless, the ambassador was highly suspicious of his man and watched him narrowly. His past service to them rendered the French more suspicious than Paget.[43]

As chief of the king's foreign service and as a skilled diplomat, Paget was required to go on five special embassies during his secretaryship under Henry. This was a duty which came even to less influential secretaries. Sir William Petre, for example, Paget's junior colleague, who was completely overshadowed by him, ran at least two diplomatic errands during the same period, but these were admittedly minor affairs. The imperial ambassador was worried about a French–English rapprochement and possible alliance when he heard of a meeting at Calais between commissioners appointed by each country. He was completely reassured when told that Petre was leading the English delegation, for, as he explained to his superiors, no such major item would be treated by such a low-powered delegation.[44] But an important diplomatic errand or a special mission would very often require Paget's knowledge of 'practices', as the gambits of diplomacy were called.

One of the first of these missions was assigned him in May 1544, just after the completion of his first year as secretary. Henry had declared war on France the previous year but had left the fighting that season principally to his ally, the emperor. The year 1544 was to be his great campaign year. All that early spring he and his council had been busy with planning the campaign. Paget had been kept occupied writing down the plans for the war and writing necessary orders to local commanders.[45] Henry intended first to launch a seaborne attack on the Scots, to burn Edinburgh, and to paralyse their military potential before leading an invading army from Calais into France in order to fulfil himself his treaty obligations to the emperor. Paget was appointed to go to the emperor and inform him of Henry's plans.

On 18 May he paid a call on the imperial ambassador, Eustace Chapuys, to inform him of the purpose of the visit and to prepare the ground for it. Because of his poor health, Henry desired to extricate himself gracefully from his treaty obligations to lead his army into France, so Paget persuaded Chapuys to join Henry's council in 'urging' this course on Henry and in securing the emperor's consent. Paget stated that he was charged to reveal to Charles V a French peace overture and Henry's flat rejection of it. But the most important part of his mission he kept for the emperor alone.[46]

Armed with his credentials, he set out for Brussels, where he made his first stop to visit the Regent of the Netherlands, Mary of Hungary, and to tell her about the French overture. He began his remarks by lauding Henry's successes in Scotland and then informed her of the date Henry's armies would move against France and what supplies she should furnish.[47] By the twenty-fourth, he was again on his way up the Rhine valley to Spires, travelling as fast as his waggon would convey him.[48]

Within four days he had arrived and had audiences with the emperor and with his principal minister. After boasting about Henry's triumph over the Scots, he reassured Charles about the French overture to Henry by showing him the entire correspondence. As to Henry's desire to evade going to war in person, there was some cautious sparring. Charles was more than willing to agree to Henry's absence but refused to give up his own plan of leading his army in person in order to spare the English monarch's pride. The real purpose of Paget's trip, discreetly unveiled, was to suggest a new campaign plan by which each monarch with a smaller army might wage war on the borders while detaching raiding expeditions into France. To this Paget secured a partial approval. The emperor agreed to Henry's reduced force, but refused to change his own plan to advance on Paris. He would send an emissary to Henry to 'persuade' him to stay home from the wars. The door was thus left open for Henry to campaign as he wished and thereafter to claim in justification that the emperor had agreed to it beforehand.[49] The mission had been a success.

The trip home was less pleasant for Paget. He paused at Antwerp on 8 June and involved himself in the complex problem of hiring mercenaries for his king. The sole result was that some haggling and stalling of one of the mercenary leaders infuriated Paget to the point where he persuaded the king and council to dismiss this man for insolence to the king's agent.[50] After journeying on to Brussels, where he courteously declined to interrupt the regent's hunting trip, he passed the Channel via Calais and reached London on the twelfth where he gave the council an account of his swift travels and concise negotiations.[51] That his acts were approved may be assumed from the fact that both the king and council dispensed with their indefatigable secretary for three days while he visited his Drayton house for a well-earned rest.[52]

His brief vacation over, he plunged into the thick of the feverish activity of a court preparing for battle. After numerous delays Henry was going to war and his secretary with him. There were many preparations to make, however, and Paget was busier than ever before. He served as one of three commissioners to negotiate a marriage alliance with the Scottish Earl of Lennox which would strengthen the northern borders.[53] He toiled away over numerous drafts of a commission of regency for Queen Katharine Parr and the many other commissions for her advisers and officers.[54] And still the regular business of the king was carried out—orders to the local commanders, letters to the ambassadors, conferences with the imperial emissaries, and the levying of troops and of money. At last all the preparations were completed and the corpulent but belligerent king, guarded by an ample escort and accompanied by Paget and a few councillors, landed at Calais on 14 July.[55]

Paget had all of the zeal for war that might be expected of a well-to-do and healthy patriot in his late thirties. He had provided himself with a gaudy set of plumes, patterned on the king's decorations, to ornament himself and his retinue, and was all set to enjoy a taste of campaigning—from a comfortable spot on the king's staff.[56] He and the other councillors, Gardiner and Rich, bustled about Calais preparing for the king's advance to the English siege camp before Boulogne, where they located a suitable headquarters safely out of range of French artillery.[57]

Paget's own contingent of one hundred footmen rarely saw their doughty leader for they were a part of the force besieging Boulogne. But he himself, presumably armed and plumed to the teeth, was a part of the colourful procession which escorted the king from Calais to Boulogne on 25 July. 'First the drums and fifers, then the trumpets, then the officers of arms, then the barons, then Mr Garter next before the King's banner, then the Duke of Albuquerque, then the Earl of Rutland bearing the King's banner displayed, then the King's Majesty armed at all pieces upon a great courser...'[58]

But life in camp proved to be little different from the routine at Westminster or Hampton Court. Paget had 20s a day allowance. He drafted more orders to the besiegers and to the covering forces at Montreuil for his king and assisted the monarch and council in deciding tactical questions. But the main burden of his own work continued to be the supervision of English diplomacy.[59]

Diplomacy was to be even more important than armies to Henry VIII. Coincident with his invasion of France and siege of Boulogne was the imperial campaign along the Marne in which Charles V was pressing deeper and deeper into France. Together the two rulers could crush the French, but neither trusted the other. Each was receiving simultaneous separate peace offers from Francis and the problem of liaison between them was becoming more and more difficult.

Paget was invaluable at this critical time. He remained on close terms with the imperial emissaries, Chapuys and De Courrieres, telling them just enough of the French offers to reassure them that Henry was not making a separate peace. At the same time, the French agent was examined and re-turned to his master with a refusal to negotiate—drafted by Paget—which still left the door open for peace talks.[60] Both Henry and Charles initially repulsed the French offers and made a great show of their firm alliance. Then each began suggesting to the other that he should negotiate a peace with France which should include every claim of the other. The emperor received a list of Henry's demands which he thought exorbitant, while Henry felt the emperor's list should be arranged in order of preference. From there it was only a very few steps to 'every man for himself'.[61]

A French peace delegation came to negotiate with each sovereign. The one to Henry was led by Cardinal Du Bellay and made handsome offers to England for a peace which would isolate the emperor. They were authorised to promise money to the influential English councillors, especially to Paget.[62] The group negotiating with the emperor had offered him good terms, and he sent a trusted adviser, the young Bishop of Arras, to secure Henry's approval for their acceptance. Arras went back to the emperor saying that Henry agreed to the separate peace, which Henry denied heatedly afterwards, and the emperor swiftly concluded a peace with France.[63] The French commission negotiating with Gardiner, Paget, and the various other English councillors quickly broke off negotiations, and Henry was left alone in a war with France which each side hoped to end to its advantage.[64]

Henry was tired of campaigning. On 30 September he embarked for England, accompanied by Paget. The rest of the council stayed on at Boulogne to supervise the garrison and prepare for the winter. The English king was resolved to retain his conquest, Boulogne, even if he had to continue the war to do so. A double diplomatic offensive was undertaken —to compel the emperor to assist Henry by menacing the French with a new war and to force the French to accept a peace which would leave Boulogne to Henry.[65] Paget and his friend, the Earl of Hertford, were sent back across the Channel to head a delegation including Gardiner and two other councillors in the operation of this plan.[66]

The two hostile delegations met in mid-October with a neutral delegation headed by the Bishop of Arras and began to sound out each other. Paget had received private instructions from Henry to renew the old treaties of friendship with the French if he found them inclined towards Henry's peace terms. However, he soon found that they would not give up Boulogne. Cardinal Du Bellay, for his part, strove to convince Paget of the emperor's ill-will towards England—with similar lack of success.[67] The English king attempted to apply pressure to the French by sending Hertford and Gardiner to Charles, demanding his support as an ally. But any imperialist pressure was of no avail as Charles would not make a new war for Henry and the French knew it. The French commissioners broke off the negotiations and departed, leaving Paget to salvage what advantage he could by revealing to Arras all the French offers to him at the emperor's expense.[68] In mid-November, Paget and his colleagues returned to England to continue the war.[69]

An alternative diplomatic programme was already being

mapped out. Even before his return to England, Paget advised
that new approaches be made to the German Protestant
princes as an insurance against the emperor's new coolness
towards Henry.[70] This was in the tradition of Thomas Cromwell and quite in accord with Henry's ideas of diplomacy, so a
couple of discreet agents were sent to the Landgrave of Hesse
to suggest that England might be willing to join the Protestant
League. Even Paget's happy thought of altering the standard
proposal to suggest that the alliance should precede any
attempt at religious conformity failed to tempt the stout
Lutheran elector.[71] But, at least, discussions had been launched, and the Landgrave had offered to furnish mercenaries to
aid England in fighting France. This was doubly valuable
because of a crisis in Anglo-Imperial relations which was
growing hourly more acute.

The prime cause of difficulty was the question of neutral
trade. Henry's ships and privateers had been seizing ships
from the Low Countries carrying victuals or munitions to
France. As early as December 1544, this fact caused the
emperor to react as though he 'taketh a little pepper in the
nose'. Early in January, he ordered an embargo on all English
merchants restricting their persons and impounding their
assets as a guarantee of the release of his own subjects' ships
and cargoes.[72]

Henry was at once indignant and alarmed. Paget and Hertford had already started to inform the imperial ambassadors
that some of the arrested neutrals were being released when
the word of Charles's vigorous action came. For a few panicky
moments, when no further word came from the Low Countries, Henry and Paget feared that all the communications
were cut and Charles was preparing for war. But a few days
later they were reassured and concentrated on preparing a
strong protest to Charles for the seizure of English property.[73]
All the imperial property was released, but Charles had the
English in a corner. This was his opportunity to secure redress
for many ancient disputed seizures stretching back over several

years, and he proposed to make use of it.

A special effort was called for on the part of Henry. He made it by sending Secretary Paget as a special ambassador to negotiate a settlement of the commercial impasse which was threatening to rupture the Anglo-Imperial treaty of friendship. His instructions were drafted largely by his own hand and gave him discretionary latitude unusual for an English ambassador. He was required to state the English grievances, to ascertain what the emperor really desired, and to find out whether the treaty of friendship was to be kept by Charles. If the emperor refused to release the arrested property, Paget was to break off negotiations, but if he only stalled, Paget was to push him. The emperor was to be reproved for making a peace with France that left his ally, Henry, at war. If he felt he could get an imperial offer to mediate between England and France, Paget might at his discretion remain to push this mediation ahead.[74]

On the morning of 24 February, Paget, who was a notoriously poor sailor, was at Dover fervently praying for a smooth Channel. Ten hours later, he ruefully wrote to his colleague Petre from Calais: 'I need not tell you that I was sick, but indeed I was so sick that I would have given one thousand pounds (if I had been a rich man) to have been on land.'[75] Four days later at Brussels, he found the emperor no less stormy than the Channel. He flared up instantly at a suggestion by Paget that he had left Henry in the lurch by his peace with France, and most of the conference consisted of an exchange of denials of each other's figures on the values of goods seized. The whole atmosphere was exceedingly hostile and Brussels was rife with rumour.[76] However, the emperor sent three of his council to go over the entire problem with Paget, who began to feel more optimistic. The imperial councillors offered to release the English goods if Henry would pay all the old claims and permit their ships to trade freely with France. But Paget rejected the offer and the conference adjourned for a few days.[77]

Paget began to make discreet inquiries as to the amount of English property held, and recommended to Henry a firm policy. He felt that the net loss to English merchants would be only £40,000 if the worst befell, and in that case, an embargo on wool shipments to the Low Countries would damage the Flemish more than the English.[78] Meanwhile the negotiations dragged on slowly and Paget began a secret negotiation with France. A secret messenger was sent into France to the French king's sister to see if some amicable settlement to the war could be found which would isolate the emperor. But the French revealed his offer to the imperialists. In the midst of a conference, one of the Flemish councillors said suddenly, 'What, M. le Secretary, you are waxen of late a great practitioner with the Queen of Navarre', and Paget was thankful for the darkness which concealed his blushes. He had little to blush for as the offer perished over the French refusal to hear of any peace that did not return Boulogne.[79]

Paget began to grow testy at the continual lack of progress. He snarled, replying to a letter from Petre, asking for more news, that he couldn't penetrate the secrets of this country overnight. Part of his irritation was due to family problems. His 'most loving and obedient wife' had been desperately ill at his departure and was still in danger. But, finally, a break in the deadlocked negotiations relieved his mind. The arrest of English shipping was to be cancelled and the old merchant claims arbitrated before a joint Anglo-Imperial court in May. Furthermore, the emperor had taken a Paget hint and was conducting preliminary talks with France about a new attempt at a mediated peace.[80] For Paget this was a triumph of skilful diplomacy. 'Dissimulation, vanity, flattery, and unshamefastness reign most here,' he wrote in cipher to Petre, 'and with the same they be rencountered!'[81]

Then, just as he was preening himself on his success, he received conflicting reports, one of which said that Lady Paget was dead. It was a truly stricken secretary who took his pen on 3 April and wrote:

Ah, Mr Petre, they write unto me my wife is dead and you write me the contrary. If she be dead, I am the most unhappy man in the world and desire no longer to live, for it is the plague of God that is fallen upon me. Ah, Mr Petre, what a loss have I. This is an unhappy journey for me that hath been cause of so great a displeasure to me. Be good to my children in my absence and give advise to Mr Wendy about my things. If my wife be alive go to her and comfort her in the King's name. I trust though His Majesty knew it he will not be displeased withall...[82]

The final signing of the agreement with the emperor for the release of the arrested shipping on 6 April can have been no pleasure to Paget, who still feared the worst, that his family was bereaved of his 'obedient, wise, gentle, and chaste wife'. Not until he was en route homeward, having in all points carried out his initial instructions, did he find that Lady Paget was not only alive but well on the road to recovery.[83]

By the time of his return, the campaigning season was not far away. Paget's foreign service staff had gathered numerous bits of information which indicated that the French planned to recover Boulogne by an invasion of England. While the council was busy preparing the coastal defences, the industrious secretary was directed by the king to push ahead with the negotiations in Germany. He had received letters which intimated that the Protestant princes might be willing to mediate between England and France, and this was too good an offer to be missed.[84] The English agents in Germany were told to encourage such a mediation, for there were still difficulties with the emperor which made Henry loath to trust him entirely.

The negotiations were hampered by the inordinate slowness of travel to Germany, which often made one exchange of letters a matter of ten weeks. Paget was himself travelling about the south of England with the king, who made an inspection tour of the invasion coast in late July. This journey enabled the king and secretary to witness the completely in-effective French attack on the English fleet in coastal waters off Portsmouth. Naturally, the king remained on shore during the skirmish, which must have been a relief to the queasy stomach of his chief secretary. However, Paget was employed to draft the king's plans for a counter-stroke at the enemy into orders to the land and sea commanders.[85]

The emperor and the Protestant princes showed almost simultaneous interest in attempting to bring about an end to the Anglo-French war.[86] They received equal encouragement from both the English and French kings, who each hoped to play off one mediator against the other at the expense of his enemy. Thus, a splendid reception of a German Protestant embassy, in which Paget figured, alarmed the imperial am-bassador into urging his master to renew his mediatory efforts.[87] Paget was pleased at the renewed prospect of peace, but Henry's stubborn intransigence over the retention of Boulogne worried him. He knew only too well how shaky the royal finances were and was more than willing to exchange the expensive conquest for a substantial cash settlement from France. Most of the other councillors agreed with him but all were reluctant to urge on their testy lord such an unwelcome step. Paget felt the necessity of writing cautionary letters to the rash young Earl of Surrey, in command at Boulogne, to warn him against undertaking any hazardous feats that might fire the king's martial zeal. Surrey, however, flew directly in the face of the warning by urging the king never to let go of Boulogne—and drew down on his head a stinging rebuke from his father, the Duke of Norfolk.[88]

The first mediated peace conference to take effect was the emperor's undertaking. A French special emissary came to the imperial court and Bishop Gardiner was sent to confer with him under the auspices of Charles V. Gardiner was instructed to negotiate a new and closer treaty of alliance with the em-peror as well as to see what the French would offer for an end

Page 99: Mary I by an unknown artist

Page 100: Elizabeth I, painting on a wood panel
by an unknown artist

to the war. Of course, if he found the emperor was secretly hostile, he was empowered to ally with France instead![89]

Paget was left almost alone at the court in Windsor to keep Gardiner instructed on policy, for most of the council members had gone to their homes, to London, or to hunt. He was kept occupied. Not only was Gardiner a prolific correspondent with whom to keep pace, but the negotiations for an alternate mediation through the Protestant emissaries, Baumbach, Sleidanus, and Bruno, were approaching a crisis.[90] This posed a delicate problem. Gardiner, one of the conservative leaders of the council, detested the German Lutherans and disliked the prospect of their meddling with Anglo-French relations. But he wholeheartedly agreed with Paget that peace was necessary even at a sacrifice.[91] England's king held many good cards in the diplomatic game. The emperor, fearing that an Anglo-French peace might include an alliance at his expense, was anxious that the peace be made under his auspices. This worry was to be used to lead him into a closer and more profitable alliance with England. The Protestants, on the other hand, feared the emperor was planning a war on them and desired a peace which would free France and England to come to their rescue.

The second series of mediating conferences got under way in late November between Calais and Ardres just as the talks in Flanders broke off. Paget, Bishop Tunstal of Durham, and John Tregonwell, Master of Requests, were commissioned to participate in these talks which were held under the auspices of the German ambassadors. Although the preliminary arguments for the meeting, made by Paget, had implied an English willingness to relinquish Boulogne for a monetary or territorial compensation, the delegation's instructions, which were drafted by Paget, were more severe. The French had to give security for the payment of all their debts, had to concede the loss of Boulogne, and agree to omit any reference to their beleaguered Scottish allies from the treaty. Such were the impossible terms which Henry desired in a peace treaty.[92]

D

The Channel crossing was as bad as Paget had feared. He sailed from Dover at 7 am on the twentieth and fourteen hours later was tottering to bed in the mansion of the Deputy of Calais, clutching his 'sea stomach' and refusing a dinner invitation.[93] The next day, he was hard at work sounding out the German ambassador, Dr Hans Bruno, on the prospects of peace. He felt somewhat encouraged. By continuous pressure on the neutral mediators, he endeavoured to prejudice them in Henry's favour, with some success.[94]

Despite a fall from his horse which hurt his leg, Paget was active at the first meeting with the French. Indeed, he took the principal role among the English delegates. Tunstal was old and not in the best of health while Paget and he had had a serious quarrel over some church lands near Durham which Paget acquired over the bitter opposition of the bishop.[95] Tregonwell was a neophyte at the conference table and so the principal burden of negotiations and writing devolved upon Paget. Except for one brief visit to Boulogne, which he forbade Petre to mention lest Lady Paget worry about the plague there, he kept steadily to his work. While both sides were awaiting instructions from home, Paget busied himself with ordering the provisions of the fortresses and straightening out accounts of a deceased garrison treasurer, though he claimed to be 'the veriest ass that can be in matters of account'.[96]

Paget had a delicate task. Henry's double policy was to bind the emperor to a closer alliance and to keep him in the dark about Paget's work with the Protestant mediators. Gardiner was also to be kept in ignorance of all but the bare outline of negotiations. The secretary had to explain to the mediators the suspicious activity of Gardiner at the court of their enemy the emperor. Paget and Henry were the only people who held all the threads in this intricate web which they wove with skill by playing off the two sides against each other.[97]

The French were willing to allow Henry to keep Boulogne as a pledge of payment of the arrears of the French pensions to him and also to press the Scots to carry out their marriage alliance treaty with England, but Paget was bound by Henry's rigid instructions to reject this proposal as too little.[98] He urged accepting these terms, if, under pressure, the French refused to bid any higher. Henry moderated his terms in response by dropping his demand for additional French lands and by offering to include the Scots in his peace in return for continuation of his pensions. It was in vain. The French would not agree to forfeit the claim to conquered Boulogne unless the arrears of debts and future pensions to England were cancelled, nor would they discuss a prolonged truce that did not include the Scots. The disappointed secretary wrote to his colleague in England that he prayed God to send him 'no more to treat in so great matters for I think I am unhappy'.[99] By 6 January of the new year, 1546, Paget 'with a seasick head and stomach' was back at Dover.

In the Low Countries the king's alternate policy had been more successful. Bishop Gardiner had negotiated a new treaty with the emperor which clarified and reinforced the terms of the old alliance of 1543. He had also laid out as bait for further negotiations the prospect that Prince Edward might well be married to one of the emperor's nieces. The emperor was cautious as his council suspected the English were only raising this prospect to entrap him into lengthy negotiations which would be used by Henry as a lever to pry better terms out of the French.

He was close to the truth. Paget admitted to the emperor's ambassadors in early April that a Venetian merchant, Francesco Bernardo, was being used to carry messages into France. He did not reveal, however, that through these messages direct peace talks between France and England were being prepared.[100] On 17 April Paget prepared a commission for himself and the admiral, Lord Lisle, to negotiate with a three-man French commission. They were instructed to secure the payment of all the old pensions, including the arrears, and the retention of Boulogne pending such payments. Scotland was to be included in the peace only if the Scots fulfilled their marriage treaty with England.[101] Paget was cheerful on his arrival at Calais, hoping for a quick settlement, or, as he phrased it, that 'we shall habb or nab shortly'.[102]

But his hopes were soon proved premature, for the Admiral of France, the chief of the French mission, was long delayed in arriving. Paget whiled away the time by going to visit the English army camp between Calais and Boulogne. At a preliminary talk with one French emissary, Paget evaded his attempts to feel out the English position, but learned enough himself to advise Henry that the English demand of three million crowns was far too high. The king reduced the figure by one-third.[103]

The interminable haggling over safe conducts and meeting sites, which began when the French admiral arrived, annoyed the impatient secretary, especially when he found the English commission was inadequate to provide the necessary diplomatic immunities for the French delegates. But, at long last, on 6 May, the two groups of plenipotentiaries met in a tent on the border between Ardres and Guisnes. They had a long dispute. Paget opened with an initial series of inflated demands totalling eight million crowns, which he had drawn up with the king's approval.[104] The French guffawed at the figure but their counter-offer of 200,000 was equally amusing to Paget, Lisle and Wotton. Prolonged discussion until dusk produced only conflicting figures and a joint resolve to refer to the two kings for further orders.

Paget was anxiously pressing for peace. He wrote to Petre urging him to use all possible influence, saying that if this peace conference failed he would give up in despair. Yet, he hoped that a peace would occur 'which we will bring from hence if you send it from thence'. A French overture for the evasion of the deadlock on Scotland seemed satisfactory to him for, he pointed out, its vagueness would not preclude the king from taking his advantage afterward at a favourable time.[105] His harping on peace got on the king's nerves to such an extent that a rebuke was sent to Paget, necessitating an elab-

orate and obsequious defence from the harassed secretary to
reassure the king that he was continuing to show a brave front
to the enemy.[106]

The main cause of Paget's pacific inclinations was his
gloomy awareness of the English financial difficulties. He and
Wriothesley, as has been pointed out, had laboured unceas-
ingly to provide funds for the war, only to be continuously
behind in their provision. It was these tortures of Tantalus
that led him to write: 'Oh, Mr Petre, if we had enough of
one thing either the Frenchmen should make such a peace as
we would appoint, or else I would wish we should make war
with them, but seeing we have it not, I say no more.' [107]

In the midst of these difficulties of negotiation, the French
galleys gained the initiative in the Channel. This required
Admiral Lord Lisle to rush to sea and disperse them, a sight
which gave Paget great pleasure. But the French ambassadors
used Lisle's absence as an excuse to refuse to negotiate, and a
frantic letter of recall from Paget was rushed to the errant
admiral.[108]

Lisle and his opposite, the French admiral, got on famously
when they met. While hard-working Paget filled the ears of
the president of the Council of Rouen with a list of the
French violations of past treaties, the two admirals went hunting and hawking. Paget was in poor health during the negotiations and feared that the damp and drafty tent in which
the parleys took place would bring on a fever. But he was able
to go to Calais for treatment on 15 May, when the first indica-
tions of a firm basis of settlement were advanced in French
proposals. To Henry, Paget urged their acceptance. They
provided two million crowns' payment over eight years, at the
end of which Boulogne would be returned, continuation of
the pensions, arbitration of disputed arrears of 512,000 crowns,
and the inclusion of the Scots provided that they did not
attack Henry again. The eight-year possession of Boulogne
was equivalent to full title to it, said Paget, citing an anecdote
of a man condemned to death by a former French king. To

save his life, the man undertook to make the king's ass speak inside a year. ' "What? It is impossible," said a friend. "Hold thy peace," quoth he (in French, for it was King Louis XI). "Car ou le Roi morera, ou l'asne morera, ou l'asne parlera, ou je mourera!" ' [109]

Henry was inclined to accept the offer, but first desired a survey of the new border, which would give him a few extra acres and could be included in the treaty. He delayed a firm answer pending such a survey. Meanwhile, Paget was taking the violent treatment prescribed by his physician to avoid a fever—bleeding and purging of such a vigorous nature that he fainted twice, and left him much weakened. But he arose from his bed and hurried back to the parleys. The French admiral, impatient at the delay, was threatening to leave, and an incipient mutiny in the English army alarmed Paget, who feared this would encourage the French to break off. However, on the twenty-third, the king sent his general acceptance of the French terms and Paget burst into a paean of joy. [110]

A few days later, he was thirsting for French blood. A French emissary, Secretary Bochetel, and he went with several guides to examine the source of a proposed boundary stream and fell into a prodigious dispute over which of five springs was the source of the river. The irate Paget wrote to his colleague: 'Instead of the grace and peace which I sent you last, help to send me unto us now this side fire and sword, for other thing cannot bring these false dogs to reason...God give them a pestilence, false traitors!' [111] Once more the negotiations hovered on the brink of destruction, but Paget's keen awareness of the desirability of peace quickly reasserted itself, and certain unpalatable articles were dispatched to Henry with a strong recommendation that he make some concessions.

This advice did not please Henry. That difficult and omnipotent monarch usually blamed his ministers for unpleasant situations which confronted him. Paget's credit with him was temporarily shaken when he realised that he must accede to several French demands. Such a delicate situation evoked a

masterpiece of diplomacy from Paget's pen. In a letter to
Petre, obviously meant for the king's ear, he combined a lucid
plea for peace on logical grounds with just the amount of
humility and flattery to appease the king. Paget regretted that
he had lacked the ability to satisfy his sovereign, but vigorously denied that he had lacked stoutness in opposing the
French. In one point, the king had given way to the French
more than Paget would have desired, but the negotiations
were on the verge of collapse, 'Mr Petre, as for the war, if it
continues, I will do as much for the service of my master as
I can; and yet had I rather have peace. I see the honour of it
and the commodities so great both to be wrought at home, at
your friend's hands abroad, and at your enemies' hands also
...As for your enemies, but that I am noted too much given
to peace, else I could say he [Francis] hath now very lately
borrowed at Lyons four hundred thousand crowns...' Paget
did not need to point to the empty English treasury to reinforce his opinion.[112] On 4 June, amid a final burst of recrimin-
ation, a peace treaty was agreed on largely conforming to the
terms endorsed by Paget. The irate Henry was satisfied, and
on 7 June the treaty was signed by the commissioners. To the
weary Paget went the honour of bearing the treaty to the
king, and despite his fever and exhaustion from the Channel
crossing he hurried to bring the welcome news to court.[113]

It is difficult to analyse the exact share which William Paget
had in the formulation of English foreign policy under Henry
VIII. Henry's own wide experience in the power politics and
diplomatic balancing of Wolsey and Cromwell made him
congenial towards the diplomatic scheming of Paget. Both
Cromwell and Wolsey had sacrificed the king's favour by
losing their adaptability and adhering too closely to their own
policies. Paget was a man of less commanding mould, not in
a class with these great ministers, but his flexibility in the
face of any situation made him a trusted subordinate to the
ageing and autocratic king. There was never the slightest

suspicion in Henry's mind that his chief secretary was an overly-powerful minister. Paget was careful to keep in his mind his subordinate position as a lowly tool in his master's service. Many of the devices by which a policy was carried out were Paget's. Often the autocratic Henry could be persuaded to adopt suggestions of policy itself from his secretary, whom he rightly regarded as a 'master of practices'. Thus, it was in the major field of foreign affairs that Paget developed the intimacy which his secretaryship offered into the role of principal adviser to the king.

CHAPTER SIX

STRUGGLE FOR POWER

WHEN King Henry VIII died near the end of January 1547, there was a smooth orderly transfer of power from the hands of the Privy Council, designated by him as executors of his will and custodians of the nine-year-old Edward VI, to Edward Seymour, Earl of Hertford, who assumed the title of lord protector and head of the government. This smooth transition was in fact a coup d'état by one group of councillors, who were inclined towards continued religious changes of an anti-Catholic nature. The complete success of the coup is the more remarkable in view of the fact that only seven months earlier an opposing group of conservative councillors had been in firm control of the king's ear. The details of the actual transfer of power of 28–31 January 1547 are known. What is not clear, however, is the process by which the more radical victorious group won the control of the dying king's mind which enabled it to prepare for the bloodless and orderly transition of power. There are a few episodes known to have occurred between 1 June 1546 and the death of the king which reflected the intense struggle for power. But these are the scattered, frozen peaks which indicate a much larger 'cold war' beneath the unruffled surface of conciliar business.

One of the key figures in this hidden conflict was William Paget, the chief secretary and close confidant of Henry VIII, whose role in it has never been properly appraised. It has been assumed that his adherence to the ranks of the victorious faction occurred only in the last few hours of Henry's life.[1] However, Paget had long been on close terms with Hertford and in sympathy with his religious views. It was the addition of his administrative experience and his control of audiences with the king which were decisive factors in the triumph of the party of change. Therefore, it is of importance to evaluate his influence with the king, to ascertain his relationship with the leaders of both factions, and to analyse his views on religious questions, before attempting to chart the course of struggle between the proponents of change and the advocates of conservatism.

Previous chapters have pointed out how the secretary's omnicompetent powers were wielded by Paget. His control of correspondence and of the audiences of the king and council had made him a major influence. Penetrating observers at the court had noted the satisfaction with which the king regarded his faithful agent as early as February 1545. Chapuys and Vanderdelft observed then that his influence in foreign affairs was on a par with that of Bishop Gardiner, the leader of the conservatives, and of the Earl of Hertford, the king's favourite military leader.[2] From that date onward both the imperial and French ambassadors were agreed in referring to him as the most influential adviser of Henry. The King of France sent him a present of silver plate, while the Imperial Regent of the Netherlands regarded him almost as a member of her council.[3] Two illustrations from the events of September and October 1546 will serve to reveal this influence. First, Paget was the only councillor advised of the king's secret oral orders, contradicting written instructions, to his commander at Boulogne, which resulted in the destruction of a French fortification and nearly provoked a new war.[4] The other illustration is a letter from Lord Chancellor Wriothesley, the highest ranking secular government officer in the land, begging Paget to preserve the jurisdiction of his Court of Chancery from alterations which the king was said to plan.

Only a minister of paramount importance and a great power would receive such a missive from a lord chancellor.[5]

As one might expect, Paget's increasing political stature was paralleled by his economic gains. A brief examination of the patent rolls of 1544–7 reveals that Paget did indeed rise in startling fashion in social and economic stature. The first sign of the flood of honours and profits to come was his promotion in the social scale from esquire to knight. In January 1544, Mr William Paget became Sir William Paget, knight, just after his old schoolfellow Wriothesley became a baron. None of the numerous lists of Henry's knights gives the exact date of this event, but as he was still referred to as Mr Paget at Wriothesley's creation on New Year's Day, and on 17 January was Sir William, it can be assumed that it occurred during the first part of the month.[6]

Such a title required of its distinguished possessor a country 'seat', and in the same month Paget was granted the manors of Bromley in Staffordshire and Edleston in Derbyshire to hold from the crown at a token rent of £16. A few days later, Lady Paget celebrated her new dignity by giving birth to another son, in a house belonging to one of her husband's ambassadors.[7] Within the same eventful period, Sir William Paget consolidated his position as a country landowner by altering his coat of arms to a more distinguished and dignified form.[8]

The two great years of acquisition for Paget, however, were 1545 and 1546. In each of these years, his prominence was recognised when he was nominated to the Order of the Garter, once by Wriothesley, and the other time by his old friend, the Earl of Arundel, whose ancient lineage did not blind him to the merits of the son of a nameless '*mediocris fortunae vir*'. In both years a succession of minor sinecures continued to come to Sir William. He became steward and keeper of the courts of the royal manor of Nantwich in Cheshire, surveyor of Tutbury Manor, and master of the posts.[9]

The royal generosity was also extended to the chief secretary in the matter of wardships. In November 1545 he was given the wardship and marriage rights of the two illegitimate sons, and principal heirs, of a wealthy London alderman. This provided a prosperous husband a few years later for Sir William's eldest daughter, Ethelreda, who was married to the legally available Christopher Alen. Three months later, a double windfall came in the form of two annuities of £40 and the wardship and marriage rights of Richard Berkeley and John Dutton, each the heir of wealthy gentlemen in the western counties. Apparently, the marriage rights were disposed of by Paget for cash, which leads one to speculate that his five other daughters were both attractive and desirable enough to attract other offers! [10]

At any rate, their father had arrived socially. His son was sought in marriage by an aspiring kinsman of the lord deputy in Ireland with an eligible daughter. [11] As a respectable landed gentleman of influence at the court, Paget became the adviser *in loco parentis* to the hot-tempered daughter-in-law of another lord deputy, Lord Cobham of Calais. This responsibility seemed to consist of trying both to salvage the young lady's marriage and to reconcile her with Lady Cobham. His more distinguished social status was reflected in the frequent greetings in letters from counciilors and other magnates to Lady Paget and 'all your little ones'. [12]

The great basis for social position in the sixteenth century was that very permanent form of wealth, land. The favour of King Henry VIII yielded Paget substantial returns in this form. Until his grant of Bromley and Edleston, Paget had been an influential and highly placed member of the government, but a man dependent on his salary and perquisites. His town house and property of West Drayton were of no more value than the small estates of hundreds of obscure country gentry. But Paget was on the way to becoming a great magnate and to acquiring properties which would insure his importance whether or not he served in the government. This transitional process was effected in a surprisingly short time.

Mention has been made of his dispute with the conservative Bishop Tunstal over the bishopric's hospital of Kepier, which Paget had laid out 200 marks to acquire. The bishop's reluctance was overcome by Paget's delicate hint that the king might take it to indicate a disapproval of other royal secularisation of church property, and within a few days the hospital and all its lands in Durham, Northumberland and Yorkshire were his![13] Paget's religious views on land secularisation were, of course, completely orthodox by Henrician standards, and he had taken the precaution to associate the king's chaplain and his eldest son's godfather, Dr Richard Cox, with him in the enterprise.[14]

Having considerable possessions in the north to support his dignity, Paget was able to secure a licence to violate the laws against livery and retain in his services forty gentlemen or yeomen in his livery.[15] However, he did not desire to keep Kepier as the foundation of his landed properties. He sold part of it but returned the principal portion of the properties to the crown in exchange for the collegiate foundation of Burton-upon-Trent, with its several manors in five counties, and the manor of Nantwich, Chester, of which he was already an officer. These properties he held in chief of the crown paying into the Court of Augmentations £336 rent to secure the bargain.[16] Most of his new lands, eleven manors, were in north Staffordshire, Worcestershire, and Derbyshire, for it was there that Sir William proposed to establish his family. His father, John Pachet, was a Staffordshire man, and the son desired to establish the roots of the family again in the soil from which it had sprung.

Thus, by expending some £1,350 for Kepier and by a judicious exchange, he held lands of some extent in a desirable location near his earlier acquisitions of Bromley and Edleston. An investment of £47 in April 1546 secured the title to his home at West Drayton for the crown so that he held it directly of the king instead of from the dean and chapter of

St Paul's Cathedral in London.[17] Since his title was satisfac-
torily arranged, Sir William began to improve the plumbing
at his 'capital dwelling-house'. Its location was convenient to
London and Westminster and, while he served the crown, he
could only rarely journey north to Staffordshire. So he built
a pipeline to convey water to his country dwelling in Middlesex, and left the other estates to his servants' management.[18]
Even though he remained an absentee lord, Sir William prepared to conclude his estate-buying with the acquisition of a
mansion house in Staffordshire to which all his manors would
be satellites.

His opportunity came in September and October 1546
at the turning-point of the struggle between the council's
factions, when Henry turned decisively away from the conservative policy. The Bishop of Coventry and Lichfield was
compelled to surrender to the king six manors in Staffordshire, including the manor and mansion of Beaudesert, in
return for the promise of several church livings held by the
crown. Paget then, in one sweeping purchase, paid the king
£2,708 and to the treasurer of the Court of Augmentations
a further £3,000. For this huge sum he received Beaudesert
and its six manors and obtained the title to his Burton lands.
The £3,000 to the treasurer of Augmentations was spread
over five annual instalments as Paget was unable to raise such
an enormous sum. Since the normal purchase price of church
lands was fixed by Henry at twenty years' rent, Paget received
this striking bargain in return for his 'special good service'
to the crown.[19]

These land grants formed the greater part of the estate
which Sir William was to pass on to his heirs, but at the time
he desired to secure more solidly his title to the church lands
which he had acquired from the Bishop of Lichfield and
Coventry. Therefore, in the Parliament which met a few
days before Henry's death, he introduced a private member's
bill 'for the assurance of certain lands to Sir William Pagett,
Knight, Secretary to the King's Majesty'. On 31 January, how-

ever, the Parliament was dissolved by the lord chancellor's announcement of the king's death, and the bill was never passed by the House of Lords. Supreme power in the hands of Paget's friend, Hertford, in the new reign made it unnecessary to strive for again.[20]

In discussing the prelude to the change of government which marked Henry's demise, it is instructive to consider Sir William Paget's relationship to the leaders of the two factions in the Privy Council. By far the most important member of the conservative group was his old schoolmaster, patron and friend, Stephen Gardiner, Bishop of Winchester. From Gardiner had come his introduction into the king's service. The older man was genuinely fond of his former protégé and had not begrudged him his timely turn towards Cromwell when he himself was in disfavour. It may well have been Gardiner's friendship which assisted Paget's continued rise when Cromwell, in his turn, lost both favour and life. Certainly the distinguished scholar, diplomat and bishop believed himself to be on excellent terms with the principal secretary.

But Paget had for some time been drifting away from Gardiner. As early as November 1544, he indicated to a friend his awareness that 'My lord of Winchester hath certain affections in his head many times towards such men as he greatly favoureth not ... and when he seeth time can lay on load to nip a man; which fashion I like not and think it devilish. God amend all our faults!'[21] His awareness of Gardiner's redoubtable temper did not blind him to the real ability of his former patron. In the king's service they were thrown often in each other's company in diplomatic business,[22] and worked smoothly together. Most of the initiative in their harmonious relationship, however, came from Gardiner. He continued to write lengthy, friendly, and affectionate letters to Paget, when they were on separate missions, in spite of the fact that Paget's replies were tardy. In letters to the secretary, the fears of Gardiner about foreign policy and his personal objections to the German Protestants continued to be poured out, long after Paget's secret sympathies had turned away from the conservatives.[23]

His conduct was similar towards another would-be leader of that faction. The young Earl of Surrey had developed from a harum-scarum playboy, who might have been a leading light in a college community four centuries later, into an equally hasty military leader who aspired to guide the Privy Council and government away from the pitfalls of rule by 'new men' of humble birth. In Surrey's scheme of things there would be no 'damned nonsense about merit'. The country should be safely governed by its ancient nobility, and who was more ancient than the Howards? However, for the time he conducted himself towards Paget with friendship, although the hardworking secretary was a prime example of one of humble birth risen to high place. In return, Sir William favoured Surrey with advice and friendly actions which covered equally well his opposition towards all for which the young aristocrat stood.

While he thus passed for a conservative and encouraged this illusion deliberately, Secretary Paget's ties of friendship with the potential leaders of an opposing group were growing stronger.[24] The most illustrious of these leaders was Edward Seymour, Earl of Hertford, uncle of the king's son and heir and one of the best military leaders in Henry's court. The long war with France had afforded scope for his talents as a commander and brought him distinction. The king esteemed him highly and seemed unaware of his views on religion which were well to the left of the monarch's own ideas. It has been shown already how Paget worked with the king to secure tangible evidence of the royal favour for Hertford.[25] The frequent dispatches between the secretary and the earl give evidence of the affection with which the military men regarded his colleague at court.

In April 1544, the secretary wrote timely advice to the soldier that he 'will do well to salute now and then with a word or two in a letter', the Duke of Suffolk, Lord Chancellor Wriothesley, Mr Denny, and others. The advice was accepted gratefully and the earl's political contacts were kept fresh. A year later, Hertford had begun sending greetings to Lady Paget and exchanging banter with Sir William. 'I perceive ye find fault with me for that I have written two times and sent never a letter to my wife, as though you would be noted a good husband and that no such fault could be found in you. I would advise you to leave off such quarrels or else I will tell my lady such tales of you as you will repent the beginning; to whom I pray you I may be commended with all my heart.'[26] Paget kept the absent earl closely informed of every development at court, sending him either news-letters or copies of important dispatches from other areas. In religious matters, Hertford regarded him as a fellow-spirit. When Paget advised him of a plan to seize all church plate for the royal treasury, he endorsed it on religious grounds, 'for God's service, which consisteth not in jewels, plate, or ornaments of gold and silver, cannot thereby be diminished, and those things [are] better employed for the weal and defence of the realm'.[27] For his part Hertford kept Paget closely informed of his plans and progress as well as of news and gossip in his vicinity.[28] When there was no news at all to write, Hertford would often pause to dictate a few lines of trivia to be sent to Paget. In a note of this sort, after he had crossed the Channel in September 1546, he concluded with a quip of humorous sarcasm about what a fine sailor Paget would have been in similar weather.[29]

The other future leader of the council's Protestant faction was John Dudley, Viscount Lisle, with whom Paget was joined in making peace with France in June 1546. But Lord Lisle's talents were primarily martial, and he had served Henry ably on land and sea during the war. He, too, regarded Paget as a friend at court who would further his suits for advancement. The two men discussed carefully the great offices in the royal household to which Lisle might aspire, and laid plans to secure the first profitable place vacated by death or loss of favour.[30] Even more significantly, in July 1546 they were discussing in veiled terms a haughty communication from the Earl of Surrey to Lisle and whether or not to show it to the king.

Thus, during the years of 1545 and the first half of 1546, Paget had cemented a friendly alliance with Hertford and Lisle—an alliance which revealed its existence in their intimate letters. At the same time, though he disagreed with Bishop Gardiner's views and found fault with his disposition, Paget remained on outwardly friendly terms with the conservative leaders. Such conduct was both discreet and profitable for the wily chief secretary, since during these months his friends were away from the court and Henry followed a markedly conservative policy in religion with which Paget outwardly conformed.

However, he had given a few hints of the nature of his real opinions in his voluminous correspondence. Sir William Paget's religious views were a mystery to many of his contemporaries, and are as difficult to define now as then. It must be noted that they were never a primary motivating force in his policies, for he was not a fanatic. Yet, his feelings on the subject did influence him to a limited extent and must, therefore, be analysed.

There can be no doubt that men who were inclined towards the reformed religions considered him a fellow-spirit. Archbishop Cranmer transmitted at least two of his plans for further changes in the church to the king through the secretary's hands. Paget's discussion of possible confiscation of church plate with Hertford has been mentioned and the way in which that Protestant peer conferred agreeably on this startling project. The young prince's Protestant tutor, Dr Cox, Paget's partner in a church acquisition, urged him to continue to advance godly and honourable, that is, Protestant, people in the affairs of the realm.[31] His colleague Petre openly rejoiced with him at the prospect of an alliance with the

German Protestants, while at least one of his special agents in Germany was even more confident of Paget's 'godly' inclinations. He asked Paget to destroy one of his dispatches in which he had too feelingly condemned the Bishop of London's official zeal against Protestants.[32] Similarly, another agent, Stephen Vaughan, relied confidently and successfully on the secretary to extricate his children's tutor, held on suspicion of heresy, from Bishop Bonner's toils.[33]

Paget's own letters and drafts go some way to bear out this view of his contemporaries. They reveal a glib knowledge of the current speech of Protestant-leaning contemporaries, with their biblical quotations and frequent use of the adjective 'godly'. For example, he described his friend Lord Lisle as 'God's own knight' to a German correspondent. But the wily Sir William was not an extremist himself in his mildly Protestant leanings. In the first place, it was not advisable to reveal such rigid tendencies around a variable sovereign, whose councillors were of conservative views, until September 1546. That was why he took pains to be acceptable to those with whom he disagreed. It explains his interest in convincing the imperial ambassador Vanderdelft that he was a leader of the group which opposed religious innovations.[34]

Not all of his discretion was caused by such temporising, however. For Paget's strength, which was sometimes his weakness, was that he was a rational civil lawyer. He did not look upon religion as a cause for which to die at the stake but rather as a support for the state which might be regulated according to the principle. His logical mind could appreciate the arguments of that other civil lawyer, Stephen Gardiner, in his book against the German theologian Bucer, while it rejected the vitriolic blasts with which the conservative bishop presented his case. Gardiner himself best summed up Paget's viewpoint in religion as in other aspects of his temperament, 'ye told me once ye love no extremities and the mean is best ... who [ever] could hit it'.[35] If he leaned at this period towards a mildly Protestant position, it was more from judging it to be 'the mean' than from evangelical zeal.

It has been pointed out that Henry VIII was following a
conservative policy in religious matters to prevent himself
from being considered a rank heretic by the continental
powers.[36] Many of his council, especially Bishop Gardiner,
the Duke of Norfolk, and Lord Chancellor Wriothesley, were
in hearty accord. In the month of March, Henry had been
dangerously ill for three weeks with a fever and an ulcerous
leg.[37] Members of the council must have given serious thought
to the state of the realm in the event of the king's death. His
eight-year-old son was in the hands of Protestant tutors, including Paget's friend Cox. The possibility of a further drift
towards heresy under a Protestant regency led by Queen
Katharine Parr and the Earl of Hertford caused the conservatives to have awful visions of a peasants' revolt and total
anarchy. Thus, during the spring and summer, great efforts
were made to put the religious and political direction of the
government on a conservative basis.

There had been rumours in London as early as February
that Henry planned to dispose of his Queen Katharine Parr,
who was known as a favourer of the new religions.[38] This
groundless rumour foreshadowed a real effort by her enemies
in the early summer to achieve her downfall. Such a conservative reaction first showed itself by a vigorous enforcement
of the Six Articles. Bishop Bonner reported that Essex was
rife with heresy, when he investigated that county in May.
Many offenders were haled before the commissions or the
council itself and many heretical books were burned. Latimer
and Shaxton, both former bishops, were called on the carpet
as were several priests and preachers.[39]

The biggest fish of all to swim into the orthodox dragnet
was the unfortunate Anne Askew. Her examination by Paget
and other councillors has already been recounted. After her
condemnation, Wriothesley himself examined her on the rack
in the hope of eliciting accusations against Lady Hertford and

other highly placed Protestants, possibly even the queen her-self.[40] It must have been at this time that the famous incident occurred which is narrated by the martyrologist Foxe. In his account, Henry had gone so far as to order the queen's arrest, and only changed his mind when the guards approached.[41] Archbishop Cranmer had earlier proved to the orthodox that Henry would never forsake him, but it may have been Anne Askew's stoicism under torture which saved the queen and many other ladies of her inclination.

At this point, however, with the forces of religious reaction in control of the council, the war with France ended. This relieved the drain on Henry's finances, while the emperor's continued involvement in Germany removed the worst of his fears of a hostile combination. More important still, peace brought the return of those successful warriors, the Earl of Hertford and Lord Lisle, leaders in the council and advocates of religious change. From mid-June until the end of the year, their group became more regular in attendance at the council and more active at its board. It marked the beginning of a two-party system in a body designed to function as a harmonious unit.

During the summer of 1546, the two groups struggled for supreme power. The contest was, in fact, a battle for the king's mind, for whichever policy Henry elected to follow would bring about the downfall of its opponents. There were nineteen councillors involved. The conservatives were led by Gardiner, Wriothesley, and Norfolk, and included Bishop Tunstal, Sir Richard Rich, and Sir John Gage, the comptroller of the household. Another group, the neutrals of the council, would join whichever side prevailed. Lord St John, who characterised himself as more a willow than an oak, typified this element, but it included such lesser figures as Sir John Baker, chancellor of the exchequer, Sir Thomas Cheyney, warden of the Cinque Ports, Lord Russell, and Sir Anthony Wingfield, the vice-chamberlain.

The Protestant group was led by Hertford and Lisle, whose

followers included the Earl of Essex, the queen's brother, Sir Ralph Sadler, the lord privy seal, and Cranmer, Archbishop of Canterbury. Sir William Paget, chief secretary, though friendly with all parties, had secretly gone over to the side of Hertford, and Secretary Petre was his faithful shadow. This forward party held a tremendous advantage in the chief secretary's constant contact and influence with the king. As Paget himself described the situation after Henry's death, 'the said King devised with me apart (as it is well known he used to open his pleasure to me alone in many things)'. Furthermore, the two chief gentlemen of the privy chamber, Sir Anthony Denny and Sir William Herbert, though not members of the council, were adherents of the Hertford party with daily contact with the king.[42]

The new party's power first became evident with Paget's entry into the council chamber on 25 July with the Earl of Arundel, whom he declared the king had appointed lord chamberlain and privy councillor.[43] Arundel was the head of one of the ancient noble families in the realm and his adherence to the forward party in the council served to counterbalance the conservative sympathies of the Duke of Norfolk and his son, Surrey. The struggle between factions was not slow in becoming evident even to such an inexpert observer as Ambassador Vanderdelft. The sixteenth of August had found him persuaded by Paget that Gardiner, Paget, and Wriothesley were the leaders of a unified conservative council, but less than three weeks later he had seen the light. On 3 September, he dined alone with Wriothesley, Gardiner, and St John and deplored with them the rise in power of Hertford and Lisle.[44]

At that time Henry VIII was hesitating between two possible foreign policies, which were closely tied to the question of domestic religious policy. One of these possible courses was a reconciliation with the Roman Catholic Church, which would end Henry's excommunication and remove this possible tool from the hands of his enemies. The occasion was the arrival of Guron Bertano, an Italian, who had previously served Henry and who desired to reconcile the pope and the English king. Bertano arrived secretly at the French embassy at the end of July and on 2 August had a long private conference with Sir William Paget. Paget served as the intermediary between the king and Bertano, for a few days later the court moved from Westminster to Hampton Court.[45]

The opportunity for reconciliation with Rome must have intrigued the conservative councillors, yet unless Henry firmly accepted the proposals it would be perilous for them to meddle. It must have been a frustrating experience for them to see a policy, which would have insured the extinction of dangerous religious tendencies, being toyed with by their aged but still dominant sovereign. It is interesting to note that at this crucial period, from 12 to 29 August, the composition of the Privy Council changed noticeably. For the first time in many months Archbishop Cranmer became a regular attendant, as were Hertford, Lisle, and the Earl of Arundel. Paget and Petre were, as usual, regularly present. Most of the neutral group were frequent attenders, but among the conservatives, only Wriothesley, Norfolk, and Gage were available to press their views.[46] The anti-Roman policy prevailed. Though Bertano stayed in London until the end of September, his dismissal was decisive. Since Paget was still the sole link with him, the councillors ordered to give him his congé were forced to ask Paget for his address. By the irony of circumstance, Bertano received the unwelcome news from Wriothesley of the conservative party.[47]

While the negotiations with Rome were under consideration, the king was considering an alliance abroad with the German Protestants and flirting with further religious changes at home. According to Cranmer's secretary, Henry proposed to the Admiral of France, during the latter's state visit in late August, that both countries adopt a Protestant faith and convert the Mass to a communion service.[48] The king had actually been negotiating a league with the Protestants without

France, but it did not progress to completion.[49] For Henry's foreign policy was, like his religious beliefs, altered according to the advantage of the moment. A lengthy memorandum or 'consultacion' written by Paget in August 1546 summed up the state of Europe and laid down a policy which appealed to Henry as it did to his secretary.[50] Both France and the emperor, said Paget, were potential foes as long as England was hostile to Rome and in possession of Boulogne. Therefore, England must be cautious abroad and must promote unity and a replenished treasury at home. Paget advised against an alliance with the Protestants as it would alienate the emperor for a negligible increase in strength. If it were possible, he felt the emperor should be brought by Henry's mediation to a peace with the Lutheran princes. However, the war in Germany might end. Paget knew that the result could only increase imperial or French strength, and England's safety lay in balancing those powers in perpetual equality and hostility towards each other. It was plain, however, that Paget was, at heart, like his master, more inclined to the emperor than to France. This was the policy which Henry decided to follow.[51]

The rejection of Guron Bertano's offer of reconciliation with Rome had been decided by the king during August. In September, the emerging preponderance of the forward party in the council became clear, for Henry went on his last progress. The king left Hampton Court for Woking, Guildford and, finally, Windsor. His council was decisively split between the portion accompanying him and a group left in London. The choice of his company was significant. Wriothesley and Gardiner were left with Lord St John to conduct the council's business in London where they could do nothing but complain. For an entire month Henry was isolated from their conservative views, escorted by a council consisting of Hertford, Lord Russell, Arundel, the Earl of Essex, Paget, and Sir Anthony Browne.[52] In the middle of this progress, Henry had another serious illness in which his life hung in the balance.

Again, it was a time for every councillor to consider soberly the face of things to come.

When the council reassembled at Windsor in early October, feeling between the factions ran high. It must have been at this time that a famous incident occurred. Admiral Lord Lisle in a heated controversy with Gardiner at the council struck the bishop with his fist in a rage.[53] For this offence against decorum he was banished from the council for about a month. But the time was ripe for a decisive blow at the conservative group, which would terrify the waverers and break the spirit of the conservatives. The first shadow of the blow was discerned by the alert De Selve. He reported great unrest in high places and that rumours of dissension and 'mutations d'estatz' were current among the principal men of the realm. De Selve had heard that the mayor of London and justices of the peace throughout the land had been ordered to investigate and search for treasons and conspiracies against the king.[54]

Stephen Gardiner, leader of the conservatives, had been absent from the council during most of September and October, probably because of his quarrel with Lisle. His absence allowed his enemies to undermine his influence with Henry. As a result of Henry's progress, even councillors had to have permission to come to court, and the forward party had thus won practical control of the council's composition. Gardiner had rashly given a further advantage to his enemies by flatly refusing to discuss a proposed exchange of his episcopal lands, which Paget, Wriothesley, and the chancellor of the Court of Augmentations had informed him the king desired. From his place in Southwark, on 2 December, the Bishop of Winchester wrote Paget a worried letter enclosing an apology to the king. To Paget, he said that he wondered why he had not seen him recently, and inquired if it were true, as he heard, that in the matter of the lands his doings were not well received. His reply from Paget must have been friendly, for Gardiner did not feel himself rebuffed, but from Henry he received a cold reprimand and no encouragement in his request for an invitation to the court.[55]

One of the more ominous features of the affair was its hint that Lord Chancellor Wriothesley was tending towards the side of the Hertford group. This change was in the nick of time for his career. The Earl of Surrey's sister had informed against her brother for his pretensions to royal arms, and Paget and Hertford had convinced the king it was time to act. The blow fell on 2 December.[56] The Earl of Surrey was taken into custody in Wriothesley's house and detained there for several days before being publicly led to the Tower, charged with treason and conspiracy. His father, the Duke of Norfolk, was apprehended on the same charge and, deprived of his Garter and his office, clapped into the Tower also.[57]

The details of the remarkable collection of charges against these two men are voluminously preserved in the published sources.[58] They may be summarised as giving reasonable grounds for belief that both men considered the king's death imminent, feared and disliked the probable Protestant advisers of the future king, and may have been considering ways to obtain the chief direction of the young prince at his accession. Surrey, whose rashness furnished most of the pretexts for their fall, had assumed a coat of arms, which might be interpreted as a claim to the throne, but it was probably only his unsubtle way of 'wiping the eye' of such newly created peers as Hertford and Lisle. The old duke's principal offence was his relationship to Surrey. He had not desired a clash and, with remarkable prescience, foresaw the struggle between factions. The previous June he had endeavoured vainly to arrange a matrimonial alliance with Hertford, which would have prevented it.[59]

Wriothesley and Paget were very active in gathering the evidence on which the government's case was built. The former had made his peace with Hertford and the winning party, while the secretary took the active share which both his office and his sympathies demanded of him in this matter of internal security. Paget's most spectacular participation occurred at Surrey's trial on 13 January 1547. He was one of the panel of commissioners named as judges, who heard Surrey defend himself skilfully and violently from nine in the morning until five in the afternoon. Over his coat of arms the accused clashed with Paget, who charged him, 'Hold your peace, my lord; your idea was to commit treason, and as the King is old, you thought to become King.' Surrey replied with a venomous reference to Paget's humble origin, 'And thou, Catchpoll! What hast thou to do with it? Thou hadst better hold thy tongue, for the kingdom has never been well since the King put mean creatures like thee into the government.' The jury was so impressed with this spirited defence that it stayed in its room for six hours without reaching a verdict. Paget then left the Guildhall and went to the king's bedside. On his return he entered the jury room and was closeted with its members for an hour. His menaces had their effect, and a verdict of guilty came out with him.[60]

The triumph of Hertford and his friends was complete. From early December until 2 January the council met at his house regularly. All of the waverers hurried to give him their support. An officer serving abroad carefully explained to Paget that his earlier brusque letter to the council was not intended to apply to the dominant group 'but only the contrary party'.[61] For Paget was known to be a power among the triumphant forward party.

Unfortunately, little information exists about his activities conferring with Hertford and the other councillors during the period of the fall of Norfolk and Surrey. Most of their planning was necessarily secret. Also, Paget's duties as executor of the king's foreign policy were singularly critical during this time, since negotiations were in progress with France, looking towards a treaty of alliance, and the preservation of good relations with the emperor during this operation was no easy task.[62] But hints of his activities are apparent in the formulation of Henry's last will and testament at the end of December.

In this document Henry appointed a sixteen-member Privy Council for his heir, who were also to be the executors of his will. Except for Wriothesley, elderly Bishop Tunstal, and Sir Anthony Browne, the executors were all members of the triumphant forward party in the council, including its leaders, Hertford, Lisle, Paget, Denny and Herbert. To assist them, another group of councillors were named, consisting almost entirely of followers of Hertford. Stephen Gardiner, the only conservative leader capable of opposing him, was deliberately excluded from either of the two groups. Henry, in response to a suggestion that he be included, was said to have rejected the idea vigorously. Paget admitted in later years that he had prepared in writing a charge of treasonable activity against the bishop with the king's knowledge. From his own testimony four years later, Paget was obviously a key figure in persuading Henry to omit the bishop, though he then alleged that the initiative came from the king.[63] Certainly Paget was one of the very few people in constant attendance on the king, and his claim to have been the council's only means of access to Henry would indicate a tremendous influence on the composition of the council of executors. As he himself stated to the French ambassador, not even Wolsey or Cromwell had the freedom of speech with Henry that he did during the king's last months.[64] The draft of Henry's will showed his influence in determining the sums to be given to each of the executors, though his own bequest of £300 from Henry which Paget had penned himself was not paid until three years later.[65]

Much speculation has been expended on Henry's intent in naming a council without a leader to govern in his son's name. Paget later alleged to Vanderdelft that he persuaded the dying monarch to call Hertford in for a three-hour conference to ask him to lead the council, but Paget was very likely justifying *ex post factor* the coup that made Hertford protector.[66] It can only be assumed that the wilful Henry did indeed believe that a conciliar government would function smoothly after his death because he wanted it to! Nevertheless, the plans for a coup to make Hertford the lord protector were being made by Paget and the earl himself well before the king's death.

It was already suspected by many people. Vanderdelft saw the trend of events a month before the king's death, and, from his retirement at Louvain, the former ambassador Chapuys predicted the course of events with singular accuracy.[67] Only the last details needed to be settled. Paget announced to the council that the king desired Sir Thomas Seymour, Hertford's brother, to be added to their number, and this accession of strength to the party was duly sworn as a councillor.[68] A last sputter of conservative protest may have occurred on 16 January, when the remnants of that faction, Gardiner, Tunstal, and Gage, attended the council for the last time. On the same day, Bishop Bonner's chaplain, Feckenham, preached a strongly conservative sermon lashing out at the religious changes of the last seventeen years.[69] But the king was sinking into his last illness under the close scrutiny of Paget, Denny, and Herbert, while Hertford and Lisle dominated every meeting of the council.

On Thursday, 27 January, all shipping was arrested, and the country was placed on the war footing that accompanied the demise of a sovereign. As Henry was making his confession to Archbishop Cranmer at Westminster that night, in the gallery outside his bedroom Hertford and Paget were arranging the steps in the coup which should bring the former to the head of a new government. While Henry breathed his last the grateful earl promised Paget to follow his advice above any other man's in whatever he undertook and turned over to him the king's last will.[70] Paget took possession of the will and the instant the king died Hertford left, pounding along the roads to Hatfield to seize control of the young King Edward on the morning of the twenty-eighth. The machinery of the coup d'état was set in motion.

CHAPTER SEVEN

THE PROTECTOR'S CASSANDRA

THE accession of Hertford to power in 1547 occurred with such smoothness that historians have disagreed as to whether or not it was a coup d'état. Certainly it was a discreetly managed affair. On the day after his departure from Paget, the Earl of Hertford penned a hasty note to him agreeing to his opening the will, but urging him not to read the entire document until the two of them had arranged matters to eliminate all controversy. Meanwhile, the council kept the king's death a secret until the new king should be brought to London and his forces mobilised. Paget was in the forefront of their activity preparing the Tower of London for the boy king's use. All other questions were deferred to the Earl of Hertford, whom even the dullest councillor recognised as the most powerful of the group.[1] Hertford, on his part, had received an important accession of strength in the person of Sir Anthony Browne, a conservative member of Henry's panel of executors. Sir Anthony Browne had joined him at Enfield to escort the young king to London, and had agreed to support him as lord protector.[2]

On 31 January the news of Edward's accession was proclaimed in London. The old Parliament was dissolved by Wriothesley after Paget had read aloud the portion of the will listing the executors. That afternoon, the king, escorted by Hertford and Browne, rode into the Tower at 3 pm to be met by his council. Afterwards the primacy of Hertford was acknowledged by the other councillors, who 'unanimously' selected him to be the king's governor and protector of his realm. This unanimity was achieved only after a bitter protest against the proposal by Wriothesley received no support, for Lisle and Paget and others carried the day.[3] The protector was so designated in order that there might be a leader in the council and a chief of state to whom foreign ambassadors might resort. However, his powers were limited by the proviso 'that he shall not do any act but with the advice and consent of the rest of the co-executors'.

The next day, all of the nobles and church dignitaries did homage to Edward VI, and Wriothesley declared to them the elevation of Hertford. With one voice they all assented. Paget, meanwhile, drafted the instructions for special messengers to Francis I and Charles V to inform them of the changes in the government.[4] Following that formality and after a rash of allegiances and ceremonial performances of homage in the court, the busy Sir William was instructed to prepare new episcopal commissions under the ecclesiastical seal in his custody and to prepare new signet letters of commission for all the justices of the peace from the council. The two secretaries themselves renewed their commissions by returning their signets to the king and receiving them again from his hand, while Paget similarly renewed his custody of the ecclesiastical seal.[5]

Thus, Hertford and his allies had installed him in power, and the time had come for the distribution of the spoils. The floodgates of patronage were opened by Paget in the name of the late king. On 6 February he and the two chief gentlemen of Henry's Privy Chamber testified to the council that the king's death had intervened to prevent a great distribution of honours and rewards to his faithful servants. Fortunately, Sir William's remarkable head for detail enabled him to make known the dead ruler's intentions. It was known to all men, he testified, that his intimacy with Henry was unique and entailed many private discussions. In one of these chats, Henry and he had discussed the division of Norfolk's and Surrey's lands and offices. Henry had ordered Paget to draw up a list of promotions and a distribution of land to accord with it. Hertford was to become a duke, Wriothesley, Lisle, St John, and Russell, earls, Essex to be a marquess and many knights to become barons. Naturally, most of the deserving were allies of Hertford in the council. Other stalwarts of his party, like Denny and Herbert, were to be rewarded with land grants worth several hundred pounds a year. Although Henry later changed his mind and decided to keep all Norfolk's lands for the prince's use, he appointed that the equivalent be given them from other sources. Paget modestly confessed that he had secured the king's assent to increase most of the grants in the revised list. Denny and Herbert, for their part, testified that they had seen Henry place the list in his nightgown pocket. 'I, Sir Willm Herbert said that Mr Secretary had remembered well all men saving one, and his Majesty answering, therewithall you mean himself? We, the said Sir Anthony Denny and Sir Willm Herbert answered yea, and so praise the said Mr Secretary and so did also His Majesty saying that he remembered him well enough and that he must needs be helped.' The king then ordered them to put Paget down for land valued at 400 marks a year.[6]

Aspersions have been cast by modern writers on Paget's convenient memory, which so rewarded all of the victorious forward party in the council. But, as A. F. Pollard pointed out in refuting his earlier doubts, Paget and the protector would not have included Wriothesley's name in an invented story, for they planned his fall. Nor would the names of St John and Russell, who did not then receive earldoms until 1550, or of seven others, who did not ever receive their baronies, have been included in a counterfeit list.[7]

The councillors virtuously renounced the monetary settlements which Henry had destined for them, but, alleging that land was plentiful, they took their rewards in this form.[8] Paget received lands in Middlesex and Buckinghamshire near his Drayton lands, and in Shropshire and Kent valued at £280 as substantial evidence of the profits of a keen memory and of the virtues of being on the side of the winning faction.[9]

It may be asked why Paget was omitted from the list of proposed peers. His influence with Hertford was surely great enough to secure this reward, but Henry VIII apparently did not consider him for it. The king may have felt that Paget's influence and his roots in his county of Staffordshire were not secure enough to support the dignity of a peerage. Paget received a reward for his service to the protector, however, when on 18 February he was installed in the Order of the Garter.[10]

His election had occurred two weeks earlier for his testimony of 6 February already referred to him as 'knight of th' order'. The elevation in the peerage of Hertford, Lisle, Wriothesley, Sir Thomas Seymour, and others occurred on the seventeenth. Hertford became Duke of Somerset, Essex Marquess of Northampton, Lisle Earl of Warwick, and Wriothesley Earl of Southampton, in the king's presence, while Paget busily read their patents of creation. So large was the number of creations that Garter King-of-Arms was incapacitated by hoarseness from crying aloud their titles.[11] The young king's coronation festivities the same weekend concluded the division of the mantle of Henry VIII among his successors in power, while it pleased the people with spectacular pageantry. Paget escorted the visiting Duke Philip of Bavaria in the procession, preceding his nine-year-old sovereign, 'the lively sight of whose most stately and royal person was to the inestimable rejoicing and comfort of all us his grace's true, faithful, loving, and obedient subjects'.[12]

By the beginning of March, Protector Somerset and Paget were ready for the next step in the former's advance to unlimited authority, which the latter saw as his own road to greater power. Somerset's legal position was based on the council's selection of him as protector, but in this role he was only the leader of that body, a *primus inter pares*. The campaign to cast off this limitation began, of necessity, with the elimination of Wriothesley, who could be expected to oppose strenuously any further elevation of Somerset. His support of Somerset in disgracing Norfolk and Surrey had been based on loyalty to Henry's wishes and not on affection for the man who profited from their fall, as his opposition in the Privy Council to the creation of the protector clearly showed. His known ability and his conservative views made him a dangerous enemy. Unfortunately, he failed to realise his danger. He gave his enemies an opportunity to strike at him by using the Great Seal in his custody to commission officers in Chancery who could substitute for him in that court and free him for affairs of state.

A protest from common lawyers jealous of the Chancery Court promptly appeared. Upon investigation, it was found that Wriothesley's act had been without authority. The protector and council dismissed him from office and confined him to his house awaiting the imposition of a heavy fine. As Paget worded their thoughts, it would never do to let the Great Seal remain in such 'stout and arrogant' hands. The seal was temporarily given to Lord St John, although rumour falsely mentioned Paget as a likely successor to the lord chancellor's dignity. As for Wriothesley, within a few months he was released from confinement and restored to the council by the amiable Somerset who felt that the earl's opposition no longer mattered in view of his own advance to an impregnable power.[13]

At the time of Wriothesley's disgrace, Stephen Gardiner also learned abruptly from Paget that the new government eyed him with disfavour, and that Paget himself wanted little to do with his old patron. The realisation came abruptly. In early February the bishop had written a friendly letter to Paget which must have been answered politely, but on 1 March he wrote a lengthy protest against Paget's wording of his new episcopal commission. Apparently feeling sure the secretary was a religious conservative, Gardiner warned him against becoming known as a 'pincher' of bishops. Gardiner acknowledged his own exclusion from government cheerfully, saying he intended to study the law to keep occupied. Paget's reply was cold and blunt. The slur at his becoming a perse- cutor had annoyed him greatly. He praised his own restraint in religious matters in Henry's time, saying,

> In his days that dead is (God save his soul) I never did that I might have done. I never loved extremes; I never hindered any men to him but notable [misdoers]...for private respects I will not do anything wherein the pub- lic cause may be hindered and in public causes I will say and do (as I have done always since I have been in this place) according to my conscience without bending ... I malign not bishops but would that both they and all other men [were] in such order as might be most to the glory of God and the benefit of this realme, and much less I malign your lordship, but wish you well and, if the state of bishops is or shall be thought meet to be reformed, I wish either you were no bishop or that you could have such a pliable will as could well bear the reformation.[14]

Thus, the long friendship of the two men ended abruptly over religion. Paget's rejection of his old master may have grieved him, but, like many a man playing a discrediting role, he ascribed the break to a change in Gardiner's atti- tude.[15]

On 12 March Paget's new master, the Duke of Somerset, consolidated his powers in a patent from the king, which ostensibly confirmed his oral appointment as lord protector. In fact, the patent conferred sweeping new powers upon him. The protectorate was to last until the king's eighteenth birth- day, and during that period Somerset had absolute powers. He might consult any of the twenty-six councillors listed in his patent, but he was not bound to do so, and he might appoint other councillors at will. Thus, his status was changed from that of chairman of a governing committee to that of a viceroy with a panel of advisers, whom he might consult or not as he pleased.[16] The protector was quick to demonstrate his freedom of action. He intimated to the imperial ambassador that audience should be sought with him alone and not with the council. Vanderdelft noted that everyone treated him with reverence and that he was confident of his power. Somerset granted himself an annuity of 8,000 marks to support his dignity, and in the summer of that year his arms were altered to resemble the royal ones his sister Queen Jane had borne.[17]

How did these changes affect Paget? He must have viewed with pleasure the advancement to supreme power of one who had promised to observe his advice above all others'. It seemed to him and to others that he was indeed the first minister to one who exercised royal authority and, accordingly, his favour was sought even more assiduously than when he had stood beside Henry VIII.

Paget's economic status was by 1547 the equal of any noble's in the eyes of the law, for he was assessed at ten light horse and ten demi-lances for the defence of the realm like the other leading councillors and the nobility, while for subsidy purposes he was rated with the same group.[18] But his influence in the country depended on his influence with the protector, which was evident to all. For Somerset never allowed his adviser to stray far from his side. Except when the duke made his campaign in Scotland in the summer of 1547, Paget travelled with him constantly, escorting him three days' journey northwards even on that occasion, while he was the only council member to accompany him on inspection tours to Portsmouth and to Dover in 1548.[19]

It was evident to the other councillors that Paget and Somerset were keeping the handling of foreign affairs largely in their own hands. When foreign ambassadors negotiated with the council it was Paget with whom they spoke, and during his temporary absence to visit his Staffordshire estate they experienced difficulty in transacting business. Vanderdelft even asked Paget to stand godfather to his newborn son in order to increase their intimacy and thus smooth the path of Anglo-Imperial negotiations.[20] Both Vanderdelft and his French colleague De Selve testified in their reports that Paget was, of all the councillors, the man most in authority and the 'principal manager here now'. Although they reported Somerset's power was absolute, he was ruled by the advice of Paget.[21] These estimates of the secretary's influence were reflected in personal letters to him from the emperor and at least one from Francis I, designed to enlarge his ego and make him incline towards their magnanimous authors.[22]

Sir William was, of course, careful to inform foreign emissaries, naturally in strictest confidence, of his own importance! He told De Selve that no man in the realm knew Somerset's plans and power so well as he. One of the best illustrations of this intimacy was the New Year's gift which he gave the protector on 2 January 1548. 'Because the determination to renew gifts of the new year was sudden I could not prepare such a new year's gift for your Grace as the fashion of the world required ... yet, considering the favour of your Grace to be special towards me, and my love the reciproque towards you, methought it best to send ... a token of my heart.' The token was a list of admonitions which Somerset was urged to consult daily, like a mirror. Paget already had seen flaws of character in his friend of the sort which eventually caused his fall. Some of the injunctions were: 'Make assured and staid wise men minister under you ... Punish the disobedient according to their deserts ... Reward the King's worthy servants liberally and quickly ... Be affable to the good and stern to the evil. Follow advice in council, take fee or reward of the King only. Keep your ministers about you incorrupt. Thus God will prosper you, the King favour you and all men love you. W.P.'[23]

Among the men who noted his influence was the Earl of Warwick, the other leader of the forward party in the previous reign, and the dominant figure of Edward VI's last years. He made use of Paget's intimacy with the protector to seek a grant of Warwick castle and park. Other solicitors cannily enlisted Paget's influence to outweigh that of the lord chancellor, knowing that his hold on Somerset's esteem would prevail. The University of Cambridge, with a quick eye for its interests, named their distinguished alumnus, Sir William, to be High Steward of the University and entrusted its future to his powerful protection.[24]

Paget felt secure enough in his unofficial post as Somerset's special adviser to feel overburdened with his duties as chief secretary, and to desire to free himself from the post in order to hover close to the protector's ear. The secretary's office had placed him close to Henry, where his grasp of detail and ability to follow the king's tortuous path had made him a power, but with a boy king on the throne he felt that he had outgrown that strategic nerve centre of administration. It may have been this desire to avoid weighty routine duties that led him to refuse the lord chancellor's post, if, as Vanderdelft reported, it was offered him.[25] At any rate, on 16 June 1547 he was said to be planning to give up the secretariat for two or three profitable and easy offices. By 29 June he had made the change and become comptroller of the king's household and, two days later, sole chancellor of the Duchy of Lancaster, a post he had shared with Sir John Gage since September 1546.[26]

These two offices were sinecures as far as the labour they entailed but were not without influence. The comptrollership was described a few years later as the second in the 'compting house' by place, but most in charge by office. The lord great master of the household was the ranking officer of the counting house and was assisted by the treasurer and the comptroller who controlled the three masters of the household, two clerks of the greencloth, and six other lesser officers.

As comptroller, Paget maintained the accounts of all moneys allocated for the expenditures of the royal household, which in his first six months in office amounted to £18,000. For his service, he was entitled to £107 a year and a table at court.[27]

As chancellor of the duchy, he received £142 a year and allowances for his expenses. He had great powers of patronage, having seventy-three church benefices and dozens of offices throughout the kingdom in his gift. A list of the twenty-two receivers and three surveyors of the duchy, from this period, which shows the names of many of Paget's friends and retainers, indicated that his patronage was employed with effect. The gross income of the duchy was over £18,000 a year at this time, but its many highly salaried officers at the same time reduced this total revenue while they supplemented Paget's.[28]

As chancellor of the duchy, he had great influence over the parliamentary choices of the eighteen duchy boroughs which reinforced his own influence in Staffordshire. Lichfield was later given parliamentary representation at his request and he controlled its elections and those of the county as well under Somerset and later under Queen Mary and Queen Elizabeth. For the Parliament of 1547–52, returns survive for only half the duchy boroughs, but two-thirds of them named government officials who were friends of Paget's. In addition, he managed the entire election of 1547 for Somerset, though he had left the secretariat before it took place. To judge from the meagre references of the Common's Journals, he also served as the leader of the house for the government in the second session of this Parliament.[29]

But Paget's desire to drop out of the administrative side of the government proved constitutionally impossible for him. He had spent too many years in the secretariat to be able to leave it entirely. Letters from English military leaders and English ambassadors abroad asking instructions continued to come to Paget.[30] The French ambassador noted, two months after his departure from the secretariat, how Paget was still

turning over to the council for action many letters addressed
to him. At almost the same time, Vanderdelft commented
that although Paget intended to retire from active management of affairs, he still held the chief place in managing all
manner of business, an opinion with which De Selve still
concurred a year later.[31]

His share in the formulation of Somerset's policy is difficult
to establish, but some clues exist to reveal his feelings in
matters of high policy. Although he was acknowledged as the
chief adviser, in most cases Somerset's own inclinations guided
the government's actions. Perhaps the most congenial field for
the two men was religion. Somerset, though inclined to further
religious reforms, was above all a moderate man, and with
that Paget was in hearty agreement. The evidence for Paget's
views on Somerset's moderate religious changes exists principally in the reports of Vanderdelft to Charles V. They
must be used with care for Paget consistently exaggerated
his moderation to the imperial ambassador. The emperor,
who was waging war on heresy in Germany, was very sen-
sitive to its encouragement in England. Vanderdelft rarely
talked to Paget without warning him against Zwinglian tendencies in religion. The wily Sir William usually took these
admonitions agreeably, but he strongly supported the use of
the Paraphrases of Erasmus when this innovation was criti-
cised. He also pointed out to Vanderdelft that the images
which had been removed by Somerset's order from the country's churches were only the idols which were mistakenly
venerated as miraculous by the populace.[32]

But Paget was nervous at the continued gradual religious
changes being undertaken by the protector's fiat. On 2 February 1548 he included a plea for caution in one of his frequent
'remembrances' to Somerset of various government policies
that needed implementing. The protector was advised 'to
appoint the number of learned men as well for the consideration of the laws which are to be continued and which
abrogated as also for the decent orders to be observed in the

church and staying all things unto the parliament time; then with advice and consent of the body of the realm to continue or alter such things as upon great and deep consideration and foresight shall be thought convenient and agreeable both to God's love and preservation of the policy of the realm ... otherways be uncertain, sudden and dangerous to you and yours'. Whether or not the duke was swayed by this warning, the administration of the sacrament in both kinds and the election of bishops by letters patent were both established by act of the Parliament before its dissolution in April.[33]

In the summer of 1548 Paget began to hang back increasingly in religious matters, not because he disagreed with Somerset's theology, but for reasons of state. He had already noted that Somerset's hand was unduly light on the populace and must have felt that the protector was promoting discord and unrest by the manner in which religious changes were effected. Paget certainly encouraged the imperial ambassador to remonstrate with Somerset over his religious policy. Yet he was still a Protestant in his own religious preferences for he told Vanderdelft, 'we will consider God's service; and although we have put down several services, we hope no one will accuse us of having acted against Him'. His glibness in reference to 'the living God' in his letters would certainly have persuaded Gardiner or Bonner of his opposition to the old religion.[34]

As the months passed, Paget was finding his post of chief adviser to Somerset more difficult, for the protector was ignoring much of his advice. In foreign affairs, particularly, Paget was unhappy over the trend of English policy. At Henry's death, the country was allied with the orthodox Charles V, while it was carefully negotiating a defensive alliance with France. But the hostility to Scotland which Henry bequeathed to Somerset, and the accession in France of a bellicose Henri II, brought the new treaty which Paget negotiated to nothing. As Somerset started north with an army to invade Scotland, relations with France deteriorated badly.[35]

The solution for the problem which Somerset and Paget sought was to negotiate the return of Boulogne to France earlier than the stipulated date, 1554, for some tangible gain. Paget began a 'practice' by secret talks with the French ambassador. The talks were kept secret from everyone in England save Somerset, for Paget explained to De Selve that he was the only one among the councillors who dared mention such a project. After cautious sparring in Paget's chamber, the French raised the delicate question of 'How much?'[36] Somerset replied through Paget that the French must open the bidding so that he would have a firm offer with which to win over Lord St John and his brother, Lord Seymour. Sir William did his best to stir up the matter, hoping the French would agree to an English conquest of Scotland in exchange for Boulogne. But the French demanded Calais as well, and seemed to be using the negotiations only to distract the English attention from the French aid which was being prepared for Scotland. By the end of the year the 'practice' had failed and Anglo-French relations became increasingly tense.[37] At the same time a growing coolness was discernible on the part of the emperor towards his heretical allies. This state of affairs was alarming to a veteran diplomat like Paget.

He took occasion to address a long memorandum to the protector urging him to look to the finances of the government and to the defences of the realm. But fortifications were of little use to England unless there was a field army available, and he urged strongly that the nobles and gentry of the country, especially 'every man of the Council and of the Chamber ... shall be ready to serve either about the King's Majesty's person or to be sent to any place for relief upon any sudden ―― [word omitted] of the enemies'. The worried comptroller also urged, with great foresight, that every quarter of the realm have appropriate dignitaries designated as responsible for 'the stay of the countries', who should be required to remain in their home areas.[38]

Paget was not alone in his uneasiness at the protector's government, for the first signs of discontent on the part of the duke's brother, Lord Seymour of Sudeley, dated from the early autumn of 1547. Lord Admiral Seymour was dreadfully jealous of his brother and felt that his own equal degree of kinship to the boy king and his marriage to the queen dowager, Katharine Parr, gave him an equal claim to supreme power. His first attempts to promote trouble occurred in August and September when Somerset was absent with the army. Although Vanderdelft had expected Seymour to head the Council of Regency, he was merely one of its members. In case of invasion or revolt, however, he was to share with Warwick the captain-generalcy of the realm. Seymour began trying to organise a party of opposition, but Paget, who was recognised as 'the spirit and soul' of Somerset, immediately detected this activity. Paget urged him to be reconciled with his brother for the honour and safety of his family, but the rash admiral desired to follow the precedent of Bedford and Gloucester during the minority of Henry VI. Why should not he have the custody of young Edward, while his brother ruled the realm? In spite of Paget's reminding him that he had consented to the present arrangement, he did not abandon his plans.[39]

Closely related to Seymour's scheming was the strange episode of Somerset's second patent as protector, which he received in Parliament on 24 December 1547. This patent duplicated the earlier one in every respect, except that Somerset's protectorate, instead of running until the king's eighteenth birthday, was to last only until the king should declare otherwise in his own handwriting under the Great Seal. Whether or not Somerset deliberately accepted this chink in his legal armour in return for a parliamentary confirmation of his title, or whether he felt so secure that he regarded it as an opening to prolong his rule past October 1555, the new patent put a premium on control of the young king. Seymour redoubled his efforts to win Edward's affection and informed a confidant that Edward had thanked him for forcing through the new patent.[40]

The one policy of Somerset's which caused more enmity among the ruling class than any other was his attempt to enforce the laws against enclosures. The agrarian lower classes had long suffered from this evil. Enclosure might be the 'engrossing' or concentration of many holdings into one large farm, the enclosure of common lands, either pasture or arable, by the lord of a manor, or the conversion of arable land to pasture. Any of these enclosures might uproot the yeoman and peasant families which had worked their own holdings, but the last was particularly disruptive and was the source of constant complaints particularly in the eastern Midland counties. The Tudor government by statutes and proclamations attempted periodically to check the trend but with negligible success, since each gentleman of the ruling element in the country usually felt that the laws should apply only to everyone else. But the protector began to enforce the statutes effectively, motivated by his keen sympathy for the lower classes, by his humanitarian principles, and partly by his desire for the plaudits of the masses. In so doing, he diametrically opposed the profit motives of the enclosers who were increasing their income as much as one-third by pasturing sheep or by large-scale enclosed farming.[41]

The real dislocation and extent of this economic movement was naturally exaggerated in the minds of the sufferers, and it varied widely in different parts of the country. Under Somerset's rule, a small group of politically conscious men were active in attempting to check the evil practice. This 'Commonwealth' party, including Latimer and John Hales, its chief agent, was aware that popular temper was nearing the explosion point in many of the counties where enclosers were active. In June 1548 Somerset commissioned Hales and five others to inquire into violations of the laws against enclosures.[42] They found many cases. But the offenders with some justice accused Hales of stirring up the people by his biblical exhortations against the rich for their greediness, a charge Hales denied to Somerset. Most significant of all, the Earl of Warwick himself bitterly opposed Hales on this ground,[43] possibly because his park was ploughed up as an illegal enclosure.

It became clear that all of the councillors disliked the new policy. Paget, the duke's closest adviser, was himself accused of enclosing lands in Northampton and the record of his enclosure of 150 acres of West Drayton Common is preserved in the manuscripts of his descendants. Though his Drayton tenants consented to this operation in return for free use of the land after the harvest, at his manor of Great Marlowe, the tenants apparently rose at their first opportunity and took possession of the new fields.[44] The other councillors were equally inclined towards the new economic practices represented by enclosures. But the duke continued to press forward as he said, 'Maugre the devil, private profit, self-love, money and such like the devil's instruments'.[45]

The entire group of councillors were begining to feel that Somerset was too much inclined to his own counsel and that he was turning for advice to a private group of his personal retainers. Even Sir Thomas Smith, one of his staunchest friends in the council, complained to the duchess of how 'they come to kneel upon your Grace's carpets and devise commonwealths as they like, and are angry that other men be not so hasty to run straight as their brains crave'. Paget also was annoyed at the cabal of advisers in the protector's household though he contained his ire until the summer of 1549. The protector's steward, Sir John Thynne, particularly aroused him then for discriminating against one of Paget's servants, revealing, said Sir William, 'his dishonesty and the disclosing of his greedy covetousness'.[46]

As Paget surveyed the state of the world in July 1548, he found little to encourage him. The defeat of English troops in Scotland and the capture of their leader Palmer was the occasion of the first of a remarkable series of warnings he wrote to his heedless friend Somerset about his increasing brusqueness and immunity to advice from his council:

> Sir I beseech your grace most humbly to pardon my departing from you this night ... but I assure your grace, my heart is and was so great for the loss of Sir Thomas Palmer that I should rather have troubled your grace than otherwise ... I love the man in particular friendship, which had beginning of this aptness to serve the King's Majesty, but the loss of him for the service of His Majesty grieveth me ... we have provoked him so much forward with letters accusing his stillness, slackness, and sleeping without doing anything. But sir, for God's sake let us never prick the stirring horse more than needeth from henceforth, and think, sir, that you supply the place of a king and to every wise man every letter, every word, every countenance of yours is enough to cause the dull horse to enter the fire and the quick horse to be busy. Sir, you are now not the Earl of Hertford nor the Duke of Somerset but governor of the King's person and Protector of his realms and subjects and even so, weigh all things in yourself. And remember by times past how the words of a King or cardinal might have moved you and so think yours move other men. I beseech your grace to pardon me; you know my true heart and meaning to your grace ... I am loth to offend your grace, glad to please you, and desirous to tell you the truth because I believe you trust me.[47]

On Christmas day, 1548, the comptroller wrote a great plea for revised policy to Somerset. In a humble introduction referring to the numerous times that 'in sundry consultations apart with your grace' his advice had been rejected, Paget reminded the duke that at the termination of the protectorate the country must be at least as well off as at its beginning. He then analysed the conduct of Somerset:

And the first degree is to look backward whether at your first setting forward you took not a wrong way, as (saving your favour) I think you did, for you have cared to content all men (which is impossible and especially being subjects in such a subjection as they were left) and be loth or rather afraid to offend any. The extremities be never good and for my part I have always hated them naturally. Too much in our old Majesty's time (I speak with reverence and in the loyalty of a true heart to my sovereign lord that was and that now is) and too much in our Majesty's time that now is hath and doth hurt. Then all things were too straight, and now they are too loose; then was it dangerous to do or speak though the meaning were not evil, and now every man hath liberty to do and speak at liberty... Marry, then the prince thought not convenient for the subject to judge or to dispute or talk of the sovereign his matters and had learned of his father to keep them in due obedience by the administrations of justice under the law. And now the ministers of the prince mislike not that every man judge and dispute of their doings upon supposal that all men shall be pleased... What is like to follow your grace knoweth better than I if it be not amended. I know what your gracious and gentle nature can say in the excuse hereof. But alas, sir, you hear not all things nor all men (I would to God you could), and also so soon believe the things to be true that yourself desireth which many times may cause your grace to leave undone things that needeth. If your grace look backward then shall you see that at the first entry of your way, being but in an entry to war with Scotland, in peace with France, in amity with the Emperor, and an indifferent concord with all the world (except Rome), you are now in open war with Scotland, entering into war with France, ready to have the Emperor fall out with you, and in discord with all the rest of the world, besides dissension at home now at liberty to burst out, which yet before was by fear kept in and constrained.

How might this lack of allies, dearth of money, and rise of domestic unrest be ended? Petty economies would not help, said Paget.[48] The protector's first care must be to secure the cooperation of the gentry and nobility to fill the treasury and insure order. Their co-operation would bring far more money than the new tax on sheep which the Commonwealth party had persuaded Somerset to levy.[49] His policy of settling religious matters in the Parliament by an act of uniformity was ill-advised, as that body should first pass a subsidy. Paget urged that his reliable auditor in the duchy, Sir Walter Mildmay, be put in charge of the levying of money. Most important of all, Somerset's reforms should be slowed, advised Paget, 'for your matters of policy at home (although many are meet to be amended if times served) yet now [ought] not to embrace more than needs'. The religious changes of the proposed act of uniformity should be weighed to see 'whether it may be so set forth as God be pleased and the world little offended . . . Let the greatest sort be brought in credit abroad in your realm for the stay of good order among the people and appoint us of the Council to attend upon your grace and discharge us of foreign offices in particular to the intent we may be the abler to assist your grace for the over sight of the whole in general.' This advice ended with an apology for its 'presumptuous, rash, unadvised, and *outrecuidant* nature'.[50]

Within a few days of this warning, Somerset's government was shaken by the arrest, condemnation, and ultimate execution of his brother the lord admiral, whose persistent petty scheming against the protector had thrived on the increasing dissatisfaction of the great nobles—nobles whose importance in government was being ignored by the duke.

Seymour's jealousy had fed upon a dispute over precedence between his wife, the dowager queen, and the arrogant Duchess of Somerset. Warwick may have encouraged the latter in stirring the protector's anger, but Seymour gave plenty of cause. He continually attempted to win Edward VI by presents and to secure secret letters from him, while his scheming after his wife's death for a marriage with Princess Mary or Princess Elizabeth was intolerable. Paget was very active in interrogating the admiral and the witnesses against him. It was Paget's hand, too, that drafted a harsh letter to Princess Elizabeth informing her of a change in her household. And when, in the Parliament, the case was discussed, Paget was deputed by the Commons to request the House of Lords to furnish them details on the case, since Sir William himself had initially explained Seymour's offence to them.[51]

In Seymour's execution the nobility and all the councillors agreed, since those who disliked the protector could see it was a damaging blow to his prestige. For Somerset's policies had alienated many who formerly supported him, while his disposition had made him increasingly difficult to serve. His tendency to supervise every detail of government himself had increased alarmingly, and his cavalier treatment through his own Court of Requests of nobles whom he felt had mistreated the poor did nothing to reconcile them to him. His strict interpretation of the marriage vows alienated the Marquess of Northampton, who was forced to put away his new wife. It was these early signs of an autocratic spirit that had moved Paget to warn the duke against hot words to subordinates in July 1548.[52] The protector, however, did not change his character. Vanderdelft noted the infrequency with which he held council meetings, and his travels to the south coast accompanied only by Paget and one other councillor.[53]

The duke's tart manner was made worse by his wife. Anne, Duchess of Somerset, has already been noted as arrogant in her dispute with Katharine Parr. Every indication of her disposition is unfavourable. Sir John Cheke, a loyal follower of her husband, was forced at one time to humble himself to her because of a fancied insult from his wife. The secretary, Sir Thomas Smith, similarly found himself in her disfavour for his fancied opposition to the Commonwealth party. In his exoneration he strongly condemned the clique of hotheads who hovered around her defaming busy executives for being faint in religion and greedy of land, two charges of which Smith was singularly innocent. It was disconcerting to a loyal councillor to have 'your grace showed me certain of my faults, the which you said, men noted in me. It was no little discouragement to me after watch and care, wherewith I was then a little vexed, to have such a rere-supper, and a clapping of the back after my travails.' [54]

Comptroller Paget owed his own temporary alienation from Somerset in the spring of 1549 to the heavy hand of the duchess, whom he freely admitted to Vanderdelft was a nagging and bad wife.[55] His first intimation of the august lady's displeasure he passed on to Somerset in a letter, which he concluded with thanks for the continued esteem of the protector and the words 'and until now I believed my lady's grace had thought the same'. Most of the disagreement occurred over a suit Paget was pressing which Somerset had rejected. Sir William in his disappointment left court and went to his West Drayton estate, but troublemakers reported to Somerset that he was disaffected. 'I have been informed that your grace hath conceived some displeasure towards me for certain communication to [sic] which hath been reported to your grace of my mouth,' wrote he. Though Paget admitted his disappointment freely he also wrote that he understood why the request was impossible. He had been hurt only because he had heard that the duchess had opposed him, which 'went to my heart like a dagger'. Paget was a dissimulator in many things, but he was genuinely attached to Somerset, and he was greatly relieved when his relations with the duchess and her henpecked husband were again upon the old terms of affectionate esteem. Paget explained to his friend that the many times he had been squelched in the council by the duke, though they had wounded him, would not prevent him from continuing to advise freely, so long as he knew he kept Somerset's regard.[56]

It was against Somerset's sharp tongue that Paget wrote one of his boldest protests two months after their reconciliation. Somerset's heavy hand in the council had caused people to avoid giving him advice. Paget himself confessed that in private the duke was gentle and gracious but in the council 'as I am more liberal to speak than others ... your grace nips me so sharply sometimes as, if I knew not your conditions well and were not assured of your favour, I might many times ere this have been blanked for speaking frankly'. But other men were often hurt as he knew well, having spent the afternoon consoling 'poor Sir Richard Alte', who had felt the rough edge of the protector's tongue.

> Your grace peradventure thinks it nothing, but by God, sir, if you would, as I wrote once to you, call to your remembrance how that as you spake some times to men in saying their opinions contrary to that which you conceived, if a king or cardinal in times past should have spoken to you, it would have pricked you at the stomach. ... However, it cometh to pass, I cannot tell, but of late your grace is grown into great choleric fashions whensoever you are contraried in that which you had conceived in your head ... A subject in great authority (as your grace is) using such fashion is like to fall into great danger and peril of his own person besides that to the commonwealth. Which for the love I bear to your grace, I beseech you, and for God's sake, to consider and weigh well, and also when the whole Council shall move you, or give you advice in a matter (like as they did of late for sending of men to Boulogne) to follow the same and to relent some time from your own opinion. Your surety shall be the more and burthen the less.

Six weeks later, however, it was evident to Paget that his words had not been heeded.[57]

The comptroller was already well launched in his role of

Jeremiah to the unheeding ruler of the chosen people. He was not only concerned with Somerset's brusqueness to the servants of the crown. He continued in a mounting crescendo of warnings which grew ever more strident to urge the duke to change his foreign and domestic policies. These letters were at once a tribute to the protector's tolerant affection and to Sir William's piercing insight into the contemporary science of government.

In foreign policy he urged most strenuously in January 1549 that someone be sent on pretext of explaining the proceedings against the lord admiral to 'decypher' the emperor, 'For God's sake, sir, follow things when time requireth and whiles time serveth', for unless the emperor were solidly behind England, the country was dangerously isolated. Simultaneously, spies must ferret out the French intention, while the country's treasury and defences were prepared against the contingency Paget feared. On 2 February he wrote a searching estimate of the European scene prefaced by a plea 'to weigh and ponder my writing again and again and make me not to be a Cassandra, that is to say, one that told the truth of dangers before and was not believed... And now, sir, lift up, lift up the eyes of your heart and look in what terms and in what compasses you stand...' France was on the verge of war to aid the Scots; the emperor was hostile and England was without money. There were no allies available in Germany nor might the realm stand alone.[58]

'What then, sayeth your grace, all in desperation? Nay, by Saint Mary, sir, but where strength faileth essay what art will do... Wherefore methought yesternight your grace began to devise well to feign friendship with the Emperor to seem to yield to him, to dally with him, to win time of him...' The things which had been done in religion should be stayed, said Paget, for the Act of Uniformity of 1549 and the Prayer Book were too drastic for the emperor. The previous changes were only forms and could be explained to him. If Somerset felt that one should seek first the kingdom of God, Paget replied, 'you may lie long enough in the ditch or God will help you if you help not yourself'. While the emperor was being courted, the nobility and gentry should be sent throughout the realm and into the restless counties of Suffolk, Norfolk, Kent, Sussex and Wiltshire to keep order. The laws should be vigorously enforced, 'For so shall you bring in again obedience which now is clean gone...the noblemen shall be regarded and every other man in his place abroad in the world reputed as he ought to be. Whereby quiet shall ensue among ourselves... We shall no more say "thou papist" and "thou heretic", for your law the last year for the sacrament and this year for the ceremonies will help much the matter if they be well executed.' [59]

But no embassy went to the emperor and the Parliament dragged on, busy with the debates on the Prayer Book. Paget begged the duke 'for God's sake to end the Parliament' so that the energy of the nobles and gentry might be turned to the quiet of the realm and its defence. The unhappy comptroller felt that religious matters at that crucial period were non-essential items and should have been deferred, and since money had been voted the Parliament should be dismissed. Wotton and Mildmay should be named to supervise money matters and Wriothesley's experience should also be employed in this, he advised. As for the peace of the realm, Paget urged the protector to send Russell to the west and Warwick to the north to keep order. He might have saved his ink, however, for though the Parliament was ended none of his other recommendations, which might have saved Somerset much grief, were adopted.[60]

Sir William Paget remained Somerset's chief adviser, almost his sole adviser from the Privy Council, but his copious advice was ignored. Indeed, if the duke heeded any advice at all, it was that of his 'new council' of young men who urged his economic policy ahead. Paget made an attempt to return Somerset to conciliar control on 17 April 1549. It was a subtle plan. He wrote a series of questions on diplomacy which he suggested 'in my poor opinion were good to be proponed to the whole council'. The paper was prefaced by a new analysis of the European scene and of the dangerous state of the realm, particularly of the bold and disorderly tendencies of the common people. The questions for discussion were whether to make a peace with the Scots after eight years of war or to make open war on France as well by continuing to attempt the conquest of Scotland. There could be no doubt that Paget favoured peace as the sole alternative to national ruin.[61]

However, it was too late to revise English policy even had the obstinate duke so desired. For in the latter part of May a series of popular uprisings began all over the south and west of England, which paralysed the English freedom of action and afforded an opportunity to its enemies. The rebels were motivated by extreme annoyance at the lack of a remedy for their economic difficulties and, in the extreme west, by religious conservatism. In May the commons rose in Somerset and Wiltshire and the counties thereabouts and 'plucked down Sir William Herbert's park' and many other enclosures. In June, Cornwall and Devon rose in arms and rejected the Prayer Book, and later a revolt in Norfolk followed, which captured Norwich and set up a commonwealth of its own. Even the peaceful counties were in a state of 'quavering quiet'. In spite of Paget's desire for prompt repressive measures, Somerset at first attempted to appease the rebels by proclamations and offers of pardon. He did at long last send the nobles to their home counties to preserve order as Paget had for months besought him, and sent Lord Russell with troops against the religious rebels in the west.[62]

In this critical circumstance the protector finally adopted another Paget plan, to send someone to renew the old alliance with Charles V and secure his support for England if France began a war to recover Boulogne. Even while this necessary measure was being attempted, the emperor was further outraged by Somerset's sending two Privy Council members to put pressure on Princess Mary to accept the Prayer Book.[63]

Somerset, however, sent his best diplomat to try to effect the desired Anglo-Imperial rapprochement. He sent Sir William Paget.

Paget's task was exceedingly difficult, for the emperor, even before the revolts began, had expressed to Vanderdelft his aversion for a stronger tie with England. Fearing that Paget's trip was only a ruse to scare the French, he hoped he would not come. Sir William, as was his custom, drew up his own instructions, ordering himself to renew and confirm the old alliance, and above all to bind the emperor to defend Boulogne against France even if he had to offer to sell it to him. In addition, he was authorised to arrange a marriage between Princess Mary and the Infante of Portugal in order to strengthen the ties between the Hapsburg and the Tudor families.[64]

Paget left England in early June for Brussels with the idea of delaying his talks with the emperor until after separate English–French negotiations should have collapsed. At his first interview with Charles V on 22 June he succeeded in keeping to a general discussion of the renewal of the existing treaty. However, in his private talks with the chief ministers, Granvelle, Arras, and Alva, the following day, he should have been conscious of lack of enthusiasm on their part for the English alliance.[65] He was quite hopeful of success for he felt that the emperor personally was inclined towards a new French war. But, appraising his mission in a letter sent to Somerset, Paget stressed that renewing the old treaty was far less important than insuring a war between the emperor and France. Accordingly, on 26 June, he suggested to Arras in a secret talk that Boulogne should be included in the defensive alliance.

Then ensued a long suspense. The imperial court showed its coolness towards England by a lengthy delay under pretext of its moving to another city. Paget, accompanied by Lord Cobham's son, William, who was in his service, went to Antwerp in search of a good pastry chef, who would brighten his table with marchpane and fancy sugarwork.[66] But his heart was sinking for he knew why Charles V delayed his answer. The revolts in England were spreading. Paget addressed a final heartbroken plea to Somerset to amend his policy. In a moving letter, he recalled to him that he had long feared such disasters as were now come and besought in the name of the affection between them and the promises of the protector before Henry's death to heed him:

> which promise I wish your grace had kept... I was a Cassandra, I told your grace the truth and was not believed. Well now your grace seeth it... Marry, the King's subjects out of all discipline, out of obedience, caring neither for Protector nor King and much less for any mean officer. And what is the cause? Your own lenity, your softness, your opinion to be good to the poor. The opinion of such as sayeth to your grace, 'Oh, sir, there was never man that had the hearts of the poor as you have. Oh, the commons pray for you, sir; they say God save your life.' I know your grace's heart right well, and that your meaning is good and godly. However, some evil men list to prate how that you have some greater enterprise in your head, that lean so much to the multitude...[67]

'Consider... that society in a realm doth consist and is maintained by means of religion and law, and these two or one wanting, farewell all just society, farewell king, government, justice, and all other virtue and in cometh commonalty, sensuality, iniquity, raven, and all other kinds of vice and mischief.' Both religion and law were lacking in England, said Paget. The old faith was illegal and the new not yet accepted by eleven-twelfths of the realm. As to law, 'the common is become a king' and dictated terms. To Paget, the worst error of all was to offer rebels a pardon instead of crushing their first revolt harshly and pardoning the other offenders. He had no sympathy with the rebels' grievances over prices, and as to taking pity on the poor, 'Alas, sir, alas, take pity of the king of your wife and your children and of the conservation of the state of the realm.' Paget felt that much of the trouble was caused by the duke's industry. 'Put no more so many irons in the fire at once, as you have had within this twelve month: War with Scotland, with France...commissions out for that matter, new laws for this, proclamation for another, one in another's neck so thick that they be not set by among the people.' The high prices and enclosures that outraged the poor were common throughout Europe, and if the commons' ancestors had endured them for fifty years, so might they. 'What is the matter then, knoweth your grace? By my faith, sir, even that which I said to you in the gallery at the Tower the next day after the King's first coming there. Liberty, liberty, and your grace would have too much gentleness, which might have been avoided if your grace would have followed advice.' Sir William grieved particularly over the way his advice given in private was ignored and that offered in the council rebuffed, especially when the whole council agreed with him, as in the treatment of the commons. For, he pointed out ominously, not the duke alone was answerable to the king for his conduct, but also those of the council who gave him his power.

This powerful condemnation was concluded with Paget's offer to retire from the council, if Somerset desired, and with several pages of encouragement and advice. The example of Henry VIII was held up as a model of an orderly governor and the German Peasants' Rebellion as the fruit of gentleness. By using the mercenaries at Calais, the Welsh horse, and by rallying the gentry, order might be restored. A liberal use of hemp on the ringleaders of each county and pardons for their followers was Paget's formula for the quiet of the realm. Though Somerset lost poor men's love, he would not forfeit the esteem of honest men, he felt. Finally, he should abolish his private Court of Requests and allow the normal course of justice to function. Paget agreed that enclosures should be punished, but urged that they be handled quietly one at a time without affording a spectacle for the common people.[68]

His outburst to Somerset did not relieve his mind; Paget knew the emperor would do no more than renew the old treaty for reports of revolution in England were widespread. However, he had a lengthy interview with the gouty Charles before he returned to England. He found the emperor fully minded to maintain the old alliance intact, although he would not take Boulogne into its terms.[69] In response to a private and secret request from Paget, he inveighed against the recent religious innovations of Somerset. The adept comptroller carefully memorised the royal objections to reinforce his own advice to the protector. Charles also remonstrated with Paget at the attempt to alter his cousin's religion, and received Paget's assurance that such practices would be stopped. Then the comptroller was free to return to his disturbed country from his unsuccessful mission. He arrived at court near 1 August to try once more what he could do to lead the protector out of his difficulties.[70]

Things seemed somewhat improved. The siege of Exeter had been raised by Russell, Lord Grey, and Herbert, and the western rebellion nearly extinguished. In a burst of energy, Paget pressed the duke to concentrate on assembling money and planning his expenditures for the future, even if some of the military precautions against Scotland had to be diminished. The disaffected councillors had rallied to the government temporarily in suppressing the rebellion, and Paget, Warwick, Arundel, Russell, and several other nobles had contributed heavily to the crown's financial needs.[71] But Paget must have been aghast at the zeal with which Somerset adopted his advice for severity against one rebel, for his own brother Robert Paget had been an acknowledged ringleader in the west. One might almost suspect the much-advised duke of irony in writing to the western commander, 'For Robert Paget, considering his offences...we think him an evil instrument of this commonwealth and to have deserved death with the worst and therefore we have now resolved.' But Russell delayed the execution, motivated perhaps by his regard for Sir William Paget, for a month later Somerset rebuked the western commander that the matter was 'touching our honour, for as we have been credibly informed divers have not left unspoken that we should consent to [the] death of our own brother and now would wink at him'.[72]

Then suddenly the situation of the government worsened. The Marquess of Northampton was defeated in Norwich by the rebels, and the French declared war on England as Paget had so long feared. He was ready with his advice, however, in the last of his letters to Somerset still extant, urging him to abandon Haddington in Scotland and to recall his garrisons there.[73] Once again his advice was followed, but the situation continued to deteriorate. The French were taking the outlying defences of Boulogne one by one, and even though Warwick crushed the Norfolk rebels near the end of August only gloom pervaded the English court. As the month ended, Paget, with his usual uncanny sense of impending disaster, bewailed the state of the realm with tears in his eyes. He may well have sensed what the next five weeks had in store for his dearest but most exasperating friend, the protector.[74]

CHAPTER EIGHT

PEERAGE AND PRISON

BY early September 1549, the Earl of Warwick was laying his plans for a coup d'état which would unseat the protector. The earl was one of the craftiest politicians of the Tudor age, and until 1549 he had co-operated loyally with Somerset. He had, with Paget, helped engineer the duke's establishment in power at the death of Henry VIII and was recognised as a leader in the new government. Although Vanderdelft in February 1547 had predicted a Warwick–Somerset feud because of the former's proud and haughty spirit, the ambassador had swiftly revised his forecast when he saw him loyally serving the duke. Probably the fact which roused the spirit of rivalry in Warwick was Somerset's commission to investigate enclosures in the summer of 1548. The acquisitive earl was a notable encloser and bitterly opposed Hales and his cohorts, accusing them of stirring rebellion among the commons. Yet, despite the protector's stubborn continuation of the anti-enclosure policy, Warwick seems to have been loyal to him in assisting at the elimination of his rebellious brother, the admiral. However, this faithfulness may have been inspired by his reluctance to replace one uncle of the king by the other.[1]

The popular uprisings of 1549 must have convinced Warwick that Somerset should be removed. From that time he began to plot the deed. His own prestige with the gentry and nobility was heightened by his victory over the Norfolk rebels, for Somerset forfeited the credit for the triumph by sending Warwick instead of taking the field himself. By 1 September, the earl was conferring with the religious conservative and dissident Earl of Southampton, Thomas Wriothesley, and with Arundel and St John, seeking means of proceeding against the duke and his 'new council'. Paget was aware of the Warwick faction's withdrawal and sought to get Vanderdelft to reconcile Warwick. He took occasion to reveal his own differences with Somerset to the imperial ambassador. Paget's hint that other means of governing the realm must be found was doubtless conveyed to Warwick at Vanderdelft's secret meeting with the earl a few days later. It may have been the basis of the secret understanding between Warwick's party and Paget, which seems to underlie the events of October, which ended the duke's office of lord protector.[2]

Warwick's faction was skilfully organised in blending the religious conservatives and religious extremists, who opposed Somerset's economic and social policy. The sharpness of temper which the protector had revealed in the council and his obstinate immunity to advice, two qualities against which Paget had repeatedly and vainly warned him, made it very easy for many of the twenty-six original councillors to avoid his presence and to nurse their growing opposition apart. The duke's high-handed 'poor men's' court and his anti-enclosure commission, against which Paget had also inveighed fruitlessly, convinced these dissidents that Somerset was deliberately courting the commons' favour in order to overturn government and society and establish himself as a popular dictator.[3] From the execution of Admiral Lord Seymour until his fall, the number of councillors with the duke never approached the number which had consorted with him in the early months of his protectorate.

When the protector, the king, and a few councillors left London for Hampton Court in mid-September, Warwick remained behind. He had already won the mercenary troops by his battlefield leadership and by his support of their claims for reward in a dispute with Somerset. In the absence of the duke, he was able to persuade the nobility and the city government to enter his camp. No less than nineteen privy councillors joined forces with him. Only Paget, Petre, Smith, Lord St John, and Cranmer were with the protector, and St John and Petre joined him when the conflict became open, while Paget remained as an ally in the protector's camp.[4]

Somerset on 25 September finally indicated that he was aware of his isolation by requesting Herbert and Russell to return to him from the west, but he apparently felt no immediate danger as he gave them until 8 October to join him.[5] On 5 and 6 October, however, his growing alarm was translated into feverish activity. Secretary Petre, whom he distrusted, was sent to demand of Warwick's group the cause of their assembly. The common people were roused by a proclamation calling on them to rally to the king's defence at Hampton Court and by sermons to the same effect. Russell and Herbert were ordered by Somerset and the king in no less than five separate letters to come to the protector's aid, and the urgency of the occasion was indicated by Somerset's son, who served as a courier. A royal letter was also directed to the Mayor of London to provide troops for the king's defence.[6]

The reaction from London was swift. Secretary Petre and St John had joined the conspirators. It was the latter who seized the Tower of London for them. The Mayor of London was directed to obey only the orders of that part of the council in London, and a flood of propaganda against the protector was released, alleging that he was betraying Boulogne to the French and was planning to subvert the new reformed religion. When his appeal to the common people was known it served as fresh evidence of his sinister designs to overturn the social order.[7]

Somerset's sole advantage was his possession of the king's

person, but unless the western army of Russell and Herbert joined him he could not hope to prevail. His untrained peasant levies would be of little use against Warwick's mercenaries and the followers of the London councillors. And he strongly suspected that Paget was disloyal.

Evidence of Paget's understanding with the leaders of the opposition is shadowy. It rests on only three points. His continued and unavailing forecasts of doom during the last eighteen months had been fulfilled to the last degree, and the distress over the state of the realm, which filled his eyes with tears, could only have been heightened by his knowledge that most of the calamities could have been averted if only his advice had been followed. Secondly, the reward which he received from the victorious rebels would not have gone to a last minute convert to their cause. To fill the gap between these points there exists a remarkable letter from Secretary Smith to Paget, written from the former's prison after the fall of the duke. It is preserved in the Northampton Record Society's Fitzwilliam Manuscripts and is worth quoting: [8]

Sir, I first commend me unto you as humbly and heartily as I possibly may. And whereas I had thought that ye had taken that already I had opened all my heart unto you, I perceive by a word cast out to my wife that ye do not even fully take it so. First, that I ever conspired your death or heard of any such thing in my presence, I do fully deny it and renounce God if ever I did, who now at this time hath most need to help me. I do not deny that on the Sunday in the morning, I trow it was, or Saturday late at night, when my lord's grace first opened this broil unto me (for ye knew before I was away) I told him if it were so, that you did know what it was, no doubt. Then he told me that he had sent you and Mr Petre away. To that I said, 'Alas, Sir, then have you done evil. For there is no man so able to help it in the world as he is, and could better do it, and if you had had more of the Council about you, it had been better. For the love of God, stay him about you, and I would wish Mr Petre too. And herein use their advice; all that remaineth here else hath no experience, and ye shall be sure they will less attempt violence against you having them here.' 'No,' saith he, 'I think he be as evil as the best of them.' 'Though he be, Sir,' quod I, 'yet I am sure he will invent something for you.' 'Well,' sayeth my lord, 'go your ways, and help Cecil to make some more of those letters which he is amaking, and if he be not gone already, I will have him tarry here.'

This is the most that ever I spake of any such matter, which I did then because I thought it true. Any conspiring or motions to kill you or any other, or that you should be committed to Mr Cotton, or any other, I know not, and surely it was not my devyse, nor I was not made privy ... I ever said (I can not deny) that you know the lords' intent, and to what extremities it would come, and what could be already done. The which I did guess of your natural wisdom, long experience, and great familiarity that ye have with them all, who I thought would not hide so great a thing from you ...

Somerset had communicated his distrust of Paget to his duchess, who, from her place of safety, wrote to the suspect, 'Ah, Mr Comptroller, I have ever loved and trusted you, for that I have seen in you a perfect honest friend to my lord, who hath always made the same account and assuredly bare you his good will and friendship as you yourself hath had best trial ... Ah, good Mr Comptroller, for Christ's blood's sake, spare not for pain, study, and writing ...'[9]

On 6 October Somerset had armed about 4,000 peasants, but late that night he took the king, and, accompanied by Cranmer, Paget, and Smith, rode hastily to Windsor to await reinforcements there from the west.[10] But the war of words was going badly for him. As Edward VI noted in his journal, the council at London published their grievances against the duke, 'after which time few came to Windsor'.

On the seventh, each group of councillors addressed long letters to the other wondering at their militant preparations and ordering them to desist. But both factions were willing to negotiate. The city of London refused to support either side with troops, and this inclined the Warwick–Southampton group to seek a peaceful solution, while Somerset knew he lacked the force to resist.[11] Paget, Cranmer, and Smith were all doing their utmost in the cause of peace. Cranmer's gentle nature was averse to conflict, while Paget was almost certainly in communication with the rebels, while even Smith, thoroughly loyal to Somerset as he was, was writing to his colleague Petre in London that Somerset would accept good terms. But it was Paget's hand that drafted a letter for Edward VI informing the London faction that Somerset would agree to mediation, and that he had meant well in his government and did not deserve the death penalty. The gentleman who bore this letter also carried the protector's proposed articles of mediation, and a lengthy and gentle plea for a guarantee of the duke's life if he agreed to surrender, which was probably written by Cranmer, but bore the signatures of Paget and Smith as well.[12]

Somerset's surrender was undoubtedly influenced by the advice of his three councillors. But when he received a letter of 8 October from Russell and Herbert he knew there was no succour from them. They informed him, 'Your grace's proclamations and billets sent abroad for the raising of the commons we mislike very much.' As Paget had known, the love that Somerset had for three years been bent on arousing among the commons had awakened sentiments of quite a different nature among the gentry. Had not Sir William Herbert's park been one of the first victims of the rebellious commons in May?[13]

The receipt of the protector's articles of surrender and of his council's letters of 8 October stiffened the terms of

Warwick and his allies, as did Russell's and Herbert's adherence to their cause a few days later. Ambassador Vanderdelft, who hoped Warwick's success would bring a return to more orthodox religion, wrote to his sovereign that nothing could save Somerset's life, and that he wondered at Paget's delay in deserting. However, he assured the councillors to whom he had spoken of Paget's integrity, which they significantly assured him they knew well. The Warwick–Southampton faction, confident of the protector's surrender, proceeded to publish twenty-eight articles condemning his pride, misgovernment, ignoring of advice, and encouraging of rebellion, which proclaimed him a traitor.[14] To the king and the protector, however, and to Paget, Smith, and Cranmer they wrote in more amiable fashion.

Their letters were delivered at Windsor early on the morning of the tenth[15] by Sir Philip Hoby, who declared to the king the London councillors' loyalty. The duke, he assured, would not be hurt in any way, while to the three councillors he delivered their letter instructing them to restore the king's own servants to his chamber. In Sir Thomas Smith's account 'all the aforementioned there present wept for joy and thanked God and prayed for their lords; Mr Comptroller fell down on his knees and clasped the Duke about the knees and weeping said, "Oh my lord, oh my lord, ye see now what my lords be" '.[16]

Paget might well rejoice at the duke's safety and his decision to surrender. For him, it meant the end of a government obstinately blind to his advice, and, at the same time, the safety of its leader, whom he liked personally. He had, however, carried out his own part of his private understanding with Warwick and Southampton by dispatching his servant Bedill to them secretly the day before. Bedill's message was that the duke would surrender and that he, Paget, was in a position to arrest the duke. Paget was immediately thanked for these 'wise and stout doings' and ordered to take Somerset, Secretary Smith, and the duke's household officers, Thynne,

Whalley, and Cecil, into custody. These instructions Paget acknowledged in a brief note to Warwick and Southampton.[17]

The council quickly dispatched the vice-chamberlain, Wingfield, with two other officers and a strong force of guards to take custody of the prisoners. For Paget's secret letters had been substantiated by the official letter of Cranmer, Paget, and Smith on the tenth saying that the protector had surrendered. The victorious faction was invited to Windsor. It only remained to punish the adherents of Somerset, to restore order by proclamations, and to reward the victors.[18]

The duke, with his followers Smith, Thynne, Stanhope and others, was moved to the Tower on the fourteenth, being led through the city under heavy guard. This decision may have been the occasion of a crisis for Paget. It was reported that he was worried that the council showed him no favour when it reached Windsor, despite the fact that he had removed the king from Somerset's influence and had taken the latter into custody. It may have been the council's sending the fallen protector to the Tower contrary to its earlier promises which disturbed him, but in any case, after several long conferences with Warwick, Paget came away reassured. Warwick's conduct during the next four months confirmed his optimistic feeling.[19]

The carefully contrived alliance, which had pulled down Somerset, had been based on an alliance of Southampton's religious conservative friends, Vanderdelft, the Earl of Arundel, Sir Thomas Arundell, and Richard Southwell, and of the nobility displeased by the protector's enclosure policy, but who were inclined to favour religious innovation. Warwick had been all things to all men, but it was obvious that he would ultimately have to favour one group at the expense of the other. He distributed equally one immediate reward of victory. Herbert, Russell, Arundel, Dorset, Paget, Southampton, and several others were allowed to reimburse themselves for their expenses by over £6,000 apiece from the profits of the mint. Similarly, the new commissions to the privy councillors made no distinction between the executors and the assistant executors in the late king's will.[20] Other favours, however, went almost exclusively to the party of innovation.

Only Arundel among the six noble attendants of the king was a conservative, while the gentlemen of the Privy Chamber were all Warwick adherents. In the committees of the council named at this time for special tasks, no important activity was supervised by groups not controlled by strong Warwick supporters.[21] In the first half of December 1549, Lord Cobham and Sir William Herbert were given the Order of the Garter, while Paget received the wardship of a youth who had earlier been betrothed to one of his daughters.[22] Indeed, the most evident token of Warwick's favour to the erstwhile followers of Somerset and religious change was his attitude towards Sir William Paget.

As early as 7 November Vanderdelft had heard that Paget would lose the comptrollership to Sir Thomas Arundell and would be exiled to Wales as president of the council there. This rumour was still current a month later, presumably encouraged by the crafty Warwick to persuade the conservatives of his orthodoxy. Wanting in perception, Vanderdelft was quite convinced that Warwick was returning to a more Catholic doctrine, but on the twenty-sixth he found Paget and Warwick deep in private conversation at the earl's house. For the first time, the emissary began to suspect that Warwick might maintain the religious policy of Somerset. The result of the Paget–Warwick parley was initially that the former abandoned the comptrollership. On 3 December, however, he received the reward for his desertion of Somerset and for his current adherence to Warwick. He was summoned to the House of Lords as Lord Paget of Beaudesert.[23]

Warwick's undermining of his conservative allies began with the admission to the council of his staunch ally the Marquess of Dorset and of the Protestant Bishop Goodrich of Ely. As the irate imperial ambassador described it, Warwick betrayed his Catholic allies by packing the council with friends of Somerset and young nobles. In the middle of January 1550, he struck down the conservatives, confining Sir Thomas Arundell, Southwell, and others, restricting the Earl of Arundel to his house, and banishing the ailing Southampton from the council after similarly restricting him.[24]

To strengthen his attenuated party, Warwick distributed wholesale rewards. Russell and St John became Earls of Bedford and Wiltshire respectively, while the young Lord Ferrers was promoted to Viscount Hereford and added to the council. Another young lord, Lord Stafford, was given a large grant of land. The great offices of state, which had been taken from Somerset, were redistributed among Dorset, Wiltshire, Northampton and Warwick himself. But the greatest manoeuvre of the Machiavellian earl was to add to his supporters the imprisoned Duke of Somerset. Deprived of his offices and lands by act of Parliament, the duke had confessed to all manner of misdeeds in office, but on 6 February he was released from the Tower. That night he dined with Warwick at the house of one of the earl's followers, Mr York, sheriff of London. On 10 April, the duke was restored to the Privy Council and to the possession of much of his land.[25]

Warwick continued to follow this dual policy for the next year and a half, temporising with Somerset to retain his support and assiduously wooing the younger nobles. Although he was careful to associate himself with the council, his leadership was clear to all. His first act of foreign policy was to negotiate a peace with France. In November 1549, the initial steps in that direction had been taken when a conference was proposed to the French king by a neutral merchant in the English service. Henri II, when he found that the papal election in Italy had gone in favour of Charles V, was inclined to come to terms with England in the north. On 8 January he commissioned four of his ministers to meet with the English. The English council selected the Earl of Bedford, Lord Paget, Secretary Petre, and Sir John Mason to represent them.[26]

Their instructions were singularly loose. They were not given any limit of concession, but were instructed to find out how much the French would offer and then await the council's instructions. The commissioners left London on the evening of 21 January, Paget having been extremely busy his last two days in the city attending Parliament and apprehending a Flemish criminal who had murdered one of the English mercenary captains.[27] He and his colleagues were delayed at Dover for some days and at last put to sea in bad weather, only to be driven back to Dover from the middle of the Channel by a storm. There they received a council letter urging them to advise the young Earl of Huntingdon, the commander of Boulogne, and commiserating with them on their stormy return to Dover, 'whereof we be sorry... [knowing] the dis-ease of some of your company that are no seamen!'[28] Paget's weakness was a standing joke in the council.

Not until 19 February, however, did the English and French peace delegations meet. The intervening period of three weeks was devoted to haggling over the site of the conferences. The French desired to meet between their forts and Boulogne, while the English were desirous of luring the French to Guisnes for reasons of prestige. The settlement of the issue required much writing back and forth. Meanwhile Bedford and Paget were troubled by vague reports of the fall of the conservatives Arundel and Southampton. Paget cautiously wrote a friendly letter to the all-powerful Warwick about his health and received a reassuringly friendly note that the earl's digestion had so improved he could eat 'good and wholesome meats again'. In the issue of the meeting site, however, the English council attempted to shift the responsibility to their commissioners. Paget was too shrewd to give his enemies such a handle by which to seize him, and the Privy Council at last directed the acceptance of the French demands. That surrender was a preview of the future course of negotiations.[29]

As usual in negotiations in which he participated, Paget took the lead in the English delegation. At the very first meeting on 19 February it became evident the French terms would be harsh. A truce was arranged between the armies of the two nations, however, before the meeting adjourned. The second day of the negotiations was devoted to each side's exposition of its most extreme claims, with Paget speaking for England. On the twenty-first he refused two French offers and proposed two sets of English terms, which would have given his country all of its financial claims in return for the immediate cession of Boulogne. The French were adamant and both sides agreed, the French with reluctance, to consult their sovereigns.[30]

That produced the first major break in the deadlock. Henri II authorised his commissioners to increase by fifty per cent his offer of money for Boulogne. Before his new instructions arrived, Paget had written his advice to Warwick. Paget revealed he had had a private talk with one French delegate, 'thinking to have practised somewhat' but to no avail. He blamed the war as the principal cause of high prices, social discontent, and all other English difficulties. Paget admitted freely that the French terms were intolerable, but nevertheless he urged strongly that Boulogne had best be sold for what it would bring. Possibly Edward could renew the war at a more favourable time when he was grown. The Privy Council reached the same conclusion and instructed their commissioners to drop the question of the old debts and take what they could get from the French for Boulogne.[31]

Paget gave way to most of the French demands, only putting up a successful fight to evacuate the English artillery and provisions from Boulogne before its return. For its return, the French were to pay 400,000 crowns in two payments. Paget was so demoralised by his knowledge of the English weakness that he failed to preserve two English fortresses in Scotland, which the French would have conceded, in spite of their inclusion of Scotland in the general peace.[32]

As Paget wrote to Warwick, however, the terms might have

been improved 'if peace and war had been so indifferent of us as we might have adventured sometime to have broken off. . .'. Nevertheless, Paget and his fellow commissioners 'have following our instructions, taken what we may, seeing we can not have that we would, contenting ourselves 'til God send better, whereof by His grace for my part I doubt nothing, utterly persuaded to myself that peace is the first degree to it and as for the other degrees, if your lordship and the rest of my lords shall please to step, there is no doubt but you may shortly get up to the highest step. I mean the commonwealth and estate of the realm may be brought to a perfect and happy estate. . .' At his recommendation, his protégé and friend Mason was named as the new ambassador to France.[33]

It only remained for Paget and Bedford to look to the defences of Calais and to settle a few minor points there for the council. By 29 March they were back in London, and their peace with France was officially proclaimed.[34]

On his return, Paget suffered progressive disillusionment about the regime of Warwick. It was true that Somerset was shortly readmitted to the council, but both the duke and his former adviser found that the earl paid little heed to their advice.

At first, Paget assumed that his role in the Warwick regime would continue to be as important as in Somerset's days of power. Even while he was yet abroad, he favoured the earl with a lengthy essay on conciliar government and the efficient use of that body's time. His suggestion for a secret ballot in the council must have amused Warwick, who desired to know the actions of every councillor. However, in April 1550, Vanderdelft attributed his good treatment at the council board to the return of Paget from the peace negotiations. The protector and his friends expected soon to return to greater power, as Paget's friend Mason informed the ambassador. In June, the duke's daughter was married to Warwick's eldest son, but this was the last encouraging sign to Somerset from the real ruler of England.[35]

For in all his policies, Warwick went contrary to the prece-
dents of his former superiors. In religion, he encouraged the
extremists and promoted such zealous reformers as Ponet and
Hooper to bishoprics. This policy might not have been dis-
agreeable to Somerset, but the zeal with which Warwick proceeded against Bishop Gardiner occasioned a dispute between
them. Somerset, after conferring privately with the Earl of
Arundel, who was still in disgrace, attempted to secure Gardiner's release, and thus incurred Warwick's wrath. The earl's
reply was to banish Arundel to his county and to initiate
measures leading ultimately to the bishop's deprivation.[36]

In his foreign policy, Warwick was not content with seeking
the favour of France, a policy anathema to Paget, but gave
gratuitous annoyance to the emperor by his attempts to enforce on Princess Mary conformity to the new religion. The
persecution of the princess was also contrary to Paget's desires.
He and Somerset had informed Charles it would cease, but
under Warwick the pressure on her grew steadily more intense, despite the protests of the emperor. At the same time
every demand of the French ambassador was being conceded.[37]

The only encouraging feature of the new regime for Paget
was Warwick's land policies. The laws against enclosures were
repealed by a re-enactment of the Statute of Merton, while
the tax on sheep was abolished. The new laws of treason and
felony made it treason to plot against a privy councillor.
Various peasant uprisings were mercilessly suppressed as the
victorious councillors took precautions against a repetition of
the risings of 1549. For the first time, a peacetime standing
army was organised by the council under Warwick's tutelage,
as the garrison of Boulogne was divided among the counties.
Thirteen councillors were to maintain 950 horses at government expense from May 1551 at £50 for each ten horsemen.
But Paget, with fifty men-at-arms, and Somerset with one
hundred, were the only armed councillors who were not
Warwick's whole-hearted followers.[38]

In the spring and summer of 1550 Paget was still active in

the Privy Council, taking the lead as he was accustomed in negotiations with foreign ambassadors. It was rumoured in Paris that he would be sent there to accept the French ruler's ratification of the peace treaty, and his friends and protégés continued to write him letters of news and gossip from abroad. But in reality, his activity at the council board was being relegated to minor tasks such as the auditing of accounts from the various courts of revenue. And while it was not possible to omit Somerset, Paget, Arundel, Shrewsbury, and other lords outside the Warwick fold from the list of lords lieutenant, in most cases they were associated in those offices with dependable allies of the careful Dudley.[39]

As he became more conscious of his exclusion from the inner circle of Warwick's friends, Paget began to avoid the Privy Council. In the summer of 1550 he was away from its meetings more often than not, and once was absent for over a month. During these absences he was able to devote more time to managing his estates.[40]

He had passed in the last Parliament a private bill by which he had acquired part of the churchyard of Drayton parish to increase the garden beside his house, in exchange for an acre of ground at the far end of the village. The only grant which he received from the king under Warwick's tutelage was one petty wardship, but by judicious purchases and leases he acquired small properties in Staffordshire and Derbyshire, while in his capacity as chancellor of the duchy he granted his son, Henry, the rent of one of its properties. The funds for these expenditures he secured by the sale of his house in Chanon Row and by giving up his office of clerk of the Parliaments. Since July 1548, he no longer needed a house in the city, for he had then been granted the noble mansion of the Bishop of Exeter between the Strand and the river, which was owned successively by Lord Paget, the Earl of Leicester, and the Earl of Essex. So active was Paget's ubiquitous estate agent, Fletcher, that such diverse personages as the Bishop of Chester and Princess Elizabeth were forced to beg his master to check the ardour with which he sought new leases.[41]

As Paget became increasingly aware of his loss of influence in the Warwick-dominated council, he made an effort to come to an arrangement with the earl. It was rumoured in September that he had vainly tried to become lord chancellor.[42] In November and December, he became almost as regular an attendant at the council as in the days of his power. At this time, the government was busily preparing for the trial of Stephen Gardiner, prefatory to deposing him from his office. The trial was the occasion of a glaring breach of faith by Paget—the only one of his numerous transfers of allegiance which brought him no reward. One is tempted to believe that on this occasion he fell into the error of supping with the devilish earl without a long enough spoon.

Paget's role in Gardiner's trial was that of witness for the prosecution in its charges of obstinacy and defiance of the council against the bishop. Undoubtedly the majority of the government's charges against the stubborn ecclesiastic were substantially true yet Paget's evidence enraged him. On 23 January the trial held its eleventh session at Paget's house in the Strand. He testified boldly against his old master, alleging, among other things, that Henry VIII on his deathbed had toyed with the idea of bringing him to trial as a traitor. Of this testimony, which was partially confirmed by Somerset, Wiltshire, and Northampton, Gardiner asked several questions of Paget designed to prove Henry VIII had respected him to the end. These questions Paget flatly contradicted. What annoyed Gardiner was that Paget was obviously hostile to him, that he had tampered with the facts in his testimony, and that as a councillor and peer he had testified unsworn. In his concluding remarks, however, he could only charge that his former pupil had neglected honour, faith, and honesty, and had shown himself an ingrate. From that time until the eve of Gardiner's death, there was bitter enmity between the two men.[43]

In pursuance of his attempt to ingratiate himself with the

wily Warwick, Paget had not hesitated to turn on his first patron. If the French ambassador can be credited, he made a great effort to interest himself in the marriage negotiations of Edward VI and the French princess, an alliance he must have disliked intensely. His efforts were without success. Although Warwick for a time considered including Paget among his allies by making him lord chamberlain, the post ultimately was given to another.[44] Paget remained in the wilderness with Somerset.

There were abundant signs that a conflict was growing between the fallen protector and his astute successor in power. For every reward to a Warwick supporter and every advancement of such a minion to the council weakened the influence of the duke. There were many such rewards and promotions. Warwick made himself warden of all the Scottish marches and had granted himself lands in Northumberland, Yorkshire, and Worcestershire to the yearly value of £660. His friends profited too. Lord Clinton was made lord admiral and admitted to the council, while Bedford and the Earl of Rutland were forgiven large debts to the crown, and Sir Thomas Palmer, erstwhile friend and future betrayer of Somerset, was given a yearly pension of £100. As Vanderdelft's successor, Scheyfve, wrote in July 1550, although Somerset and Warwick were both present in the council, the latter was in complete control.[45]

Warwick used his control to pack the Privy Council with friends. Although Paget's protégé Mason was made a councillor, he was packed off to France as ambassador. Lord Cobham, the Earl of Huntingdon, Lord Darcy, Sir John Gates, were all admitted as allies of the earl. Conservatives like the Earl of Derby were similarly courted, and even Arundel's fines were cancelled, and he was re-admitted as a potential ally.[46]

Secure in his strength at the council, Warwick followed a policy of gratuitous insult and rebuff towards Somerset, designed to drive him either to revolt or retirement. Since he

knew Somerset had many friends in Parliament, he successively postponed that body's meeting for over a year. In addition, he must have watched carefully the old conservative
nobles, Derby and Shrewsbury, and Arundel for signs that
they intended to ally with his enemy Somerset. But in October
1550, Somerset was told to bury his mother—and the king's
grandmother—without pomp or ceremony. A few weeks later,
during a serious illness of the king, a foreign ambassador
noted that the council was deeply split between partisans of
Somerset and Warwick.[47]

In February 1551 Somerset's chamberlain, Whalley, was
accused of planning a parliamentary restoration of the protector and of wooing the Earl of Rutland and other nobles in
this cause. But the Parliament was prorogued again and the
scheme was delayed indefinitely. Both Somerset and Warwick
competed fiercely to marry a daughter to the young Duke of
Suffolk, and they nullified each other's efforts. In March there
was an open dispute between the two in the council, and
there were rumours that Somerset favoured a return to the
Henrician religious settlement and was negotiating with
Derby and Shrewsbury. In April one of his henchmen, Vane,
was imprisoned in the Tower, and a rumour spread as far as
the French court that Paget had been sent to the Tower and
that Somerset had rebelled. Even Somerset's friends knew it
would be fatal to proceed to such extremes, however, while
Warwick controlled the north. Sir Richard Moryson, who was
in disfavour with the council, wrote to his friend Secretary
Cecil that he could cast off the dog of disfavour let loose on
him, 'if it be not the mastiff himself'. He also urged Cecil to
persuade Somerset to bow to the superior force of the mastiff
Warwick.[48]

Somerset did moderate his attitude temporarily, though he
conferred privately with Herbert in an attempt to win him
away from Warwick at about this time. Nevertheless, the
aggressive earl abolished the duke's separate table at court
ostensibly for 'economy', and at the Feast of the Garter he had

inserted 'on his mother's side' into the statement of the duke's relationship to the king.[49]

During the summer months of 1551, Paget's withdrawal from the business of government became complete. He was directed by the council to stay away from the court. Only once during August was his attendance noted in the council register. Somerset continued to attend occasionally until the end of August and then he too ceased the useless labour. During his absence, Paget wrote Secretary Cecil several letters asking for news. Cecil was reputed to be a friend of Somerset, so Paget favoured him with fragments of advice and kept him informed as to his whereabouts.[50]

Warwick was preparing to eliminate the danger to his rule implicit in Somerset's existence. As long as the king's uncle was alive and popular with the lower house of Parliament, he furnished a rallying point for popular discontent and for the old conservative nobles, equally displeased with the Dudley regime. Even Warwick's precaution of having the boy king attend council meetings to reinforce his own control could not ensure him against a new Somerset coup. Some form of effective revolt was almost assuredly in the duke's mind, to make use of the growing opposition to Warwick. The duchess had been heard to say she hoped some changes would soon occur. It was alleged by his enemies that he planned to attack the council's troops on their muster day, 8 November, and to raise London, and also that he intended with Arundel and Paget to arrest his enemies at a banquet in Paget's home. The imperial ambassador thought both these charges were false, but Arundel confessed that he and Somerset had discussed a plan to arrest Warwick and his ally Northampton at the council. The duke himself admitted that he opposed a French marriage for Edward VI and that he had tried to get the conservative Earl of Derby's son, Lord Strange, to suggest instead to Edward a marriage to the duke's third daughter.[51]

Warwick was obviously aware of his danger. His first step was to rally his followers by an unprecedented shower of titles and rewards. He took for himself the title of Duke of Northumberland; Dorset became Duke of Suffolk, Wiltshire became Marquess of Winchester, and Herbert Earl of Pembroke. These creations were scheduled on 4 October for Sunday the eleventh. In addition seven gentlemen were knighted, including Secretary Cecil, who soon proved to the new Duke of Northumberland his fidelity to the new hand which paid him. Northumberland and Suffolk received annuities of 50 marks, the new Marquess of Winchester had the same annuity and a fee-farm worth over £200 a year, while Mason, Cecil, and Pembroke had land grants to the annual value of £100, £150, and over £200 respectively.[52]

Northumberland was none too soon. When his ducal patent was read giving him credit for the battle of Pinkie, Somerset's friend and dependant, Lord Grey, boldly denounced this filching of his master's laurels. According to the imperial emissary Scheyfve, popular discontent with Northumberland was reaching a crescendo. Almost simultaneously with his distribution of political largesse to his friends, however, Northumberland struck a shrewd blow at his enemies. Lord Paget was confined to his house for having contradicted the emperor, who alleged Paget had in 1549 promised him religious freedom for Princess Mary. This subtle pretext, which removed from Somerset's party the shrewdest schemer available to it, was typical of the plausible Northumberland. Paget's own reputation for political trickery was such, however, that there was considerable doubt whether he was detained for the reason alleged or for plotting with Somerset, because of Northumberland's coldness to him, or for protective custody after he had betrayed a Somerset plot to Northumberland.[53]

On 7 October, Northumberland set in motion the machinery for crushing Somerset. On that day, Palmer, former henchman of Somerset and Grey, whom he had bought with a pension, 'revealed' to Northumberland in his garden a plan of Somerset's to attack the 800 soldiers maintained by the

council on their muster day, 8 November. Since the muster
had only been scheduled that very day by the council, it was,
to say the least, an incredibly rapid formulation of a plot
on Somerset's part, and a highly unlikely story. What leakage
did occur seems to have been concerning Northumberland's
plan against Somerset, for, by the tenth of the month, Scheyfve
had heard his rival's arrest was being planned.[54]

Somerset took alarm on the fourteenth and asked Cecil
to come to him for a conference, only to be refused by the
freshly bought secretary. On the sixteenth, he came to court
and was arrested and taken to the Tower with his friends
Lord Grey, Sir Thomas Arundell, Vane and Palmer. The day
after, his duchess and another half a dozen of his followers
joined him there. On 21 October, Paget was moved from his
house to the Fleet prison. After examinations of Somerset
and the Northumberland-inspired witnesses, Palmer and
Crane, had implicated the Earl of Arundel, Paget and he
were moved to the Tower on 8 November.[55]

The examination of the prisoners was hurried forward
during November. Arundel, who had been arrested for his
impertinence to Northumberland—when accused of treason
by this son of the decapitated Dudley of 1509, he replied
pointedly that the Fitzalan earls of Arundel had never been
traitors—confessed that he and Somerset and discussed arresting Northumberland. On 1 December, Somerset was tried
for treason and felony before a packed court. His spirited
defence completely discredited Palmer's 'confession' of a plan
for armed revolt, but he was condemned for felony. The
far-sighted Northumberland in the parliamentary session of
1549–50 had passed a law, making it a felony to plan the
death of a councillor. In the midst of a popular demonstration
Somerset was returned to the Tower, to leave it only for his
execution on 22 January 1552.[56]

Paget's detention in the Tower was less rigorous than that
of Somerset and the 'conspirators', for he enjoyed the ques-
tionable privilege of providing his own diets, lights, fuel,

and servants.[57] During his confinement and interrogation, the council protected his steward in the administration of the Paget household, but Lord Paget was deprived of his office as chancellor of the Duchy of Lancaster. The seals of that office were taken from him and given to Sir John Gates, one of Northumberland's most faithful followers. From early December 1551 until May 1552, Paget remained a problem for the council. The real cause of his disgrace was his friendship for Somerset, but he was not involved in the conspiracy charged against the unhappy duke. The difficulty of finding a suitable pretext for punishing him is attested by the frequent notations in Cecil's memoranda, 'L. Pagett's matter'.[58]

While yet he remained in the Tower with the other prisoners, there were signs that his life was in no danger. On 27 February, Lady Paget was given permission to visit her husband in the Tower.[59] This permit was revoked on 11 March but no one feared for his life any longer. Ambassador Scheyfve reported that there was no danger he would be executed with Somerset's followers. Shortly afterwards, Lady Paget was allowed to repossess her husband's property from the royal receivers.

Although Paget's head was safe, his dignity had still to undergo grave trials. Just before the annual feast of the Order of the Garter, the heraldic officer of the order was sent to the Tower and took away his Garter, as the king said 'for divers his offences and chiefly because he was no gentleman either on his father's side nor mother's side'. His name was also erased in the parchment book of the Garter, and he was succeeded by Northumberland's brother, Sir Andrew Dudley.[60]

The offences to be charged against the imprisoned Paget were finally decided, however. He was to be punished for malversation in office as chancellor of the duchy. Wisely he co-operated in confessing to all that was desired when 'the mastiff himself', Northumberland, disapproved of his first submission as being framed 'with subtlety and dissimulation only to abuse the King's Majesty's clemency'. The wolfish duke approved whole-heartedly of the second draft in a letter to Cecil, as he well might, for Paget as secretary of state had learned the glib phrases of humility in the chambers and palaces of a lion. This submission was signed by the offender on the last day of May and approved by the king's attorney and solicitor. In it Paget 'confessed how he without commission did sell away my lands and greater timber woods, how he had taken great fines of my lands to his said peculiar profit and advantage, never turning any to my use or commodity, how he made leases in reversion for more than twenty-one years. For these crimes and others he surrendered his office and submitted himself to those fines that I or my Council would appoint.'[61]

The youthful king's description of Paget's offences is not born out by the financial records of the Duchy of Lancaster. The net receipts of the duchy for the year ending Michaelmas 1543 were slightly more than £10,000, while eight years later, despite the land sales of Henry and the grants of Edward's council, it was still well over £9,000. And in Northumberland's own survey of the duchy in 1552, his commissioners found no such peculations as Paget had confessed. It is highly probable that Paget's financial administration was as irregular as other nobles' in that day, and that he regularly treated royal funds as his own as was customary of fiscal officers, yet it is also evident from the records that his offences were minor and of little effect on the royal revenues.[62]

In any case, Paget was wise to bow to the superior force. His compliance was rewarded by the restoration of Lady Paget's visits to the Tower and by permission for him to pace the gallery outside his prison and to visit the garden of the governor of the Tower. Meanwhile, the victor Northumberland amused himself with prospective divisions of Paget House and West Drayton among his followers. Lord Paget appeared before the council on 16 or 17 June to make his confession orally and was then ordered released from the

Tower and confined to his house. He was summoned to the council again on 20 June and told that his fine was set at £5,000 and the loss of all his stewardships and keeperships. In addition, he was to depart within six weeks to his Staffordshire estates. He accepted the fine with good grace, but to the rustication he 'made very lamentable and humble suit, with the effusion of many tears', alleging many excuses. He had no provisions in Staffordshire and Beaudesert was so small that his large family within one month would cause it to become 'unsavoury' for him. Lady Paget's 'stitch in her side' and her liver complaint required a London physician's service (she lived until 1587) as did his own fistula which troubled him so he 'rots as he goes'. By such graphic and moving pleas, Paget secured permission to tarry indefinitely in the vicinity of London.[63]

For three months he remained quietly inconspicuous at Drayton. In October 1552, however, Paget felt the time was propitious for securing some moderation in his fine. In a letter to Cecil he asked the secretary's and Lord Darcy's help, while Lady Paget besought the council directly for the king's clemency for her family. Accordingly, he was summoned to the council and his fine reduced to £4,000, for which the government would accept land of the yearly value of £200. Northumberland desperately desired more land with which to purchase allies and supporters. Thus, land, valued officially at twenty times its annual value, would settle Paget's debt. But the canny Paget had not been a financier under Henry for nothing. He succeeded in persuading the government to accept part of his fine in cash. Paget would have preferred to pay the whole amount in that manner for he knew that lands were undervalued at twenty years purchase and desired to cling to his lands and pay his fine in a debased coinage. According to an undated summary of his properties in his papers, the yearly value of Paget's lands was about £1,250, but he had large debts. The king accepted his manors of Appleby, Ilam, and Alcester in Derbyshire, Leicestershire,

and Warwickshire, valued at £100 a year, and his bond to
pay the remaining £2,000 in cash at the next two Christ-
mases. By an exquisite irony he was also required to pay Sir
Thomas Palmer, Somerset's betrayer, for the gold chain
Palmer gave Northampton at the moment he 'confessed'
Somerset's 'plot'.[64]

This great settlement of his fine improved Paget's status.
Scheyfve even heard that he was being considered for the
office of lord chancellor, though he doubted such fortune for
the emperor's favourite Englishman. He reported, however,
that Paget's health, which had suffered from imprisonment,
had improved. Lord Paget received his full pardon for all
offences early in December 1552, and promptly set about paying his fine in full. What means he used to raise such a sum
in so short a time are unknown, but by the end of February
1553 he had paid the first £1,000 and had delivered to the
king an obligation owed Paget of £744 which was accepted
as payment in full, since it came ten months before the last
payment was due. Sometime in early March he was admitted
to the royal presence to kiss the king's hands in thanks for
his complete restoration to royal favour. The Paget coat of
arms, which had been taken from him on the pretext that it
was an illegal grant, was restored to him, and Lord Paget and
his family were free to take their places in society again.[65]

He chose to make himself inconspicuous in the mad pursuit
of titles and lands among Northumberland's allies during the
remaining five months of King Edward's life. While Northumberland completed his plans to oust Princess Mary from
the succession, Paget was busy suing the stepfather of his
ward and son-in-law Henry Lee. As the young king grew
weaker and his coughing began to leave ominous crimson
stains, the powerful duke sought allies. After vainly courting
Princess Mary, he betrothed his son Guilford Dudley to Lady
Jane Grey, daughter of Suffolk and granddaughter of Henry's
sister Mary. He added Westmoreland to the council, forgave
and restored Arundel, and put his brother Andrew in charge

of strengthening the Tower. In spite of occasional temporary improvements in his health, the king grew steadily weaker. Northumberland organised the final reinforcements to his following, and from a brief, packed Parliament in March (from which Lord Paget was absent) he extracted a subsidy.[66]

The busy duke arranged a series of marriages to strengthen his party. Lady Jane's sister Catherine was betrothed to Pembroke's heir, and still another sister was said be be pledged to Lord Grey of Wilton's son. A Dudley daughter was engaged to Huntington's son, and Sir Andrew Dudley was allied to the Earl of Cumberland. With the French ambassador Northumberland conferred privately to arrange for French support. These alliances were made more binding by a shower of gifts to Westmoreland, Pembroke, Clinton, Darcy, Lord Lawarre, Huntington, Shrewsbury, Bedford, and Gates. In the first six months of the year, over £4,000 worth of land was granted to his followers for a meagre £1,000 payment.[67]

In the last half of June, Lord Rich, Sir Thomas Cheynie, and other lesser magnates were summoned to court to give their adherence to the duke's violent plan for altering the succession. The judges and law officers of the crown attempted to balk him, only to see him fly into a rage and offer to fight them in his shirt. The dying king himself directed them to draw up a will leaving the crown to Lady Jane, which all the nobles and magnates were required to witness on 21 June. Paget added his name far down amid the lesser knights of the realm and carefully apart from the others of his estate. The reluctant Privy Council, meanwhile, was bullied into signing a pact to stand by the will. The way was clear at last, and the French ambassador Noailles found the councillors looking relieved after the stormy session just concluded. France offered Northumberland its complete support and all things waited for the death of Edward.[68]

Edward obligingly passed away on 6 July, secure in the knowledge that his will had saved the reformed faith in England. All that was needed was Princess Mary's person secure in the Tower and the reign of Guilford the First would dawn brightly, but the mighty duke discovered that all his plans and bribes were helpless against a popular revolt. Princess Mary fled from the vicinity of London to a house sixty miles away, where she was warned by a staunch Protestant follower of Northumberland that her brother was dead. She promptly proclaimed herself queen under the terms of her father's will, and the commons flocked to her standard. The nobles, however, generally held back.[69]

Meanwhile in London on the tenth, the proclamation of Queen Jane was made to a surly crowd. The forceful personality of Northumberland held together her supporters and troops were raised to follow him against the 'bastard' Mary, as he termed her. His allies, however, were reluctant. On the sixteenth they heard that 10,000 men led by Huntington's brother were gathering at Paget's house at Drayton, while the six ships sent to cut off Mary's retreat had joined her. 'Each man then began to pluck in his horns,' says the chronicler, but Northumberland held all the council prisoner in the Tower, haling back the reluctant Winchester from his city mansion under guard. He himself led his troops out through Shoreditch to apprehend the rival queen.[70]

No sooner was his back turned than the allies who had sworn fidelity began eyeing each other, wondering who would be first to desert. Cecil, Winchester, and Bedford whispered in one corner hoping that they could secure Windsor Castle and desert to the popular Mary. As Noailles confessed, the hatred even the nobles felt for the bear and ragged staff of the new queen-maker impelled them even more than esteem for Mary. On the morning of the nineteenth, Paget was summoned to the Tower by the desperate councillors. His name appeared for the only time as a supporter of Queen Jane in a letter to the Lord Lieutenant of Essex urging him to stand fast for Queen Jane as did the council. With that item of business dispatched, the conciliar rodents began scuttling from Queen Jane's ship of state under the leadership of

Paget and Arundel.[71]

Both nobles had good cause to hate Northumberland, for both had suffered in dignity and property at his hands. Arundel opened the door for a revolt by suggesting to Pembroke, ostensibly the duke's chief ally, and to Bedford, and perhaps Cecil, that the council should adjourn to Pembroke's mansion of Baynard's Castle. Mason, Cheynie, and Shrewsbury were at once in agreement. As they rode along the wharves they met the mayor, who with the sheriffs of London and several aldermen joined the conference at Pembroke's mansion. Arundel boldly denounced Northumberland as a tyrant, and charged that if the duke succeeded he would be omnipotent. His plea for a unanimous revolt was powerful. Even more weighty was Pembroke's hand on his sword seconding the argument. Queen Mary carried the meeting. Then Mason and Shrewsbury announced the decision to the imperial ambassadors and at four o'clock in the afternoon the councillors reassembled at Cheapside.[72]

There the Lords Arundel, Bedford, Shrewsbury, Pembroke and Paget in the presence of the mayor and most of the Privy Council caused Queen Mary to be proclaimed. A scene of indescribable popular joy followed. Pembroke scattered a capful of gold angels, money was thrown from the windows and caps from the ground. 'Men ran hither and thither, bonnets flew into the air, shouts rose higher than the stars, fires were lit on all sides, and all the bells were set apealing, and from a distance the earth must have looked like a Mount Etna. The people were mad with joy, feasting and singing and the streets crowded all night long.'[73]

The Duke of Suffolk in the Tower tore down his daughter's royal insignia and the council, after a *Te Deum* in St Paul's, decided Arundel and Paget, the two nobles least soiled by the embrace of the 'ragged bear', should carry the queen the news. Bearing a letter excusing the other councillors' lapses, Paget and Arundel, escorted by thirty horse and carrying the Great Seal, set out at nine in the evening for Framlingham.

As they rode they cheered the commons banqueting about
the bonfires, asking them if they rejoiced not at their good
news, and all thanked God and cried 'God save Queen
Mary'.[74]

As the two nobles clattered through the Essex countryside
with their escort, their conversation no doubt concerned the
hated Northumberland and their joy at his fall. But Paget
may well have opened to his friend Arundel his hopes for a
substantial settlement in Queen Mary's reign in which 'the
noblemen shall be regarded' and government by a minor be
replaced by a firm hand on the reins. Lord Paget already
had ideas as to whose hands would be most apt.

CHAPTER NINE

POLITIQUE VERSUS CATHOLIC

AS they posted towards the new queen, Paget and Arundel undoubtedly worked out a harmonious plan for joint action under the new government. They realised that their strong position as notable foes of Northumberland would lead the queen to rely heavily upon them. The new sovereign did indeed turn to them for advice. During the first two weeks of her reign, there is abundant evidence that the two nobles carried on the government almost alone. Both the imperial and French ambassadors wrote their sovereigns to that effect. Paget and Arundel utilised their position to reconcile to the triumphant Mary as many of their fellow councillors, who had not been overly zealous for Lady Jane, as they could.[1]

After their visit to Mary, Arundel went to arrest Northumberland while Paget apparently returned to London. When Arundel rejoined him, they endeavoured unsuccessfully to persuade the queen not to arrest Lady Jane's father, the Duke of Suffolk, and Paget's friend, Sir John Cheke. The queen's reply to this suggestion reminded Paget of the 'deep and weighty considerations' they had discussed privately for arresting Suffolk and wondered at his 'sudden mutation'. The probable cause was Paget's early perception that Mary would be relying much for advice on his enemy Bishop Gardiner and her old household servants. If a strange and religiously unproven councillor like Lord Paget was to remain chief

adviser, he would require support from the great magnates
and the nobility of the realm. The emerging composition
of the new council established considerable hope for him.[2]

Several members of Northumberland's council were admitted to Mary's favour almost immediately. Bedford and Sir
Edmund Peckham were sworn as her councillors on 29 July
at Newhall, while Petre and Mason were formally admitted
the following day. Pembroke and Lord Treasurer Winchester
were admitted only after a delay during which they were confined to their houses. Cheynie, Gage, and the northern earls,
Shrewsbury and Westmoreland, completed the tally of the
veteran statesmen whose careers were prolonged by the new
queen.[3]

Within a few days, however, the council was enlarged
by the addition of many servants from the loyal household
of the erstwhile Princess Mary. On 3 August, while Paget
and the French ambassador watched, she entered London in
triumph and, going to the Tower, released the old Duke of
Norfolk and Bishop Gardiner, her cousin, Edward Courtenay,
and all those whom Henry's and Edward's council had imprisoned. Norfolk and Gardiner were almost immediately
added to her council with Rochester, Waldegrave, Englefield,
Jerningham and other loyal members of her household.[4]
The bishop had already indicated from his prison that he
knew the tide was running strongly for him, by evicting
Northampton's family from his former episcopal palace and
depriving Pembroke of other loot from the see of Winchester.
While the other councillors toiled in London, Norfolk and
Gardiner escorted the queen to Richmond. By the end of
August it became evident that the Earl of Derby's earlier
complaint of Mary's neglecting her loyal servants had no
validity, for that noble was admitted to the council while
Gardiner was recognised as Paget's rival for leadership of the
council.[5]

The two diverse elements of the council ranged themselves
behind their leaders. The old household servants were loyal

to the Catholic faith and had proved their steadfastness like
their mistress under Edwardian persecution. To them and
to their leader Bishop Gardiner, who had realised in his
prison that Erastianism led to disorders and Protestantism,
the major objective of English policy, was the restoration of
the Roman faith. The magnates, on the other hand, were
wary lest such a reaction deprive them of their monastic
spoils and favoured caution in religion. Their leader, Lord
Paget, whose chosen sphere of action was diplomacy, was concerned primarily with the restoration of English prestige
abroad and the maintenance of order at home. To achieve his
ends, he turned to England's ancient ally, the emperor.

In 1553, the French king and the emperor were in the
fourteenth round of their perennial prizefight in which each
strove to check the other's aggrandisement. This situation
in an earlier round had preserved Henry VIII from their
unwelcome attentions, and he had often taken a handsome
profit from the sale of his friendship to the highest bidder.
His successor, Northumberland, had bought absolutism at
home by a shameful peace with France, and in July 1553
both continental powers were prepared to exert a maximum
effort through their embassies to win England as an ally. The
issue over which Simon Renard and Antoine de Noailles
clashed decisively was the problem of finding a consort for
Queen Mary. The imperial emissary was desirous of match-
ing her with one of the imperial family, preferably Philip
of Spain, while his rival sought to bar such a match by
pushing for a marriage between Mary and her cousin Edward
Courtenay.

Paget, almost alone of the councillors, advocated the Spanish match. He apparently felt in his heart that England could
not stand alone without allies, for he had so warned Somerset
repeatedly in his masterly analyses of the European scene.
His emotions turned him against the ancient enemy, France,
while his reason was influenced by the old commercial ties
with the Low Countries and his recollection of the victories

which Charles V and Henry VIII had wrested from France in 1544. As De Selve interpreted Paget's mind to his master —with the emperor, England could dictate terms of alliance, but if England fell under French domination it would be utterly helpless.

The middle course of a strong and independent English policy, which Queen Elizabeth was to develop, was for Paget impossible. Allied to his sentimental leaning towards an imperial alliance was his distrust of the 'monstrous regiment of women'. He had seen how a boy king's rule brought English pride low, and he expected even worse from one whom he termed a gentle and inexperienced queen. She could not 'penetrate their knavish tricks nor weigh matters of state' concerning her subjects. Therefore Paget pinned all his faith on the talents of Prince Philip, whom he prayed God 'to send us hither with all speed, for then all will go well; and, 'til then, things will take the course you see them running now'.[6]

Supplementing Paget's reasoned and instinctive motivation was the undoubted ambition for power and pelf, which had brought him in twelve years from the signet office to the House of Peers. Ambassador Renard alleged that Lord Paget was interested in assuring his own and his family's future, but this interest, if true, reflected considerable credit on his perspicacity in placing himself in the driver's seat of the nuptial chariot of Philip and Mary long before it became a bandwaggon.[7]

He correctly foresaw the imperial plan within the first two weeks of Mary's reign. While all London was cheering the Queen's entry into the city on 3 August, Lord Paget slipped away from the French ambassador, whom he was escorting, to exchange a few words with Renard hinting at an imperial marriage for the queen. Charles V and his minister Arras, in great alarm, warned Renard to beware of Paget, 'who is more than a match for you', and forbade him to show his hand to the queen too hastily. Actually, of course, Paget was as eager for the match as was the emperor, for he was increasingly

jealous of Bishop Gardiner's growing power in the council
and with the queen. On 23 August Gardiner had been made
lord chancellor and his zeal in religious matters had met with
the queen's approval. There were even rumours that Paget
planned to retire in disgust at his enemy's prosperity. Actually, he was stretching every nerve to insert his practised hand
into the complex negotiations between the emperor's ambassador, Queen Mary, and the Privy Council, which a foreign
marriage for the queen would require.[8]

Lord Chancellor Gardiner was opposed to a foreign marriage and hoped that if Mary chose to wed it would be his
protégé Courtenay, newly created Earl of Devonshire. With
this intent and to turn immediately to religious restoration,
he was urging the queen to call a parliament without delay.
But Renard had already had a secret conference with the
queen and learned that she was disposed to a foreign marriage
and particularly inclined towards her cousin Philip of Spain.
Paget, too, was in contact with Renard on the subject. The
queen had named him to the ambassador as one urging a
foreign alliance, and sometime before 4 October the two men
held two lengthy secret conferences. Paget, in response to a
flattering message from the emperor, indicated he did indeed
favour a Hapsburg marriage, but he outlined all the objections which such an alliance would meet—French hostility,
Spanish arrogance, and English distrust of aliens. After Renard had answered these points and evaded a direct inquiry
whether Philip were being proposed, Paget promised to outline a plan of campaign for an imperial marriage offer.[9] The
next day Renard came to Paget House in the early morning
by the back-garden door. Paget advised that after Mary had
been secretly won over, the emperor should formally urge her
to marry for the sake of the realm, and secretly write letters
to Arundel, Shrewsbury, Gardiner, Rochester, Tunstal, Petre
and himself. Then Paget and Renard would work with the
individual councillors to win them over, and accept the formal offer of a Hapsburg prince. Renard refused to say this.

Philip was to be the candidate of his master, but it was obvious that Paget knew and welcomed the fact. The emperor adopted this programme with alacrity, authorising Renard to carry on secret negotiations with the queen and Paget to bring about her marriage to Philip. Letters were sent to the people named by him and six unaddressed letters were furnished Renard for use at his discretion.[10]

Paget was able to serve the imperial cause well. For one thing, in early October he completely deceived the French ambassador Noailles into feeling that Courtenay was the favoured candidate with the queen and her council. Noailles had received the early and accurate information of Renard's progress from a Courtenay supporter in his pay, and had suggested a parliamentary party to be gathered to oppose a foreign marriage. In addition, he had stiffened Gardiner's hostility to it, although the cautious chancellor did not reveal his feelings to Noailles. Despite the gossip that Courtenay had threatened to revenge his sufferings under Henry on the former secretary, if he won the matrimonial sweepstakes, Noailles swallowed Paget's report of the council's hostility to the emperor and believed Paget was the friend of Courtenay and France.[11]

Triumph came to Renard between 12 and 29 October. In secret conferences with Mary he overcame her lingering scruples against the Spanish marriage—which were those Paget had rehearsed to him a week earlier—while Paget joined him in urging its advantages. On the twenty-seventh, Renard formally urged Mary, in the presence of her council, to consider matrimony and then began to work on the individual councillors, presenting them their letters from the emperor. That day the queen gave her tentative decision to marry Philip of Spain. Paget and Renard met secretly at the former's mansion on Sunday the twenty-ninth, and planned their next steps. Paget took advantage of his opportunities to intimate to Renard that Gardiner's intemperate religious zeal was inflaming public opinion, and also hinted that Gardiner's years in the Tower had affected the bishop's mind. That evening, in a moving interview with the queen, Renard received her solemn pledge on the sacrament to marry Philip. The crucial victory was won.[12]

Two great tasks remained to consolidate the victory. The council must be won over and popular opinion must be swung to the side of Philip. In both these undertakings, Paget was active. The enemies of foreign marriage and the friends of Courtenay, the Catholic religious zealots and the heretics, had prepared a loyal address in the Parliament against a foreign match. Paget, who had supplanted Gardiner in the chief control of state business under the queen, planned a brilliant stroke of policy to torpedo both elements of the opposition. At the same time that Mary wed Philip, he urged that Elizabeth be married to Courtenay and recognised as heir to the throne. This would conciliate the Courtenay faction and appease the Protestants by adopting their favourite scheme. This faction would be compelled to oppose France, which favoured the Queen of Scots as next heir to Mary Tudor, and would enable a unified realm to restore the Henrician religious settlement and repair its depleted treasury, while Philip's arrival and marriage could be carried through peacefully. Gardiner and the Catholic extremists, who disliked Elizabeth, would be excluded from power and Paget's own influence would be supreme. Unfortunately, this measure, which might have eliminated the disturbances of Wyatt, Carew, and Suffolk two months later, was rejected by the emperor, who was suspicious of Paget's motives.[13]

Paget and the queen worked out a technique for applying pressure to Gardiner to win him to the Spanish match. Mary informed him she had decided in favour of it. Renard urged the chancellor to accept the imperial offer, and on his evading the issue informed Paget. The latter gleefully worked the queen into a fury at the bishop, and when the parliamentary petition, which she suspected him of sponsoring, was presented, the daughter of Henry VIII exploded. Cutting off the chancellor's formal reply for the crown, she rebuked the Lords and Commons harshly. The next day she gave Gardiner a tremendous 'wigging' which brought the reluctant bishop to complete obedience to her will.[14]

During the remainder of November, Paget devoted himself to winning the council to the marriage agreement. He urged Renard to have it drawn up by the emperor in such generous fashion as would silence opposition. Paget appointed himself the 'opposition' and rehearsed in advance with Renard every conceivable objection to the terms. The emperor followed Paget's suggestion, and his generous offer met every point raised by the opponents of the marriage. In a meeting of the council on December, Renard and the key councillors, Paget, Arundel, Gardiner, Thirlby, Rochester, Petre, and Winchester, settled on a final draft. The negotiations were revealed to the mayor and the members of Parliament and a struggle for popular support began.[15]

Paget again attempted to persuade the queen and the omnipresent Renard that a match between Elizabeth and Courtenay would completely win the uneasy public to the Spanish marriage. Mary toyed with the idea, but her dislike for the daughter of Anne Boleyn and her reliance on Renard's advice quickly stifled her interest. The gravity of missing this opportunity was indicated by Renard's own reports to the emperor that the bare rumour of such a popular match and the report of the handsome terms of the Spanish marriage allayed much of the popular discontent. It was probably already too late to have adopted it, however, for Courtenay's friends were deeply involved with Noailles and plots of revolt, and Paget himself, near the end of December, abandoned the idea.[16]

On 9 November, Noailles had informed his king that the Spanish match was resolved on by the English. He asked what his reply should be to the prospective rebels' request for aid. Although his optimistic nature occasionally persuaded him that the negotiations would collapse, he concentrated on

Page 197: William Cecil, Lord Burghley,
a portrait by Arnold van Brounckhorst

Page 198: Simon Renard, a portrait by an
unknown artist

encouraging the plans of the anti-Spanish plotters. He realised that Paget had been the chief proponent of the marriage, but the master of practices in a private interview wove such brilliant dialectical rings around Noailles that the dazzled ambassador seriously requested approval for a handsome bribe to Paget, which would lead him to sabotage the marriage negotiations! [17]

Paget, however, informed Renard of the offer, and busied himself with the final negotiations of the marriage treaty along with Arundel and Petre and the converts Gardiner and Rochester. The final treaty was substantially the work of Paget and embodied his desires. Philip was to assist the queen in governing but was not to favour foreigners, while the queen was to receive a dower of £60,000 a year if she survived him. The Low Countries should go to their heir and in default of issue of Philip's son Don Carlos, their male heir would inherit Spain and Naples also. Philip was to take an oath before the ceremony to keep Englishmen in his household, to preserve the laws and customs of England, not to promote aliens to office, not to involve England in war with France, not remove the queen, their children, or jewellery from the realm. On 14 January 1554, Gardiner proclaimed to the realm the conclusion of the treaty. [18]

Lord Paget had many reasons to rejoice at his share in the marriage arrangements. He had warded off Gardiner's influence with the queen which had been a threat in August and had seen his own influence with Mary become paramount. His service had brought him considerable rewards. The queen had restored his Garter ceremoniously, holding it was taken from him 'neither justly, nor in due order', and had restored to him the three manors which he had given up to Northumberland in 1552 as part of his fine. Although the youngest of her barons, he had taken a prominent part in her coronation, bearing the sword of state before her part of the day, while Lady Paget was one of the few barons' ladies to escort the queen in her procession, a service for which she received a handsome diamond brooch. His son and heir, Henry, received the order of knighthood in the accompanying festivities. Even more important than the honours were the promises of a handsome imperial pension which he had received from Renard and which the emperor's own letter to him confirmed would be presented to him by Philip.[19]

But the fruit of success quickly proved to have a sour pip, for Renard, Paget and the queen had failed to sway opinion to their side. Even in the council, the scarcely reconciled Catholics, who had opposed the Spanish match, were taking their satisfaction out of opposing Paget, whom they envied for his power and detested for his low birth. They began undermining his influence with Renard by calling him a heretic, and to the queen they urged the speedy recall of her cousin Pole, hoping that he might prevent her marriage or at least oust Paget from first place in her confidence. In January 1554 also, the rumblings of popular disapproval burst into open rebellion.[20]

Paget and Renard had feared such a disaster since early December, when a groundswell of mutters, pamphlets, and rumours against the marriage began rising. Paget's large corps of 'good spies' were busy searching out plots, which were blossoming rapidly under the careful nurturing of Ambassador Antoine de Noailles. Even though the nobles were largely won over to the queen's support, Noailles counted on a popular revolt to repeat the miracle of July 1553. Actually, there were four revolts planned. Peter Carew was to raise the south west, where Plymouth had offered its service to Noailles. Suffolk and his brothers were to raise the Midlands, Sir James Crofts Herefordshire, and Sir Thomas Wyatt Kent. Paget's or Renard's spies exposed Carew early, and then Gardiner prised a confession from his protégé, Courtenay, of the western rising and hints of others. Carew was summoned to court and his rising never materialised.[21]

Wyatt left London on 19 January, forced by Courtenay's betrayal to take arms six weeks early, and by the twenty-fifth

Kent was up in arms. A few days later, Suffolk and his brothers fled to raise their standard too. The government seemed paralysed. The bitter opposition between Paget's group and Gardiner's in the council had prevented any effective repressive measures before the revolts broke out, as each side was more concerned with embarrassing the other than with the safety of the queen. Even when Gardiner had seized the dispatches of Noailles which implicated—erroneously as it turned out—Princess Elizabeth, this only divided the council more deeply. For Gardiner attempted unsuccessfully to conceal Courtenay's name which occurred in them, and he succeeded only in rousing Renard's and Mary's suspicions of his own loyalty. Some councillors advised her to take refuge in the Tower or in Windsor, and the only person she could confide in seemed to be Renard, for Paget admitted in despair that all his defence measures were sabotaged in the council. He implied that many in that body were turning against Philip.[22]

In this crisis it was only Mary's courage and the coolness of Renard which saved her. Paget was ordered by her to raise troops, and himself provided thirty horse and a hundred foot. The Marquess of Northampton was sent to the Tower, and Huntington was sent with a strong force (and many more of Paget's servants) against Suffolk. With Wyatt, the more dangerous menace, Mary stalled for time. Two of her councillors went to him to offer a pardon if he would lay down his arms, but Wyatt, cheered by his defeat of Norfolk, demanded that the queen abandon the Spanish marriage, place herself in his custody, and hand over Paget and Gardiner as hostages. The queen's Tudor blood was up. She went to the Guildhall and addressed the quavering mayor and the citizenry, telling them Wyatt's shameful terms. The city's loyalty to the crown overcame its heretical sympathies and when Wyatt's force reached Southwark, the bridge was up and the Londoners in arms.[23]

Wyatt wasted three days in Southwark on the incidental felicity of looting Gardiner's episcopal palace. Meanwhile,

Mary had appointed Pembroke and Clinton to head her army
of nearly 7,000 men. Since she was not entirely sure of Pembroke's loyalty, she kept her forces on the defensive. On 6
February, Wyatt moved upstream in a wide flanking movement and crossed the Thames at Kingston to advance on
London and, as he thought, his allies there. On Ash Wednes-
day he and his 3,000 rebels came at about nine in the morning
to 'St James field, whereat was the Earl of Pembroke, the
Queen's lieutenant, and my Lord Privy Seal, and my Lord
Paget, and my Lord Clinton...with divers other lords on
horseback, which Lord Clinton gave the charge with the
horsemen by the park corner...'. Wyatt and a remnant of his
forces broke away past Charing Cross towards Temple Bar,
where he penetrated into the city. Meanwhile, Courtenay and
Worcester fled to Mary and reported that all was lost! But
Wyatt and his 500 men held Temple Bar for only an hour
before Wyatt surrendered to a Mr Barclay. On the way to
court with his captor, he met Lord Paget who bore him in
triumph to the court.[24]

Lord Paget's contingent of troops, 'who with divers others
did very well', received their reward for their services, for the
queen gave them 200 marks, but their master was to fare less
well, receiving only a grateful letter from the emperor. Wyatt's
near success had shaken the queen badly and the revolt's after-
effects gave Gardiner his chance to oust Paget from her confidence for the first time since the marriage question had been
broached. The problem of punishing the rebels became a
political football. The obvious rebels and previous offenders
such as Suffolk, Wyatt, and Lady Jane were duly executed,
but the widespread tentacles of the plot with all its heretical
and anti-foreign implications had touched the families of
many potentates of both Gardiner's and Paget's parties. Each
side was eager to punish its rival's friends and spare its own.
The bewildered Renard and his master, the emperor, in
vain attempted to persuade Mary to inflict an impartial and
severe justice. Her council failed to heed her wishes.[25]

Within a week after Wyatt's defeat, Gardiner and Arundel had a violent dispute in the council with Paget and Petre supporting the earl. Gardiner, as chancellor, supervised the grilling of the rebel prisoners and carefully excluded Paget's friends from the investigating groups. The two men were bitterly at odds over the treatment of Princess Elizabeth. Paget regarded her as the heir to the throne to be won over or neutralised by a marriage to some imperial sympathiser, but Gardiner succeeded in forcing the reluctant council to commit her to the Tower in the middle of March. The chancellor and his followers Gage and Rochester tended to avoid the council meetings and they and their allies began undermining Paget to the queen and Renard. They had considerable success for they selected Paget's weakest spot—he was a former adviser of Somerset and Henry VIII. Both the suave ambassador and the pious queen showed increasing awareness of Paget as one with heretical leanings.[26]

Gardiner planned to follow up his advantage by holding the next parliamentary session in Oxford and turning to his (and the queen's) dearest project, the reconciliation of England with Rome. Such a programme would leave the layman Paget on the outside of the queen's circle of advisers. Paget's retort to this programme was ostentatiously to avoid the council when Gardiner's parliamentary plan was broached and to persuade Renard to oppose it as conducive to disorder. In the matter of punishing the rebels, Paget retaliated on Gardiner by persuading the queen to pardon six gentlemen sentenced to hang as rebels, alleging that bloodthirsty men, ie, Gardiner, had already shed enough of the best blood in England. This induced some of Gardiner's followers to free eight accused gentlemen including Northampton and Lord Cobham to escape the charge of cruelty. This impasse in the council was ended temporarily by a shrewd scheme of Paget's.[27]

The scheme was a simple plan to reduce the council to its most experienced members and end the factions and difficulties of an unwieldy council of over thirty members. This plan for harmony and efficiency was adopted by Renard and the queen, while Paget agreed to the exclusion of his supporters, William Lord Howard, Pembroke, Derby, Shrewsbury, and Sussex, except on special occasions. The clever Paget knew that most of Gardiner's own time would be consumed by his duties as chancellor and that all his followers except Rochester would be excluded for lack of experience. Thus, Arundel, Petre and he with the moderate Thirlby would control the inner council. In the last few days of March, the plan was put into effect and, as Renard said, more business was dispatched in the week thereafter than in the previous two months. Harmony reigned supreme; Gardiner and Paget were outwardly reconciled, and Paget devoted himself to the examination of the remaining rebel prisoners and to the rehabilitation of Elizabeth.[28]

The harmony proved to be illusory. By 20 April the two factions were locked in a more bitter struggle than ever before. The clash came in Parliament. Gardiner had abandoned his plan of holding it at Oxford, but he was prepared to raise the question of the papal supremacy despite his agreement under pressure to restrict the Parliament's business to confirmation of the marriage treaty. Again, as in the first Parliament of the reign, the disappointed faction in the council carried its grievances into the High Court of Parliament, which met on 1 April 1554. In the first week of its session, besides the non-partisan bills to confirm the marriage treaty and to protect Philip by a new treason law, measures were introduced to repeal the queen's title of Supreme Head of the Church, and to forfeit to the crown all the lands of rebels and fugitives. Opposition to the religious measure at once materialised, led by Paget's faction of nobles. This split in the government was reflected by the virtual cessation of other government business. Paget told Renard that Gardiner intended to re-establish the bishops' powers and set up an inquisition against heresy as soon as the papacy was re-established. He blamed Gardiner for breaking the agreement to restrict parliamentary business to the marriage confirmation. To add insult to injury, the chancellor had even sought Paget's aid in disinheriting Elizabeth. Paget besought Renard, 'for the love of God, persuade the Queen to dissolve Parliament instantly ...for the times begin to be hot, men's humours are getting inflamed, warmed, fevered, and I see that this person [Gardiner], for his own private respects and affection has resolved to hurry forward such measures as will create too much heat, with no regard to the circumstance in which we are placed...'. Paget was 'at my wits end and know not what to do except to pray God to send us hither his Highness with all speed, for then all will go well, and, 'til then, things will take the course you see them running now'.[29]

The chancellor's party had also negated the limited council's operation by its complaints to the queen against Paget and Petre as heretics. Then Paget in his turn deserted the council and took up the cudgels in Parliament. The bills on religion and fugitives' lands were defeated by his procurement. Renard tried to save the day by urging the queen to stand by Paget, but she was persuaded he was an obstinate and heretical man. Paget, however, made a serious error by leading his followers to eviscerate in committee the treason bill designed for Philip's protection, and this the royal bride-to-be could not forgive. Although Gardiner and Paget cooperated in ending the parliamentary session, Paget's credit with the queen was ruined.[30]

On 1 May, he confirmed her worst suspicions of his unsoundness in the faith by inducing the Lords to reject Gardiner's bill for reviving the statute for the burning of heretics, which had already passed the Commons. That Paget disapproved of making heresy a capital offence was to the single-minded queen clear evidence of unreliability. Renard was in a quandary. Paget had been of inestimable service in carrying through the marriage plans, but he was of no value if the queen distrusted him. To his credit, let it be said the ambassador stuck by Paget until Mary made her dislike plain, but he then persuaded himself that Paget was too much in company with Hoby, a notorious Protestant, and Sir John Mason, who was related by marriage to many of the Wyatt party. Renard convinced himself that Paget's action in scuttling the anti-heresy bill was part of a new conspiracy. Gardiner and Renard were soon as intimate as Lord Paget and he had once been.[31]

Renard blamed Paget's actions on his hatred of Gardiner and on his ties with heretics. In this respect he was unjust. For William, Lord Paget, was motivated as much by a states-manlike desire to rise above sectarian wrangling in the government as by a desire to surpass his enemies. A few years later, men of this nationalist stamp in France were called *politiques*, 'who preferred tranquillity to salvation, and would rather have godless peace than holy war'.[32] All Paget's training in the Machiavellian diplomacy of Henry VIII persuaded him of the virtues of expediency. The queen's government must be carried on despite the religious differences among her sub-jects, and the strengthening of that government was Paget's desire. He was not an irreligious man himself, nor was he an advocate of toleration. 'Society in a realm doth consist and is maintained by mean [*sic*] of religion and law,' he had advised Somerset. This was Paget's firm conviction. The church was a prop to the crown and it was highly desirable that all the queen's subjects be united in one faith, but if the price of such unity was civil war, the master of practices preferred to work towards such unity 'by little and little'.[33]

Lord Paget was no longer a Protestant himself. Under Henry VIII he had been a member of the religious reforming group, but, in his role as Somerset's Cassandra, he had been alarmed at the swiftness of the religious changes between 1547 and 1549. Sometime during his disgrace under Northumber-land, he seems to have been converted to a Catholicism as moderate as his Protestantism had been. As he explained to Renard, one of the Henrician or Edwardian bishops had led him into error over transubstantiation, but he had long ago seen and renounced his heresy. Although his moderate Catholicism was far milder than the zealous orthodoxy of Bishop Gardiner, both of these erstwhile Henricians in their separate imprisonments had turned towards religious conservatism as a bulwark against the disorders and excesses which had marked the government of England under the two Protestant administrations of King Edward's reign. Gardiner, having started from a more conservative and religious basis and having suffered more deeply at the government's hands, returned to a purer Romanism than his former pupil and protégé.[34] That was the basic cause of the mutual opposition under Mary, underlying the rage of the bishop at his pupil's betrayal of him and reinforcing the culprit's enmity to the sponsor he had helped deprive and imprison.

Paget realised that a re-established Roman church was the best basis of real order in the realm, but he felt that the method of 'blood and fire' which the chancellor's hasty nature proposed would only make a difficult task more difficult. He knew that the nobles were worried for the security of the former monastic lands which they held. He knew the strength of the opposition too. He had pointed out to the emperor that many heretics were fully persuaded of the truth of their opinions and others had been born and bred in them. Such errors could only be uprooted gradually and moderately. The papal supremacy should indeed be restored but the rope must not be strained to the breaking point, said Paget. It was Gardiner's haste in religious matters that led Paget to maintain his contacts with heretics like Hoby. But the way of the moderate is hard. Renard was soon convinced that Paget was deep in a plot of the heretics, while the Venetian Soranzo called him 'an acknowledged anti-Catholic', and forty years later the Jesuit Persons was certain he had been a covert Protestant. Only when one compares the works of Foxe and Ponet on the Protestant side, who were equally sure he was a Catholic, does it become evident that the 'practising P' was also a *politique* P.[35]

It was unfortunate that Paget gave his enemies reason to

complain of him to the queen and to Renard over the treason bill in Parliament. He gave them even greater grounds to distrust him by revealing to the religious dissidents that Mary's appointment of bishops before the Parliament met was made under papal authority. Furthermore, it was known that he had been on friendly terms with Sir John Cheke, Northumberland's secretary of state, and had assisted him in his financial difficulties before he went abroad, both directly and through Cheke's relative, Mason. But Renard's assumption that he was plotting against the crown is not borne out by the dispatches of Noailles and his brother, who were complaining to their correspondents that Paget was the most active councillor in exposing one of their own minor conspiracies and in breaking up the ring which operated the notorious voice in the wall.[36]

In any case, Paget, the author of the Spanish marriage, found himself in early May distrusted and discarded by the queen. He came to Renard and asked his mediation to secure a permit for him to retire from court to the baths in Cornwall. Renard, however, evaded the task and was soon deep in conference with Gardiner, who had become a strong supporter of the marriage, a fact which tempted Paget seriously to wreck his own handiwork.

Nevertheless, he remained active in the council, assisting the chancellor on 7 May in catching the French ambassador exceeding his instructions. In an attempt to appease the queen, Paget sought her presence and begged her pardon for his conduct in Parliament, alleging that Lord Rich had persuaded him to oppose the bill against heresy and that ignorance had led him inadvertently to oppose the treason bill. The queen rebuked him severely and ostensibly forgave him. Actually, she was completely devoted to Gardiner, who believed Paget, Arundel, Cobham, Pembroke and other lords were plotting to seize him and put him in the Tower. The sole evidence of such a plan was Paget's brief imprisonment and interrogation of one of Gardiner's gentlemen, but the alarmed ecclesiastic sought to persuade the queen to arrest Paget and the two earls as well. Paget was at least as afraid of a new prison term as his rival. But only the knowledge that the bridegroom was en route to England prevented the unfortunate Mary from thus plunging her realm into civil war, for by far the wealthier and more influential part of her council was allied to these nobles. She took the precaution, however, of ordering the lieutenant of the Tower not to accept Gardiner as a prisoner without her personal knowledge and consent.[37]

Gardiner's support from the queen not only sustained his power but recoiled upon Paget, for Mary directed the council to leave her chancellor alone and reproved Paget so harshly that he apologised on his knees with tears in his eyes. He had sought her leave to return to his home for a few days on 15 May, but she summed up his entire career with a scathing tongue condemning his inconstancy and warning against plots and light conduct. The unfortunate Paget was indeed amazed and complained to Renard that he was cast aside after greater service to the queen than any other had rendered. After a few days, however, Paget was back at the council concealing his displeasure, and more suspect than ever to Mary and Renard. Their fears were foolish for his only actions had been to draw his party of nobles more tightly together and to attempt a reconciliation with Courtenay. His principal hope, however, was in the arrival of Prince Philip on whom he relied for justice. While waiting for that happy event, he could only maintain his party's unity and await developments.[38]

Renard feared Paget's plan was to marry Arundel's son and heir to Elizabeth and raise the heretics on her behalf against Mary, but he had no evidence on which to base his alarm. Only his fear of revolt and consequent harm to Prince Philip prevented him from urging the imprisonment of Paget and Arundel, who he feared were in communication with heretic leaders through Ambassador Mason in Brussels. Late in July, Philip of Spain landed at Southampton, resolved to do his duty by a bride whom his secretary described as 'old and flabby'. On the twenty-first, Lord Paget kissed the hand of the prince and 'departed well satisfied'. All things were improved, the wedding ceremony was splendid, Lady Paget attended the queen, and Paget's ward and son-in-law, Thomas Willoughby, was knighted as an earnest of his guardian's future restoration to royal favour.[39] The process of rehabilitation, however, took some time for the new king consort to effect. One of his first moves to reconcile the Paget faction was the wholesale distribution of pensions.

The subject of rewards and pensions had long been discussed between Renard and the emperor. The ambassador had been instructed not to give out any pensions before Philip's arrival, though he had been directed during the negotiations to give out several thousand crowns in gold chains or in coin to the lesser dignitaries, who had served the imperial cause. Only Paget among the major luminaries of the court had received a firm promise before the beginning of 1554. He, in turn, assisted Renard as did Gardiner in drawing up a list of those others deserving remuneration. It may have been Philip's telling Lord Paget that his promised 1,500 crowns annual pension would be paid him that caused him to be well satisfied with his first audience with the prince.[40]

Paget's faction of the council, Arundel, Pembroke, Darcy and Cobham, had retired to his house at Drayton after the marriage ceremony to discuss their relationship to the new king. It was thought by the worried Renard that they were planning to work on Philip to free Elizabeth from her seclusion under guard. The Queen Regent of the Netherlands, however, very sensibly advised the emperor that she thought Paget had a legitimate grievance at being cast out of Mary's confidence, and the emperor agreed that Paget should be won over by Philip and restored to power. Philip's secretary, Gomez da Silva, was in hearty agreement and blamed Renard severely for taking sides with Gardiner and driving Paget into resentful opposition. Accordingly, after his entry into London, King

Philip presented over a dozen pensions ranging from 500 to 2,000 crowns a year to the officers of his bride's household and to the great lords of Paget's following. As part of his quest for popular approval, the conscientious groom ordered his Spanish followers to go native and set them an example by gulping down manfully a pot of English beer. His efforts were partly successful for Pembroke and Arundel went away contented and Paget avowed himself 'extrement tres content', while the first rumours of the queen's 'pregnancy' allayed the anti-Spanish sentiments of his reluctant subjects.[41]

During September 1554, however, Paget avoided the council and the still cold gaze of his queen. He then began to build upon the imperial support to interest himself in the question of restoring the papal authority in England. On 12 October he was again in consultation with Renard urging that the return of Cardinal Pole to England on this mission must be prefaced by a complete general dispensation to all holders of monastic lands, if it were to be successful. Although he had been given four months' leave by the queen, Paget let Renard know that he was only awaiting a summons to come to court. Within a week, he was deep in conference with Philip directing the plans for the return of Pole and assuring Arras, Charles's chief minister, of his entire devotion to the imperial family.[42]

After a flying trip by Renard to the impatient cardinal, Paget and Sir Edward Hastings were sent to escort him from the Low Countries to Westminster, where a reliable Parliament, 'as well catholic as comfortable to the King and Queen's Majesties' pleasure and their godly reformation', had been summoned. Their instructions called for haste, but directed them to see the emperor first to advise him of their actions. They were to inform Pole that a complete dispensation for holders of monastic lands must accompany him to England. On 7 November the two men set out in haste. The emperor was pleased to hear of Paget's coming, saying, 'My lord Paget I would be glad to see for old acquaintance whose affection I have always found very good towards my affairs besides his service lately done for the bringing of my son and daughter together.' On the eleventh of the month, the two emissaries saw the emperor briefly, and that night Paget supped with Pole for the first time in over twenty years. Doubtless they avoided the subject of their last trip together, soliciting university opinions in France for Henry VIII to prove the invalidity of his marriage to Queen Mary's mother![43]

The cardinal proved to be amenable to all their instructions as well as being 'Godly, Virtuous, and humble'. On the twelfth he received his congé from the emperor and started for England as fast as his poor health would permit. Paget, however, had a long, important, and private interview with Charles on the evening of the twelfth, in which the two men were as completely frank with each other as their secretive natures would permit.[44]

After a few delicate moments discussing Paget's recent disgrace, which he characteristically blamed on Gardiner, the canny statesman discussed with the cautious monarch the condition of England. According to Paget, the weakness of the government was caused by the queen's inability to reduce the size of her council. The best remedy was for Philip to take over the government subtly and reduce the council to its essential six or eight members. Gardiner, he said, was better at stopping a hole than preventing its being pierced, but Paget's friends Arundel and Petre were invaluable, the latter for his knowledge of conciliar business. To these men should be added Clinton as a military man, and Howard as lord admiral, with Bishop Thirlby serving as a man of good will. Paget's recommendation for policy was for firmness to 'bridle the insolence' of the commons, who, he felt, were still factious and unruly. Religious changes must be made moderately and gradually to be successful, he convinced Charles. The problem of finances might be coped with in eighteen months of firm and consistent policy. As for Elizabeth, Paget recommended that she be married to an obscure German prince, since the queen was now pregnant, while Courtenay could be discredited by sending him to Rome for a year or two. With all these views, the emperor was in cautious but sincere agreement. However, Paget's trial balloon suggesting Philip lead England into war with France, though welcome, was hastily fended off. Their long, intimate discussion convinced Paget more than ever that England's future prosperity lay in co-operation with the Hapsburg, while the emperor's conviction that Paget was his most reliable friend in the council was fully confirmed.[45]

On 14 November, Paget, with a gold chain presented him by Charles, rejoined Pole and his other escort en route to Dunkirk and Calais. Ten days later, the cardinal, Paget and other nobles came up the Thames from Gravesend to White-hall in the royal barge, escorted by Gardiner in his barge, and Shrewsbury in his with his men bedecked in blue coats, red hose, scarlet caps and white feathers. The Parliament, this time unhampered by the opposition of Paget and his friends, swiftly repealed the anti-papal legislation of Henry VIII and restored England to the fold of Catholic Christendom. As Paget on some unspecified occasion said to Sir William Cecil, who had travelled with him among his gentlemen on this very mission, the papal restoration had laid the basis for a quiet and peaceful religious settlement. The shrewd Cecil, however, pointed out that his friend's wonted vision had deserted him. 'My lord,' said he, 'you are therin so far deceived, that I fear rather an inundation of the contrary part, so universal a boiling and bubbling I see.' [46] It was to this boiling and bubbling that Lord Paget was forced to devote many of his remaining active years in the councils of his sovereigns.

CHAPTER TEN

LORD PRIVY SEAL

THE immediate concern of Lord Paget after the restoration of the Roman faith was his peripheral position in the government. Queen Mary was firm in her dislike and distrust of the man who had done so much for her marriage. The lord chancellor, Paget's bitter enemy, was her favoured minister, and had the management of all important business in his hands. The Parliament was creating trouble for the chancellor's bills, for the assurance of secularised church lands to its holders, and for the punishing of heretics, while the regency bill, to give Philip the guardianship of the heirs of his marriage and the rule of the realm in the event of the queen's death, was meeting equal obstacles. Paget was unable to oppose any of these measures of Gardiner's without forfeiting the remnant of the queen's esteem for him, but with many of his friends he absented himself from most of the meetings of the House of Lords. Only the act of restoring the Roman supremacy seems to have had his vigorous support, to judge from an early draft in his hand among his papers.[1]

Paget, however, was able to see clearly his best means of returning to power. He lashed himself firmly to the wheels of the Hapsburg chariot. Taking for himself the role of Philip's chief friend in the council, he was more often in the king's apartments than in the council. The imperial policies were congenial to his nature with their reliance on moderation.

Since he had advocated the marriage initially to bring a firm masculine hand to the wheel of the ship of state, Paget's unquestioning adherence to Philip's desires was the logical fruition of his matrimonial planning with Renard in the previous year. This route did not lead directly to increased influence in the government. Indeed, the most noticeable immediate result of his attendance on Philip was increased jealousy of Paget and annoyance at Philip by Gardiner, which threatened to paralyse the crown bills in Parliament.[2]

During March and April 1555, Paget and Arundel avoided the council almost entirely. Paget's only activity was a vain attempt to foil the French ambassador in his endeavour to secure four Frenchmen, who had escaped from imperial captivity, but his 'slowness and nonchalance' as judge in the dispute was foiled by Gardiner's intervention. King Philip was as yet unsure of his position and was advancing cautiously. Though his speech to the Parliament had been well received, an inspired suggestion in January in the House of Commons for his coronation had been unanimously rejected. Possibly at Paget's suggestion, Philip was seeking popularity by showing favour to Elizabeth, but his pursuit of favour was sorely handicapped by the simultaneous campaign of Bishop Bonner and the church to extirpate heresy.[3]

By the beginning of 1555 the English government under Gardiner's leadership was prepared to act firmly against the heretics who refused to accept the restored Roman faith. Gardiner was not the bloodthirsty persecutor that Ponet and Foxe pictured him to be. He had preferred early in the reign to scare the non-conformists into abjuring the realm. Perhaps, like Paget, he regarded the heretics more as menaces to public order than as damned souls, for the two men co-operated at first against the heretics suspected of assisting Northumberland. But Paget's rejection of Gardiner's first attempt to revive the statute *De Heretico Comburendo* showed clearly that the layman did not approve his former tutor's way of 'blood and fire'. It was one thing to order the officers in a

country to punish those who railed against the queen's religious settlement, but quite another to proceed to extremes
against people born and bred in religious error, to Paget. In
October 1554, however, Bishop Bonner had launched an inquisition into heresy in his see, which caused much grumbling
in the council and among the people. It was followed by the
first proceedings under the newly passed act for the punishment of heretics.[4]

Paget and William Lord Howard had the dubious pleasure
of representing the moderates' views to seven more zealous
colleagues on a heresy-detecting commission, which met at
Gardiner's palace on 22 January 1555. The queen was resolved to punish learned heretics who led simpler people
astray, and the Privy Council was directed to be represented
at each auto-da-fé. The first victim, John Rogers, was adamant
in the face of Paget's attempt to persuade him that Parliament's unanimity in restoring the Roman allegiance should
lead him to accept it also. Although Howard secured the
release of another suspect, no less than nine were condemned
by the commission. Rogers's cheerful endurance of his martyr-
dom and the cheers of a sympathetic crowd convinced Renard
also that the burnings were ill-advised and would only serve
to identify Philip with such actions.[5]

Although Philip's intervention served to check the zeal of
Bonner and his henchmen for a time, the problem remained
the largest unsolved one of Mary's brief reign. Heretics un-
punished were disorderly and rebellious, while executed at
the stake they served only to light such a fire as no combination of church and state could extinguish. Queen Mary's
bishops with real singleness of purpose continued the fires
of Smithfield during the rest of the reign, and the council,
urged on by its pious mistress, continued to carry out the
law, but many an English youth learned then to identify the
smell of charring protestants with the lisp of Spaniards in
their court and the chant of Latin in their churches. Lord
Paget continued to cherish a *politique's* dislike for the

extreme policy during the rest of Mary's reign, but, after his disastrous experience in her second Parliament, he intervened directly in religious matters with caution.[6]

So perplexing did the problem of religious persecution seem to Paget that he sought the advice of an older statesman. The next time he saw the emperor, he explained that the heresy hunts and executions in England were failing to restore the dissidents to Catholicism. He requested the advice of Charles as one with ample experience with the same problem in Germany. Unfortunately, the emperor's reply is not preserved. To judge from past imperial policy, it may have been a recommendation to follow a harsh policy only where power to impose it sufficed and where doctrinal compromise was unavailing. If so, it had no effect on the English policy.[7]

Although he did not risk competing with Gardiner again by offering his queen an alternative religious policy, Lord Paget was able to intervene successfully in the conduct of foreign policy. With the support of King Philip he began participating in the English attempts to arrange a mediated peace between France and the emperor. Both men agreed with their sovereigns that a peace would immeasurably strengthen England. It would cut the ground from under the feet of any potential rebel and enable Philip and Mary to strengthen their rule and repair their finances without fear of war. The English plans to arrange a peace had begun in Paget's days of power at Mary's first accession, as part of his great plans for the imperial alliance, to free it from the possibility of involvement in the war. Gardiner had co-operated with them in a fruitless offer of English mediation, and Paget had sketched to Noailles a settlement not unlike the ultimate peace of six years later between Valois and Hapsburg. The French were too suspicious of the English motive at that time, however, and the offer languished unheeded.[8]

Some months later Cardinal Pole attempted to negotiate a peace for the pope, but this time the emperor was suspicious. The actual mediation attempt finally resulted from a joint effort of Bishop Gardiner and the Constable of France in the autumn of 1554. Although the king and Renard suspected the French of trifling with England, the negotiations began to make real progress. On one side Philip did some discreet sabre-rattling in which Paget and Pembroke joined, implying that continued war would find England helping her king consort against the traditional foe. Some unnamed peer, probably of Paget's party, inspired a bill in the Commons by which Philip would be encouraged to lead England into war, and its rejection by the lower house did not entirely extinguish French alarm. The most significant action of the English government, however, was to associate Cardinal Pole in the negotiations through his factotum, the Abbot of San Salutore.[9]

Pole's intervention crystallised the negotiations. It was his suggestion that each belligerent send a peace delegation to neutral English territory near Calais, where they might meet with English mediators. Despite a rash of jealous suspicion of Pole by Gardiner, this was the ultimate basis of the negotiations. Noailles frightened Gardiner into feverish action by threatening to end the dragging talks. English pressure on the emperor induced him to agree to the mediation after weeks of stalling, which Henri II accurately diagnosed as reluctance to quit the war a loser. One factor which reassured the emperor was that Gardiner was once more in control of the negotiations, for Charles preferred to rely on the Bishop's dislike of the French rather than on Cardinal Pole's careful neutrality. The French were busily arranging their sources of information in Gardiner's retinue, but the emperor had the satisfaction of knowing that Lord Paget was to be one English mediator, a report which the French received with justifiable alarm.[10]

Actually, neither belligerent was prepared to compromise, but, thanks to the optimism in London, both thought a conference worthwhile on the grounds that the enemy might be ready to make concessions. There was no advance agenda prepared for the meetings and no agreement between

Gardiner, Paget, Pole and Arundel as to their manner of mediating. Paget took the first steps. He was sent over to Calais ahead of the other negotiators to prepare the site for the conference. With a plentiful supply of canvas from the stocks of the master of the revels, he set about erecting four tents or houses for the delegations—English, French, imperial and papal—with a conference hall in the centre of the circle. But his first action on reaching Calais on 13 May, in company with the Duke of Medina Celi, an imperial commissioner, was to write to the Bishop of Arras, chief of the imperial delegation, to urge him to come quickly for a private conference.[11]

Paget was exceedingly busy for the week before the start of the conference, journeying back and forth to the site, and conferring with French and imperial messengers. In the involved negotiations which began on 20 May, Gardiner functioned as the chief mediator, while Paget favoured the imperial cause at every chance. Cardinal Pole's honest neutrality manifested itself inconveniently in appeals to reason or suggestions that all the clergy in all delegations join in a ceremonial High Mass, a proposal which the practical Paget and Arras rejected with scorn. Paget paid the preliminary calls on each belligerent delegation, speaking to the imperials not as a mediator but as an 'affectionate servant' of the emperor, informing each of the English resolve that there be no initial face to face meetings, but that the mediators establish with each side separately a basis of agreement. In spite of the French protests, this system was adopted initially.[12]

The results of the initial conferences were that each side laid out its extreme claims which Gardiner and Pole urged them to moderate. Paget, however, accurately informed the imperial emissaries they would not get good terms from the French and that a two or three year truce was the best for which they could hope. Gardiner soon began losing his impartiality in the face of French obduracy and ended by having a violent and unseemly quarrel with the Constable of France.

The last English proposals for peace—which Paget supplied
in advance to Arras—included two dynastic marriages to solve
the problems of French claims to Milan and imperial desires
to recover Savoy. In each case, however, a French princess
would have been sacrificed to Hapsburg connubial and territorial aggrandisement. At the French rejection of the offer,
the conference adjourned for a week to allow both sides to
reflect, but it was clear the end was in sight. Paget secretly
sent word to Arras on 6 June that the French were adamant
and urged him to let the onus of breaking off negotiations fall
on France.[13]

At the final session on 7 June, all expedients failed and the
conference adjourned late in the afternoon, with the imperial
delegation successfully persuading even the neutral Pole that
the failure was a French responsibility. As Paget knew, it was
caused by their success in electing a bitter enemy of Charles V
to the throne of St Peter, but he did not know that they were
equally emboldened by the failure of Queen Mary's much-
advertised pregnancy to produce a Hapsburg heir to the English throne. The peace negotiations had failed, but Paget had
secured a solid claim to imperial gratitude by his zeal in
Charles's service.[14]

The emperor took considerable pains to show his regard for
Paget publicly. Young Sir Henry and Paget's son-in-law had
accompanied him to the peace conference, and in its closing
days paid a visit to Brussels. Sir Henry was less close-mouthed
than his father, for the Venetian ambassador wormed a good
deal of information out of him about the progress, or rather
lack of progress, of the mediation. Although the two English
youths did not plan a visit to the imperial court, the emperor
sent for them to come to court, where he showed them many
marks of good will out of his regard for his 'affectionate servant' Lord Paget. The Venetian particularly noted that no such
fuss had been made for the Earl of Devonshire, who was
socially their superior, when he was in Brussels on his grand
tour.[15]

From Brussels the two young men rejoined Paget, who was deep in conferences with the agents of the Prince of Savoy, while he waited for a fair wind. On 12 June, however, 'we took ship at Calais about six of the clock in the morning, having the wind very [fair to] us, which continued not for ... there rose a sudden storm ... [then] the wind not only decayed but turned ... so as or ever we could attain to Dover [it was] an hour past two of the clock'. After Paget's stomach had descended the next day, he rode to Canterbury and after dinner there left Pole, Gardiner, and Arundel, to hurry on by barge to London and to his house at Drayton.[16]

He returned to a government still torn by factions. It had become increasingly clear that the queen would bear no children, a fact which strengthened that group of nobles and gentlemen who supported Princess Elizabeth. They were so encouraged that this semi-heretical group attempted to hold a meeting in London, and Lord Admiral Howard, annoyed at Philip's lack of attention to him, had flirted with the dissident supporters of his royal cousin. Paget, who was interested in keeping his moderate party together, apparently clashed with the admiral over this indiscretion. He had good reason to be optimistic for himself and his associates, for there were many encouraging signs. In the first place, his role at the peace conference caused him to be included in the secret talks of Pole, Gardiner and King Philip, who were discussing a new attempt to bring peace to Europe. Gardiner's health had begun to deteriorate seriously in August, and the grave faces of his doctors must have encouraged his bitterest rival. But for Paget, the most hopeful sign of his own return to power was the keen interest King Philip was taking in the government.[17]

In the year he had spent in England as king consort, Philip had frequently exercised his influence in the government. From the time of his marriage he had received a Latin or Spanish summary of conciliar business. In September 1554, he had begun transacting business with the council to familiarise himself with English affairs, while his personal inter-

vention had made possible the speedy reconciliation with
Rome in the Parliament of November 1554. It was largely the
pressure of Philip on his father which had led the emperor to
accept the English mediation offer in the following spring,
and his cautious popularity-seeking had temporarily checked
the burning of heretics and had liberated Elizabeth. In deciding against sending Elizabeth out of the country, he had been
influenced by Paget's assurance that it would cause most
certain mischief and probably revolt. But, as Philip decided
to join his abdicating father in the summer of 1555, he took
an unwontedly determined hand in settling the government
of his English realm before he left.[18]

The first and greatest task was that of reducing the council
to its former small size and great efficiency. This plan had
been recommended by Paget early in the reign, but the jealousy of Gardiner's excluded followers had quickly negated an
attempt to implement it in the spring of 1554. He again
urged it to the emperor in his trip to Brussels in November
of that year, but the emperor's approval had not persuaded
either Renard or Philip that it could be carried out. By the
end of April 1555, however, Renard had again told Philip he
considered the plan advisable. That cautious king first attempted to win the confidence of Gardiner's faction by revealing to them his own personal belief in their plan to enforce
religious conformity throughout the land. During the summer
months, Gardiner's followers were in the majority at the council board, for Paget and his party of magnates were more often
absent than present. Early in August, Philip urged the council
to adopt three measures proposed by the chancellor, which
would have tightened the enforcement of religious uniformity
in every English parish. He simultaneously recommended the
selection of 'none but Catholics and none who are suspect' to
the coming Parliament, which he persuaded the queen to
summon in order to relieve her financial extremities. Having
thus won the chancellor's faction, he turned to the problem
of reducing the council's numbers.[19]

To the inner council he named Gardiner, Lord Treasurer Winchester, Bishop Thirlby, and Rochester; Paget, Arundel, Pembroke, and Petre represented the magnates, and Cardinal Pole was to attend whenever he desired. The new select council was urged to lay aside its internal quarrels and to concentrate on the good of the realm. It was directed to have especial care to the management of Parliament, the payment of debts, lessening of expenses, and increasing the queen's revenues by careful management of her estate and her customs. In these financial duties Paget was destined to take an active part, for he was already serving as Philip's liaison officer to the English treasury in arranging a temporary loan to finance the king's trip to the Netherlands.[20]

The select council had great difficulty in beginning its operations. Arundel and Pembroke were absent escorting Philip to Brussels from 4 to 24 September, while Paget did not bury the hatchet with Gardiner and begin attending regularly until the eighteenth of the month. His prestige, however, was increasing, for Gardiner's former friend Courtenay had begun addressing friendly letters to the chancellor's rival. Furthermore, Paget's former colleague and friend Petre was growing in influence with the queen.

In a few weeks fortune was smiling more and more broadly upon Paget. Bishop Gardiner's health was visibly deteriorating, and from early October he was unable to attend to state business. In his absence the council divided itself into four committees to handle affairs of state. On 21 October the chancellor, supported by four servants, opened the Parliament, but within three weeks Paget's chief rival and the principal obstacle to his regaining the foremost place in the government was dead. Gardiner's death-bed was as peaceful as his life had been tempestuous, for 'he hath made so good and charitable end as he hath well declared by his reconciliation with my lord Paget'. Paget was apparently sincerely moved by his old patron's peaceful end, for his subsequent references to him were always kind.[21]

The death of his rival, however, left Paget by default the chief figure in the government, but the mantle of lord chancellor did not descend upon his shoulders, although he braced them for the welcome load of honour and dignity. Queen Mary was in a quandary. Paget she would not appoint, for she believed him unreliable in religion, so the office remained vacant for nearly six weeks. She informed Cardinal Pole that he was the only man she would trust completely, but the prospect of leading her government caused that unworldly churchman to perspire visibly. During the queen's hesitation, however, government business in Parliament was meeting difficulties.[22]

Paget had begun attending the council with increasing frequency during November 1555, but Gardiner's followers were still attempting to manage government bills in Parliament. They were singularly unsuccessful. The House of Commons was crowded with young noblemen and gentlemen irritated at the religious persecutions, violently anti-Spanish, and encouraged in their obstreperousness by the French ambassador. Even Sir William Cecil, for all his careful moderation, was associated with the group, and only Paget's and Petre's favour saved him from the prison and disgrace of the other leaders. Though the queen received a subsidy, it was less than she had asked, and a third of the house opposed it. Her desire to alienate the clerical First Fruits and Annates to the Papacy was twice rejected, before she got her will by much labour, long talks and practice, anger and promises. Hastings and Rochester, the government leaders in the Commons, were helpless while Pembroke's ill-timed violence to Sir John Porret, one of the leaders of the opposition, only enraged the house. The bills for confiscating religious refugees' goods, for devising the crown by the queen's will, and for the election only of MPs resident in their districts were flatly rejected. When the Parliament was ended on 9 December, it had well earned its title of 'the most unruly and obstructive of her reign', while the enraged queen's imprisonment of several of its members did not improve her situation.[23]

It was indeed more than time to reconstruct her government by securing an able chancellor to lead it. Her absent husband was urging Paget's merits to her, for from Philip 'all favours shown him proceed, nor does he fail to seek it by all means and with all his might'. Paget had absented himself from most of the sessions of the Parliament, although his follower Pembroke had been active on the government's behalf. Arundel and Pembroke had both come around to Paget's views of the advantage of a close adherence to Philip's side, but their colleague may have been both glad to see Gardiner's men failing to manage Parliament and reluctant to alienate that part of the opposition inspired by heretic leanings rather than xenophobia. Fortunately, he was able to occupy himself acceptably to all parties and the queen in early December, discussing with Pole and Philip's representative a new effort to arrange a Franco-Imperial truce. Not until after Parliament adjourned did he begin a daily attendance at the council as faithful as it had been in the days of his secretaryship.[24]

On New Year's day, 1556, Lord Paget received a disappointment and a promotion. As Pembroke that day wrote to Shrewsbury, 'this morning we hear the King had appointed Heath Chancellor and Paget Privy Seal'. Queen Mary's veto had limited Paget to a lesser office, while the cherished woolsack had been thrust under the reluctant posterior of Nicholas Heath, Archbishop of York and an old friend of Paget's. The office of lord privy seal, to which Lord Paget received his patent on 29 January, was one of the great offices of state. Its tenant had the gift of all the posts in the Privy Seal Office in his hands, and he enjoyed a fee of £1 a day from the customs receipts of various ports, while his table in court and two messes were valued at nearly £800 a year. The routine duties of the office were not heavy. It carried an *ex officio* supervision of the Court of Requests, but it had no mandatory judicial duties of the sort that consumed the chancellor's time, and for that reason Cromwell had preferred it to the greater post. The

Privy Seal was used for letters of summons, and for royal forced loans, and for authenticating the acts of many of the lesser departments without their own seals, but its operation could be left entirely in the hands of the clerks.[25]

Paget and Heath worked well together, but Paget had little chance to devote to strengthening the government. Before all the congratulations for his promotion had been received, the queen heard of the truce of Vaucelles, which had been arranged without English mediation. Since she obviously could not blame her adored Philip, she vented her spleen at the diplomatic slight on Paget and Arundel, on whom she blamed it. In this indignant round robin, Pole blamed the queen, and San Salutore blamed Pole. Paget did not reveal whom he blamed! He must have been encouraged, however, by the changes in the council's regular participants. As the year progressed, the great officers of state and the great nobles dominated the board increasingly, although a remnant of Gardiner's group, Hastings, Rochester, Jerningham, and Waldegrave, secure in the queen's trust, remained faithful in their attendance. Except for the dragging negotiations with the Hanse cities over the loss of their trading privileges, however, Paget and his colleagues had time for little else than the queen's relation to her husband and the progressive revelations of an elaborate plot to unseat the royal pair.[26]

When Philip left his clinging wife in September 1555, it had been her intention to suggest in Parliament that there be a coronation for her husband. He had made it plain that he was annoyed at being delayed so long in England where he had so little power. But the subject of coronation was one which the queen did not dare raise with her stubbornly resisting subjects who feared that the mystic ceremony, which conferred regalian rights on a ruler, would saddle them with Philip for life. The entire realm, however, knew Philip was pressing his wife to have him crowned, and that knowledge was largely responsible for a new conspiracy, which history calls by the name of Sir Henry Dudley.[27]

The conspiracy was apparently organised during the latter part of the parliamentary session, and during December 1555 the French king, through his ambassador, gave it qualified support. France was negotiating with Philip for a truce, but desired to have such a promising prospect as ousting him from England developing as a reserve stroke. Dudley and several of his friends were given pensions and crossed to France to be ready to lead an invading army of expatriates. Far more dangerous were the allies they left in England. The commander of a fort in the Isle of Wight and other key coast defence commanders were prepared to open their gates. The leader of the parliamentary opposition, Sir Anthony Kingston, was prepared to raise 6,000 men and sixty substantial gentlemen in the west, in support of any French landing, while Edward Randall, commander of four companies of mercenaries in Philip's service, had also sworn his adherence. Indeed, the plot with ramifications in every stratum of society, blossomed more rapidly than the French desired.[28]

A plot which included much of Elizabeth's household, many leaders in Parliament, a sizeable chunk of the armed forces, many nobles, and included a plan to steal £50,000 of silver from the exchequer could not be kept secret, especially when the murmuring of the populace against the subsidy, a revolt in Ireland, and unrest at the renewal of the smoke columns of Smithfield had the government in a state of nervous suspicion. King Philip was doing nothing to help his agitated queen, for he was pressing her to have him crowned and wrangling with the council over whether Spain should precede England in the royal titles. To smooth its relations with Philip, the council resolved to send Paget and Thirlby to him. Before the two men could leave, however, the first revelations of the Dudley conspiracy cancelled their voyage.[29]

Sometime early in March the government had its first word of the plot, which was apparently betrayed to Pole by one of the lesser conspirators. By 8 March, the queen was mustering her councillors' followers in arms and preparing to strike. Ten days later, the first group of conspirators were imprisoned, and the details of the plot began to come out gradually. To the alarm of the council, more and more people, including highly placed officials and nobles, were implicated. Paget was not present during the latter stages of the examinations which were committed to Mary's faithful few household officers in whose steadfast Catholicism alone she could rely. The queen sent her lord privy seal to Philip charged with a very delicate mission. On 6 April he received his passports, and two days later he was again en route to Brussels.[30]

Ostensibly Paget was sent to congratulate Philip and his father on their truce with France, but the Venetian ambassador was convinced that he was to find out why Philip was delaying his return and to attempt to mediate between the king and his queen to the end that Philip might have more authority. Thus he was 'establishing himself in the closest confidence of both one and the other, and increasing his repute to an unlimited extent...Thus...the wish and aim cherished for a long while by this shrewd and clever statesman ...will have its full effect.' Paget thus was attempting to arrange both his own future and the continuance of Philip's authority in England. He had not given up hope of an heir for the queen, and with this intent he desired Philip's return to England. Failing a legitimate heir to the queen, he could not entertain such hopes of the rule of 'our sweet Lady Elizabeth' that he could prefer her tapering and youthful fingers holding the sceptre to the more experienced digits of Philip. On 13 April he reached the imperial court and had immediate audience with Philip, followed by daily private conferences with him thereafter.[31]

In these conferences Paget explained the difficulties preventing Philip's coronation. Together, they mapped out a plan to win over the three great earls, Westmoreland, Derby, and Shrewsbury, for with Arundel, Paget, and Pembroke they would constitute a solid Philipine party to whose support Mary could rally her household retainers. Once this had been settled, the two men, Philip and Paget, turned to a discussion of the king's return to England. Paget used every argument at his command, which he later recounted in detail to his grateful queen, but from his view the most important was to create an heir, or 'for that thing which should be comfort to all your good subjects', as he phrased it to Mary. The retiring emperor was also urged to speed Philip's return. Paget also attempted to get the elderly emperor to advise a stay to the persecution of heretics in his son's kingdom of England. Lord Paget persuaded the king to place England first of his realms in the royal title and then turned to the task of convincing Philip's reluctant Spanish gentlemen that their master should return to England. In this endeavour, he gave several magnificent dinners for Spanish cavaliers and assured them that the plots, conspiracies, and hatred of Spaniards, which they advanced in opposing it, were exaggerated. He asserted 'they might come cheerfully, as he assured them that for the future the authority they exercised in England would be of a different sort to what they have had there hitherto'.[32]

Queen Mary was well pleased with her emissary's assurance that Philip expected to return to her in June. Although she was too ill to write to him, her favourite gentleman attendant, and Paget's firm ally, James Basset, assured Paget of her pleasure. Her council, however, did not agree and found it necessary openly to assure her suspicious subjects that no one intended to have Philip crowned. The queen and her council must have agreed in being gratified also at the zeal which Paget and his friend, Ambassador Mason, showed in helping unravel the Dudley conspiracy. Although one prospective victim whom Paget had threatened 'to be set by the heels' had escaped, the two men were the channel by which Sir Peter Carew revealed some major parts of the conspiracy he had been invited to join.[33]

Carew, one of the leaders of Wyatt's rebellion, had tired of continental exile, and through the active intervention of his wife had received the promise of a pardon from Philip. Accordingly, after he informed Philip he was being solicited to join the Dudley conspiracy, Paget and Mason received from him in Antwerp the letter of invitation, which implicated Sir William Courtenay, Parrot, and other leaders of the opposition group of western gentry in the last Parliament. These plotters preceded Lord Bray, Lord Thomas Howard, and several members of Elizabeth's household to the Tower by only a few days. The alarmed government redoubled its efforts to get to the bottom of the conspiracy. Paget had told Philip that at least ten persons of quality were involved, but there was insufficient evidence to execute them. One of these was doubtless Princess Elizabeth, yet the queen could only send her trusted Hastings to apologise to the haughty heir presumptive that her name had been mentioned in the confessions of conspirators. That was one measure of the regime's weakness. Another measure, which was also a principal cause, was the execution, within a few days of each other, at Tyburn, of the swashbuckling gentleman-at-arms Captain Stanton, taken in his second treasonable conspiracy, and at Smithfield of two eighty-year-old men and three women, 'obstinate in their error'.[34]

Lord Paget had remained in the Low Countries after his week of conferences with Philip. He told the Venetian ambassador he planned to take the waters at Aix-la-Chapelle and then make a tour of Flanders while waiting for Philip to return to England. Accordingly, he had a supply of beer and other provisions sent to him. Then, abruptly, on 9 or 10 May, his plans changed. On the ninth, he had a farewell audience with Charles V, the last time the two veteran statesmen were to meet. From Philip he received a gold chain valued at 1,200 crowns—which his attendants said just equalled the amount he had spent in splendid entertaining and ostentation befitting his position[35]—and the assurance that Philip would follow him to England within six weeks. On 12 May, he left Brussels en route for England. What was

Page 231: Edward Seymour, Duke of Somerset,
a portrait by Corneille de Lyon

Page 232: Thomas Cromwell, Earl of Essex

the reason for this sudden departure?[36]

It has been alleged by various authors that his departure was connected with the celebrated seizure of Sir John Cheke and Carew by Philip's officers. One of their fellow-Protestants, John Ponet, even alleged the operation was planned 'by Mason's working and Paget's devising' to convince the queen that Lord Paget was a reliable Catholic. Much of the importance of the case depends on a recent author's conviction that Cheke's seizure was treacherously arranged by Carew as part of the price of his pardon, and that the English government desired to lay hands on Cheke as the director of heretical anti-Spanish propaganda for the English exiles. The problem is an exceedingly complex one and is seemingly insoluble.[37]

Lord Paget and Mason unquestionably had been visited by Carew and Cheke in Brussels in early May. Mason was related by marriage to Cheke—his wife's daughter was Lady Cheke—and when his stepson-in-law came into Philip's territories in April to wait for his wife in Antwerp it was natural for him to see something of his influential relative, the ambassador. Paget also was an old friend, who had been favoured in 1552 by Secretary Cheke, and who had returned the courtesy since Mary's accession. Carew and Cheke apparently had a pleasant time in Brussels for several days, well entertained by Paget. At Paget's departure on 12 May, they offered to escort him part way to Calais, an offer he courteously refused. Then, taking them by the hands, he bade them farewell. The following day, on their way to Antwerp, and between Mechlin and that city, Cheke was arrested by Philip's knight marshal. When Carew and his servants resisted, the two men were bound and gagged, lashed to a cart, and carried back to Vilvorde, near Brussels. From there they were conveyed to a prison in Ghent. The English and the foreign colony were startled and alarmed at the seizure, for Carew held the king and queen's pardon, but Philip explained to the Duke of Saxony that they were arrested on suspicion of involvement in a new plot against himself and his queen.[38]

H

Meanwhile, Paget was having encounters on the road to Calais. On the morning of the thirteenth, a courier was sent after him by Philip to have him wait for Secretary Verzosa to overtake him at Calais with messages and a gift of jewellery for the queen. Before Paget reached Calais, 'Sir Peter's man, coming out of England, meeteth him and asketh for his master. Paget smileth and sayeth nothing but his master was in health.' When he reached London on the sixteenth, presumably bearing Verzosa's messages and jewels, Lord Paget had two long and very private conferences of over two hours which wonderfully cheered the queen with news of Philip's expected return. The following day, a royal courier was sent to Philip, possibly about Cheke and Carew as well as affairs of greater moment, for on 29 May the two prisoners arrived at the Tower by sea from Flushing. As the Venetian ambassador wrote, 'One of the chief members of the Privy Council who busied himself with this arrest and was perhaps the author of it, has said that Carew is arrested because being in the company of Cheke, against whom alone the warrant was given, he together with his servants, chose to resist the provost ... and indeed *this same lord* [author's italics] had repeated that as Carew is taken, it would be desirable on several accounts to find him guilty of something to have an opportunity of putting him out of sight...'[39]

Undoubtedly the circumstances surrounding the Cheke case were rather incriminating for Paget. They are all capable of being explained, however. In the last analysis, the solution to the problem must rest on Paget's rather speckled character and on the validity of Miss Garrett's description of Cheke as a minister of propaganda for an English government-in-exile in 1556. Paget was not at all averse to betraying an old associate in the public and his own personal interest, but his proven distaste for a policy of religious persecution at that times makes it highly improbable that he would have assisted in laying a man by the heels for purely religious reasons. As for Ponet's charge that Cheke was a sacrifice he made to win the orthodox queen's favour, he had little motive for such a step after the chancellorship had been filled, especially when he had already established himself as a mediator 'in the closest confidence of both one and the other'. Inasmuch as Cheke's treatment after he reached London consisted entirely of intensive pressure to convert him to Catholicism, the success of which was followed by the queen's favour, it would seem that Miss Garrett's assumption of a political rather than a religious basis for his arrest must be taken as not proven.[40]

Paget's credit with the queen was strengthened by his cheerful news that Philip expected to see her soon. Her pathetic disappointment when he did not appear as the summer passed only strengthened her reliance on her lord privy seal. Paget consolidated his position as an acknowledged leader of her government during that summer of 1556, while the Privy Council at long last shrank to a manageable body, although only slightly less faction-ridden than the past. The lord privy seal enjoyed his usual pre-eminence in the council's diplomatic business, in spite of the long illness which confined him to his bed during October and November. He also found, as had Gardiner, that favour with the queen did not eliminate divisions in the council, for there was a new line of cleavage emerging in that body.[41]

One group was reluctant to approve a policy of closer attention to Philip's desires, fearing that such pliability might jeopardise the English peace with France or affect Elizabeth's position as heir to the throne. This element included the majority of the council. Lord Admiral Howard was inclined to be the leader of this faction and demonstrated his conservatism by courting the French ambassador and by advocating the cause of Elizabeth and the imprisoned Sir William Courtenay. Howard was allied by marriage to that successful middle-of-the-roader, Lord Treasurer Winchester. Although Arundel and Pembroke agreed with Paget in cleaving to the cause of Philip, they were not able to control the council. The queen showed her awareness of her council's views by her distrust of that body in matters concerning Philip or Elizabeth.[42]

In November and December 1556, the sorrowing queen made constant use of her husband's chief ally in the English government in her attempts to induce her consort to return to her. Paget carried on a regular correspondence with the queen through her gentleman, James Bassett, from his sickbed. In Philip's retinue, Ruy Gomez, his secretary, was Paget's contact with the king, and though the queen's pride forced her to edit Paget's 'vehement persuasions' for Philip's return, she obviously pinned great hope on these letters. The letters also included Paget's regular reports to Philip of the progress of business in the English Privy Council. One major element of that business was a determined effort by Paget and Lord Treasurer Winchester to restore the financial stability of the government.[43]

Paget's experience as one of the financial experts of Henry VIII served him well in the repairing of Mary's finances. He had been regularly employed as an auditor of accounts in previous reigns and he continued this function under Queen Mary. He was the recognised expert of her government. Early in the reign it was to Paget that Sir Thomas Gresham, the government's financial agent, wrote letters explaining his activities in detail, rather than to the Privy Council. Paget arranged through Renard for a permit for Gresham to export 300,000 crowns from Spain, and he was on the conciliar committees for raising money and reducing the number of patents and annuities. Before his loss of favour in the spring of 1554, he had taken an active part in the sporadic but earnest efforts of the council to reduce the size of the court and to effect economies in government. In November 1554 he had expressed to the emperor his conviction that England's financial problem could be solved in eighteen months of systematic work. As a result of this conference, he became Philip's source of information on English finance as well as the channel for such funds as the impoverished Hapsburg was able to draw from England.[44]

One of the first steps in improving the queen's finances was to determine the extent of her debts. Paget, Thirlby, and Petre were appointed to confer with Gresham about her foreign obligations, but the lord treasurer took pains to have himself added to their commission. In April 1556 they began gathering facts and expediting repayment of some foreign and domestic debts. That summer, with Winchester, Thirlby, and Englefield, Paget was busy studying the possibilities of recoining the currency to eliminate the debased issues of Henry VIII and Edward VI. Paget was still recommending that reform over a year later, however, and it was not actually accomplished until Elizabeth undertook it in 1561.[45]

Despite considerable opposition, he worked to induce the queen to reduce her household, to take away the 'beggary and tippling' and the 'rascal rabble' that resorted to her court. Although he differed with the lord treasurer over the question of farming the revenues, the two men worked together in reducing her household expenditures and in raising fresh loans as her military expenses increased in her last two years. Domestic forced loans were raised by Privy Seal letters and foreign loans were renewed.[46]

The greatest contribution of Lord Paget to government prosperity, however, was his activity in raising the customs rates. In December 1556, he had suggested such a measure to the queen through Bassett, and in the following May he was named to a commission to revise the rates with Winchester, Thirlby, Hastings, Petre, and the chancellor of the exchequer. The task took over a year to complete, for the rates were weighted according as it was desired to encourage exports and critical imports or to protect home industries 'lest a glut of any of those wares bring them below their rates...'. An average increase of roughly seventy-five per cent in the rates and the addition of new imposts more than tripled the customs revenue of the next sovereign.[47]

Lord Paget was also rearranging his own estate during these years. Only two additions were made to his properties—the purchase of a garden and barn near his mansion by Temple Bar, and of the much disputed manor of Great Marlow near West Drayton—but he drew up an entail for his properties. Five manors were reserved for his wife for her life and one for his second son, Thomas, but all the other properties were entailed to his heir, Sir Henry, and his male heirs. This conservative settlement of his lands, however, did not prevent Paget from taking a more adventurous course with his investments, for he was an original investor in the Muscovy Company and took an active interest in selling arms through the company to the Russians.[48]

In the autumn of 1556, however, Paget was becoming deeply concerned with a more serious use for arms. For, as the autumn turned to winter, the new pope was at war with the Hapsburg kingdom of Naples, and Queen Mary was also queen consort of that realm. Both Philip and Mary expected that France would soon break the truce of Vaucelles and Philip's queen began working to induce her council to aid the king with men, money, and, if necessary, war. The six months' struggle to induce a reluctant realm to come to grips with its ancient enemy was a difficult one, for a large proportion of the populace preferred its ancient enemy to its new master. Even in the council, more men preferred an uneasy peace to a difficult war. The original member and principal organiser of the war-hawks, however, was the rheumatic fifty-one-year-old lord privy seal. The successful result of Philip's campaign to drag England into war was his last important feat as leader of an English government.

Paget got off to a very slow start. He was ill for six weeks and absent from the council during a series of meetings in November in which Mary endeavoured vainly to get a promise of men and money for Philip. He was in regular correspondence with the king's secretary, Ruy Gomez, however, and when Paget's written advice and the queen's orders failed to win the council, he may have advised the next step. The council had intimated that it was not even bound to observe the old treaty of alliance of 1542, so in February 1557 Ruy Gomez was sent to England to press for English aid under the old alliance.[49]

Gomez was instructed to reveal his real mission only to Paget, who could then begin campaigning for it as though spontaneously. The nature of Gomez's request was indicated by an elaborate estimate of the pay and supplies necessary for an overseas army of 8,000 men, which Paget drew up a week after the Spaniard's arrival. However, the opposition to any more aid than the old treaty required was very strong in the council. Only some of the younger nobles and the experienced warriors who could profit by war—men like Westmoreland, Howard, Pembroke, Clinton, Shrewsbury's and Derby's heirs, and Lord Montagu—were willing to support Paget's belligerent plans. In spite of the fact that Gomez paid up the pensions of most of the council through the following June, Heath, Mason, Winchester, Cardinal Pole, and most of the clergy and the queen's household clung firmly to a policy of peace with France.[50]

The peace party was in communication with the French ambassador, and one of its leaders plainly informed Noailles that he cared not for Philip but only for the welfare of the realm. But Philip had used his wife's passion for him to compel her to become the most bellicose advocate of a French war with England. On 18 March he arrived in England, accompanied by Renard, to reinforce her efforts for she had promised him satisfaction. Derby and Shrewsbury were summoned to court, and on 1 April intense pressure was applied to the Privy Council.[51]

On 1 April the queen in Philip's presence pressed the council to agree on war, but two days later her only reply was that the marriage treaty and a bad harvest were reasons for avoiding it. She dismissed the council angrily and for two days it met several times a day with Renard assisting Paget in urging war. Under pressure the council agreed to a war to begin next November, but for the time being it attempted to

buy off the king by offering 7,000 troops and £200,000. At
that point, on 28 April, all resistance evaporated for word
was received from the north of the ill-advised and futile
French-sponsored attack on Scarborough by Thomas Stafford.
The French provocation enabled the king and queen to carry
their point. Well might Paget sardonically twit Noailles's
secretary that the Scarborough attempt was a flop, for it
delivered the anti-war party into his hands. Not all Noailles's
disavowals to Heath and Paget could undo that effect. By
4 May Philip could write freely to his ministers in Brussels
that war was at last decided upon.[52]

Paget did not wait to go off to war—by proxy! He fitted
out a privateer and sent it to sea even before war was
declared, and his agent at Plymouth began disposing of lucrative prizes including some luckless neutrals. Paget's personal
share in the new war was that of chief of the war council.
He had already been investigating the situation in hostile
Scotland—as it turned out, through a French agent who was
betraying his 'curious questions' to Noailles—while his spies
in France and his staff of informants in Italy were keeping
him posted just as in the great days of the war of 1543-4.
On 3 May, the war council of Paget, Clinton, Lord Wharton,
Howard, and Montagu discussed reinforcing the garrisons
and raising troops. A few days later with Philip's councillors
Figueroa and Mendoza he was revising an old plan for an
assault on Le Havre, which was shortly betrayed to Noailles.
Then, on 7 June, war was declared 'in the very best vein'.[53]

When Philip left England early in July, he was none too
sanguine about the zeal of his English subjects, but Paget was
active enough for ten in the cause he had adopted. The English agent raising troops in Germany reported to Paget as
often as to the council, while in estimating the needs of the
English army under Pembroke, Paget was more active than
any other. Plans for the northern defences, equipping his
own 300-man contingent, and the grilling of suspected information sources of Noailles occupied his time until late in

July. Then his health gave way, and he was absent from the court until late in September.[54]

The war began very well for Philip, for that summer his army roundly defeated the French at St Quentin. But the English war effort collapsed ignominiously that winter, when, in early January 1558, the French swooped down on Calais and took the entire Pale in a matter of a few days. Philip's last minute attempts to save it were in vain, and the remnant of English empire in France was eliminated after two centuries. The gallant defence of Lord Grey at Guisnes relieved some of the disgrace of English arms, but morale in England was utterly shattered. When Philip sent his servant, Count Feria, to invite England to raise a fleet and army to assist him in recovering Calais, only Paget and Arundel were enthusiastic. The rest of the council offered a fleet, but they refused on grounds of poverty to raise an army. Howard and Pembroke had gone over to the peace party, and only Paget and Clinton would actively plan a new campaign. All of the discontented were quick to point out Philip's duty to protect his English realm and recover Calais, but their chief contribution to such vigorous steps was to point out that their pensions from him were in arrears.[55]

Much of the increasing passive resistance in the council was caused by its knowledge of Queen Mary's poor health—she, poor lady, was again interpreting her dropsy as pregnancy and drew up a will naming a list of executors, from which she carefully excluded Paget. Knowing her condition, no Tudor councillor would willingly risk binding himself to the ex-husband of a late queen at the cost of thereby earning popular hatred and the aversion of the new queen. Paget, Feria, and Clinton, however, continued their efforts to rally the government to a vigorous prosecution of the war. For this the first requirement was money.[56]

Paget was still the chief expert on this subject. He had drawn up the generous subsidy, which Parliament voted under pressure of the collapse of Calais. For a time he even held out to Philip the prospect of an extra £150,000 as Gresham was endeavouring to raise £100,000 in Antwerp and the rest in London. But Antwerp would provide only £10,000, while London could only furnish £20,000, in spite of the appearance of Paget and the council at the Guildhall on two occasions. Paget blamed his predecessors in the management of the finances for his faulty estimate, but he merely convinced Feria that the English were utterly inert. Paget, Thirlby, Englefield, and others were appointed a committee of the council to study the crown revenues, but they found no bright spots. Paget made his gloom plain in meetings with Pole and Feria, and in spite of the appointment of a new council of war—Lord Paget was the only privy councillor on both the finance and war committees—it was obvious to the Spaniard that England was lacking not only in the will to win but even of a will to fight.[57]

Philip made a last attempt in May 1558 to revive England's martial spirit. Paget and Clinton drew up a plan of attack on Calais, but it quickly failed for lack of conciliar support. The queen was visibly growing weaker, and even Paget was suspected by Feria of courting the rising sun, Elizabeth, at Philip's expense. Feria himself visited her on the king's behalf. The council meanwhile relapsed into its old factiousness, obstructing Paget's efforts to send an able commander with a force of pioneers to Philip's aid. He soon turned to negotiations with the Hanse merchants, but again, Feria charged, at the king's expense. By late September peace negotiations were opened between England, Philip, and the French kingdom.[58]

By then Paget was again in his bed at Drayton, but he was consulted by the council on the choice of peace commissioners and their instructions. He gave the group little hope of regaining Calais but suggested one or two offers which might be made to the French as a basis of exchange. Indeed, few important items were attempted by the council without the ailing lord privy seal's advice. Reduction of the northern garrisons and the Irish finances were both referred to his sick-bed for decision by letter or by a delegation of councillors. But Paget's influence in the Privy Council was being reduced to an empty honour, for every eye at court was turning to Princess Elizabeth.[59]

Lord Paget was well enough to attend Parliament from 7 November until its dissolution. Perhaps his experience told him it would be well to be on the scene at what everyone saw were the closing days of Queen Mary's reign. The Privy Council had already persuaded the dying queen to recognise Elizabeth as her heir, but there is no record of Paget's participation in the action. Count Feria visited Elizabeth on the tenth. After she had firmly denied any obligation to Philip for her imminent succession, she commended Heath, Paget, Petre, Mason, Dr Wotton, Clinton, Grey, Sussex, and her cousin Lord Howard to him. When Feria attempted to exploit this amiability and suggested to Paget a new marriage practice, the privy seal remarked that he would not meddle again in such a matter, having seen Queen Mary's turn out so ill. Thus, even before the old queen's death, her husband's representative was being flouted by his most loyal friend in the English council. On the morning of 17 November Queen Mary breathed her last, and again men 'did make bonfires and set tables in the street, and did eat and drink, and made merry for the new Queen'.[60] On this occasion, however, it was not Lord Paget who rode to her bearing the great seal and the news of her accession.

CHAPTER ELEVEN

ELDER STATESMAN

THE accession of the vigorous young queen brought about the retirement of William Lord Paget from the management of government business. Elizabeth, in selecting her government, was inspired by contradictory motives—to satisfy popular demand for an end to persecution and Spanish hegemony by eliminating Mary's ministers, and to assure the conservatives that her reign did not mean a complete revolution in the government. She could neither dismiss all her sister's ministers nor appoint all of her Protestant supporters to office. In the first months of her reign, she proceeded cautiously, while all the Protestant world flocked to her presence to offer gratuitous advice.

Even before her sister's death, two would-be councillors were selecting the queen's new cabinet. In London, William Cecil was conferring with Lord Chancellor Heath 'touching the state of the realm and also the matter of religion'. Heath was also asked by Cecil to recommend his own successor since he was determined to be 'utterly disburdened of mine office'. As soon as he heard of Mary's death, Sir Nicholas Throckmorton wrote Elizabeth a lengthy and familiar letter suggesting new candidates for most of the high offices of state, but urging her to proceed gradually in effecting the changes. Such advice was never wasted on Elizabeth. Her only new appointments in the first week of her rule were Cecil, Parry, Robert

Dudley, Bedford, and William Lord Howard, while she received the chancellor and the noble members of the last government graciously. Although Paget, Lord Treasurer Winchester, and Heath had given up their seals to her, they were received into her council. Significantly, however, their offices remained in her hands. Only the Catholic extremists, the remnants of Gardiner's party, were immediately dropped from the council.[1]

From December 1558 until the following April, Paget was progressively accepting the fact of his exclusion from power. As Feria wrote to Philip, 'I think Paget is dying as fast as he can. He was very bad before, and the Queen seems not to have favoured him as he expected; indeed, I do not think she will return him his office and this no doubt has increased his malady.' Although there were rumours he might be retained if his health were better, the Privy Council's request that he turn over his papers on the financial status of the realm must have convinced him of his dismissal.[2]

In February 1559, Paget took occasion 'lying here like a beast' in his sickbed, to write Parry and Cecil his advice on the peace negotiations with France. His advice was, as always, against English isolation lest 'they make a Piedmont of us'. To Paget, the slow and phlegmatic Burgundians were a necessary ally against the swift and diligent French. This advice the queen was resolved to ignore ultimately, but for the first months of her reign she was careful to keep the friendship and support of Philip of Spain—and Burgundy. His illness and his lame hand kept Paget away from Elizabeth's first Parliament, though his son and son-in-law sat in the Commons and his interest in Staffordshire secured the return of one of Queen Mary's heresy-hunters from Lichfield. Perhaps this accounts for Cecil's courteous attention to the ailing noble at a time when the government's hand was being forced by religious extremists of Protestant views in the House of Commons.[3]

Paget supplied Parry and Cecil with an extensive plan for recoining a debased currency, a project which was not attemp-

ted until two years later, when his advice was again offered to
the queen. In addition, Paget, from his extensive experience,
advised the secretary in the finer points of phrasing the peace
treaty with France. His role of elder statesman so heartened
Paget that he solicited from the secretary the post of Lord
President of the Council in Wales, but in this suit he was
disappointed. Within a few weeks, after several fruitless visits
to court, he sought out the Spanish ambassador, Feria, and
blamed his loss of credit and authority on his record as a
friend of Philip. By this means he secured the payment of
eighteen months' arrears of his pension. On 19 July, under
suspicion of dabbling in French affairs, he received the
queen's licence to return to Staffordshire for his health—and
to hunt the queen's deer there when he recovered![4]

At this juncture, he became involved in a bitter dispute
with two of his former colleagues over his monopoly of the
wine trade. In the last few months of Queen Mary's reign, he
had received a grant for five years of the monopoly of import-
ing wines into England for 2,000 marks a year above the
normal customs. This monopoly, estimated at the end of the
century at between £4,000 and £8,000 value per year, was
not continued by the new queen, for it appeared that Paget's
profits would be too large. He blamed Lord Clinton and Lord
Hastings for working against him and attempting to stir up
grudges held by other lords. In a dignified letter to Parry and
Cecil, he sought the queen's favour in ending their attacks on
him. One of the chief glories of a sovereign was his ability to
raise to honour and dignity men of humble beginnings whom
they considered worthy. This, said Paget, her father and her
brother had done to him. However, if the queen thought him
unworthy, then he would pray for a writ of dotage to absent
himself from Parliament and all other duties of a noble.[5]

Queen Elizabeth was far from desirous of excluding Paget
entirely from an active share as a noble in the government of
the country. In November 1559, he was back at court taking a
firm stand in the prolonged crisis that marked the rise of

Robert Dudley in Elizabeth's court and his aspirations to her hand. Paget earned his pension from the Spanish ambassador by informing him that Elizabeth would not marry a Hapsburg prince sight unseen. The French court heard he had been closeted with Elizabeth for several hours advising a strong anti-French policy, and he was certainly investigating Scottish affairs in late December. The apparent desire of Cecil, with whom he co-operated, was to use Paget's reputation with King Philip to lead him to support Elizabeth's policy against France in Scotland. With this intent, Paget was offered the post of ambassador to Spain which his dubious health led him to refuse.[6]

The Privy Council was bitterly divided into factions, and Arundel and Clinton had a prodigious dispute in the queen's presence chamber, falling to beard-pulling and fisticuffs over the question of severity towards the Catholics. Philip's ambassador, De Quadra, heard that Paget's enemies had encouraged one of his servants to kidnap one of his younger daughters and carry her off. Another great cause of friction among the nobles was the question of the succession. Paget heard that Lord Darnley was the candidate of the Catholics, although others mentioned Lord Hastings, son of the Earl of Huntingdon. The Protestants suspected Paget of managing the case for Darnley, and Paget's friend Mason was implicated with him by an indignant enemy. ('God confound all Pagetyans devises with Mason and all his fellows; such arch practices against God and country... Because they may not have things go after their will and devise, they had rather bring in a foreign prince than live subject under the godly laws of their own country.')[7] Queen Elizabeth, however, defied the urgings of all sides and the succession question remained unsolved and the topic forbidden.

In the winter of 1560–1, the crisis in Dudley's relation with the queen occurred. Most of the Protestants in the council and many of the great nobles disliked his pretensions, but some of the Catholic party were inclined to support Dudley and his foreign policy. If he married the queen it could only be with the support of a tight alliance with Philip of Spain to foil France and the Stuart claim to the throne of England. Such an alliance would of necessity bring with it a domestic religious policy oriented towards Catholicism. The opponents of Dudley were by no means unified, however. Paget's former servant, Robert Jones, was a clerk of the Privy Council, and through Jones he kept in touch with Throckmorton, who had been relegated to an embassy in France rather than the high post of secretary of state in conjunction with Cecil. But in that month, Throckmorton forfeited the queen's favour by plain speech. He had heard in France of Amy Robsart's timely death, and sent Jones to the queen to urge her not to forfeit the respect of the world for Dudley's highly suspect hand in marriage. His blunt advice coincided with Elizabeth's views, but Paget and Jones shared her displeasure at Throckmorton's blunt speech.[8]

In January, Dudley offered the Spanish ambassador his absolute loyalty in return for Philip's support if he were to wed the queen. But Elizabeth was reluctant to repeat the mistake of her sister in spite of the fact that Dudley urged her forward. In this crisis, while Cecil was apparently helpless to prevent Dudley's Spanish policy from being adopted, Paget was closeted with Elizabeth for several hours and suggested an alternate policy which she grasped with relief. The young Earl of Bedford was sent to arrange an alliance with the French regent to make Elizabeth independent of Philip—and Dudley! De Quadra was furious at his pensioner's having betrayed both his Catholic religion and his Spanish paymaster in the interest of a strong and independent England. Lord Paget thus, in one stroke, abandoned his earlier views on the viability of an independent England, to return to the Henry VIII policy of balancing the continental powers against each other. And he did this in spite of his 1,500 crown pension from Philip. Did he perceive that Elizabeth, unlike her brother and sister, in 'the body of a weak feeble woman' had 'the heart and stomach of a king—and of a King of England too' like the great Harry from whom Paget had learned statecraft?[9]

It was his last great service to his sovereign. During the next two years Paget participated but little in politics. He was honoured by the queen with a leading role in the Feast of the Order of the Garter on two occasions, and his advice was sought on two occasions by the queen and Cecil in affairs of state concerning the coinage reform and the expedition against Le Havre. His old friends in the foreign service continued to write him occasional letters, and he intervened in matters of patronage on rare occasions, but he was present at only a few sessions of the Parliament of 1563.[10]

His principal attention was doubtless fixed on the care of his properties and his family. His extensive properties were valued at £1,500 revenue a year, and his iron furnaces in Staffordshire were a solid supplement to his fortune. But, like all Tudor nobles, he was perennially indebted to the crown. Paget's expensive mansions, his forty-eight household servants, his debts to the Court of Wards, and the unpaid parliamentary subsidies were a heavy burden, while the expense of his son Sir Henry's trip to Italy and of his separate establishment were an additional drain. Nevertheless, Lord Paget had good reason to be pleased with the accumulation of over thirty years of public life.[11]

On 10 June 1563, at Drayton, Lord Paget died after an absence from public life of several months. Word of his death was received with grief by at least one of his old protégés and by his old sovereign, Philip of Spain. His funeral was described with professional relish by Henry Machyn as occurring about 15 June, 'with a standard and a great banner ... banner rolls of arms and a coat armour ... garter, helm, and crest, and mantells, and sword ... dozens of scutcheons, and a four dozen of pencels about the hearse'. Although his body was interred in the parish church of West Drayton, his son Thomas erected a stately monument to his father's memory in Lichfield Cathedral. It was demolished, appropriately, by Puritan zealots of a century later, of whom Paget would certainly have disapproved.[12]

In his will which he had drawn up during an earlier illness in November 1560, Paget had provided amply for his wife, his children, and his two sisters, and £100 for his household servants. The bulk of his properties were to pass into his eldest son's hands. His property was so entailed that the widow's and younger children's portions reverted to the incumbent baron's hands at their deaths, for William, first Baron Paget of Beaudesert, was, like many a Tudor noble, a conscious founder of his family.[13]

Lord Paget would doubtless have been pleased at his success in this respect. His six daughters married (and when widowed remarried) substantial gentlemen and knights. Although his eldest son died without male heirs (his infant daughter gained unwitting fame in legal textbooks as Baroness Paget, *suo jure*), and his two younger sons were Catholic recusants and exiles soon after, Lady Anne, the dowager, brought up his grandson William as a loyal subject of the queen. The attainted barony and confiscated lands were restored to this William by the Stuarts. The family furnished an illustrious succession of diplomats and soldiers to three centuries of sovereigns, although the title of Baron Paget was swallowed up by an earldom and a marquessate.[14]

William Paget was a product of his century. Erudite but not a scholar, loyal to his country but not to his friends, he had a happy marriage in an age filled with nobles' connubial strife. Like the other great statesmen of his early years, Wolsey and Cromwell, he rose from a humble station in life to a high place in the King's Council. But he was not a statesman of the outstanding force of either Henry's great ministers or of Elizabeth's. Unlike her secretary, Walsingham, he was an opportunist and a *politique*, but his long service to four successive sovereigns revealed certain principles by which he strove to govern.

To Paget, the first care of a government was its foreign policy. Under a strong monarch he favoured an independent policy which played off his country's enemies against each other. But, under a weak and faction-torn government, he preferred to ally his nation to the supernational conservative Hapsburg empire rather than see it become a battleground for rival armies. Paget's domestic policy was reactionary. A traditional state in which a stern king meted out justice and governed through his loyal and obedient nobility, while the law protected the common people from disorder, was as much Paget's ideal tree of commonwealth as it had been Edmund Dudley's fifty years earlier. In religion, also, he would have preferred a realm which worshipped as one after its sovereign's manner, but his practical mind sought that ideal by gradual pressure rather than open persecution.

Paget contributed to many policies in his days of power. His assistance in the financial reforms of Mary's reign, and his maintenance of the secretary's powers in the exalted state that Cromwell had left them, laid two solid foundations for the success of Elizabeth's minister, Burleigh. But his fortune in attaining his greatest powers in the reign of the lesser Tudors destined Paget's greatest triumphs to be rearguard actions and negative policies. The pursuit of Henry's will-of-the-wisp Boulogne by all the arts of his diplomacy and finance, the mournful and vain exhortation of an unheeding protector, and the eventual betrayal of that ruler, the great plan for the Spanish marriage were all proven failures in the larger pattern of later English history, as many were revealed to be even in his own lifetime. Perhaps it was this knowledge which led Paget to leave to his heirs the maxims: [15]

Fly the court	Learn to spare
Speak little	Spend in measure
Care less	Care for home
Devise nothing	Pray often

In answer cold   Live better
                    And die well

In two of these maxims only had William, Lord Paget of Beaudesert distinguished himself.

NOTES

CHAPTER ONE   ANCESTRY AND EDUCATION (pp13-18)

1 C. Read, *Mr Secretary Walsingham*, Oxford, 2 (1925), pp386-424, calls the Pagets one of the 'oldest families in the kingdom'
2 British Museum, Harleian MS, 1077, f7; 806, ff83-4. (Hereafter cited as BM)
3 BM, Harleian MS, 1155, f60; S. Shaw, *History and Antiquities of Staffordshire* (1798), p215
4 M. A. S. Hume (ed), *Spanish Chronicle of Henry VIII* (1889), p147
5 W. Dugdale, *Baronage of England*, 2 (1676), p390
6 Anglesey MSS, Box 49, 1617, 1817-22; *Staffordshire Historical Collection*, William Salt Society (1939), pp85, 129-30
7 Public Record Office, C1/345/f42 (hereafter cited as PRO)
8 Anglesey MSS, 1617 (1817-22); *Staffordshire Historical Collection* (1939), pp85, 129-30
9 W. Dugdale, *Baronage of England*, 2, p390; BM, Harleian MS, 2043, f153-4
10 Anglesey MSS, 1047-51, contain several references to a Poer Paget of that date. The fact that these papers are in the hands of William Paget's descendants is not significant, as they are almost certainly part of the rich collection of medieval documents of Burton Abbey, which was later granted to William Paget
11 Somerset House, PCC Wills, 12 Godyn
12 PRO, C1/454/f12; C1/1460/f1
13 Shaw, *Staffordshire*, 1, p213, but cf S. Lee (ed), *Dictionary of National Biography*, New York (1895), 43, p60; and G. E. Cokayne and Vicary Gibbs (ed), *Complete Peerage* ..., 10 (1945), p276, for the latter date. His schoolmates Thomas Wriothesley and John Leland were born in 1505 and 1506(?) respectively. In the absence of early records, one can only speculate that this confusion may be the result of the custom of beginning the new year on Lady Day, 25 March, which, if true, would make the first three months of 1506 the time of William Paget's birth

14 Somerset House, PCC Wills, 27 Chayre

15 Leland, *Encomia*, pp100-1 in Hearne (ed), *Collectanea*, Oxford (1715), vol 5

16 *Ecclesiastical Memorials*, Oxford (1820-40), I, i, p430

17 W. G. Zeeveld, *Foundations of Tudor Policy*, Cambridge (1948), *passim*

18 J. A. Muller, *Stephen Gardiner and the Tudor Reaction*, New York (1926), *passim*

19 *Letters and Papers of Henry VIII*, vol 20 (2), 788, hereafter cited as *L&P*; Leland, *Encomia*, contains another reference to this dramatic performance at Cambridge which must have been a riotous and impressive event

20 W. G. Searle (ed), *Grace Book Gamma*, Cambridge (1908), p223; M. Bateson (ed), *Grace Book Beta* 2, Cambridge (1905), contains two other entries about a Pachett for the same year as a Bachelor of Civil Law, though it suggests, without advancing any reason, that this may be another man

21 Leland, *Encomia*, pp100-1

CHAPTER TWO   THE SERVICE OF THE KING (pp19-34)

1 Leland, *Encomia*, pp100-1

2 Muller, *Stephen Gardiner*, pp20-1

3 *L&P*, 5, 559(9)

4 *L&P*, 4 (2), 4440

5 T. F. Tout, *Chapters in the Administrative History of Medieval England*, 5 (1920-33), p227

6 Muller, *Gardiner*, p32

7 BM, Stowe MS, 571, f21, indicates that they received no official fee. But cf F. Peck, *Desiderata Curiosa*, 1 (1732-5), p58, which places the fee at £5 per annum in Queen Elizabeth's time. The regular recurrence of monthly payments of 41s 4d to 'Paget clerk of the signet' (BM, Arundel MS, 97, ff3b, 56b, 133b, 171, and Stowe MS, 554, f12b) seems conclusive that he, at any rate, received a stipend

8 G. R. Elton, *Thomas Cromwell, Aspects of His Administrative Work*, unpublished thesis, University of London Library (1948), pp285-315; PRO, DL 42/133/ff1-4, gives the full text of Cromwell's reorganisation of the office

9 PRO, PSO2/4-9. These bundles contain authority for issues of the Privy Seal from 1540-2 with scattered bills from the period 1529-32. Even after Cromwell's fall the plan which he initiated remained in effect

10 BM, Additional MS, 35815

11 The date of his resignation is uncertain, but the coincidence of his trip to France then as ambassador with a grant of the next vacancy in the signet office to William Honnyng in October 1541 (*L&P*, 16,

1308(28)), and Honnyng's appearance as duty clerk in the office soon after (PRO, PSO2/7/bundle January 1542) seems suggestive. However, as late as May 1542 Paget was still receiving his monthly fee (BM, Stowe MS, 554, f12b). There is some evidence that he had earlier relinquished the clerkship while secretary to Anne of Cleves, but, if he did so, he received it again soon after the end of her marriage. (*L&P*, 16, 503(13))

12 A. F. Pollard, *Thomas Cranmer* (1927), pp38-9
13 *L&P*, 5, 6; Herbert of Cherbury, *Life and Reign of Henry VIII* (1672), p329
14 *L&P*, 5, 363
15 Strype, *Ecclesiastical Memorials*, I, i, p219
16 *L&P*, 5, 337
17 *L&P*, 5, 378, 393
18 Preserved Smith, 'German Opinion of the Divorce of Henry VIII', *English Historical Review*, 27 (1912), p675
19 *L&P*, 5, 427
20 *L&P*, 5, 548; BM, Additional MS, 25114, f49
21 *L&P*, 5, 791; BM, Additional MS, 25114, f1
22 Muller, *Gardiner*, p45
23 BM, Cotton MS, Vitellius, B, xxi, ff152-5; *L&P*, Addenda, I (1), 767
24 Pollard, *Cranmer*, pp48-9
25 *L&P*, 5, 1292, 1531; 6, 89. Chapuys remained convinced that Paget had been to see Melancthon and believed that on the basis of this acquaintance Paget wrote to him in January 1533 expressing to him Henry's desire to have him visit England
26 Muller, *Gardiner*, pp46-8; *L&P*, 5, 1019
27 *L&P*, 6, 465
28 Elton, *Cromwell*, pp101-4
29 Muller, *Gardiner*, p54
30 PRO, SP1/82/ff201-2; (*L&P*, 7, 220)
31 Strype, *Ecclesiastical Memorials*, I, i, pp231-4
32 BM, Cotton MS, Titus, B, i, ff414, 422; *L&P*, 7, 137
33 BM, Cotton MS, Vitellius, B, xiv, f68; Additional MS, 29547, f1b; *L&P*, 7, 21
34 H. A. L. Fisher, *Political History*, 5, pp359-60
35 PRO, SP1/82/ff201-2; *L&P*, 7, 220
36 PRO, SP1/82/ff291-2
37 *L&P*, 7, 584; BM, Cotton MS, Titus, B, i, f495
38 P. Friedmann, *Anne Boleyn*, 2, p23; *L&P*, 7, 710
39 *L&P*, 7, 546, 1282; *L&P*, 16, 4n
40 BM, Stowe MS, 599, f82b; Additional MS, 5524, f164
41 Stebbing Shaw, *Hist & Antiquit of Staffs*, I, p213
42 Leland, *Encomia*, pp101-2
43 This document (*L&P*, Addenda, I(1), 466), is dated Michelmas 1525. But as it refers to several trips by 'My lord of Winchester'

who in 1525 would certainly have been cited by his primary title as 'my lord Cardinal Wolsey', and as in 1535 Bishop Gardiner was on an embassy to France, the latter year seems almost certainly the correct date for this manuscript

44 BM, Cotton MS, Vitellius, B, xxi, f155; *L&P*, 9, 242
45 *L&P*, 13 (1), 1520
46 Nicolas, *Proceedings of the Privy Council*, 7, p3
47 Cooper, *Athenae Cantabrigensis*, I, p223
48 *L&P*, 15, 642(1&2); 16, 380(f138b); BM, Arundel MS, 97, f133b
49 PRO, Wriothesley letters, 13; *L&P*, 12(2), 1238, 1245
50 BM, Cotton MS, Vespasian, F, xii (2), f263. This letter, given both in *L&P*, 5, App 37, and *L&P*, 14 (2), App 54, must of necessity be later than June 1537, when Paget acquired the house at Drayton from which this letter was written
51 *L&P*, 12 (2), 1008(31); 14 (1), 1354(11); 15, 47b; 18 (1), 100(21)
52 *L&P*, 13 (2), 986; Deputy Keeper of the Public Records, *Third Report*, Appendix II, p251
53 Anglesey MS, Box 1, 3
54 *L&P*, 14 (2), 472, 616; Anglesey MS, Box 50, 1824; *Staffordshire Historical Collection* (1939), p130
55 *L&P*, Addenda 1 (2), 1457; 15, 728
56 M. Bateson (ed), *Grace Book Beta*, 2, p175; Cooper, *Alumni Cantabrigensis*, I, p554, feels this is William Paget, but the strong probability that he did not marry before 1536 and his relatively insignificant station in 1533 convinces me that this present noted in the proctor's accounts for the latter year was for one of the other Pagets who had attended Cambridge
57 *L&P*, 13 (1), 1427
58 W. R. Douthwaite, *Gray's Inn* (1886), p193; BM, Harleian MS (1912), f167, gives him as James Padgitt, but gives a correct coat of arms, while a list of Cecil's in the state papers of Elizabeth's time refers to him as Lord Pagett
59 *Calendar of Patent Rolls*, Philip & Mary, 4, p181; W. M. McMurray (ed), *Records of Two City Parishes* (1925), p259a
60 Anglesey MSS, Box 47, 2158
61 Anglesey MSS, Box 13, 808-11
62 BM, Cotton MS, Vespasian, F, xiii (2), f263
63 F. Peck, *Desiderata Curiosa* (1779), I, Book 2, p70
64 *L&P*, 5, 559 (9); 7, 1352 (21); 13 (1), 1520, f26

CHAPTER THREE   THE KING'S AMBASSADOR LIEGER IN FRANCE (pp35-54)

1 Elton, *Cromwell*, pp409-11
2 Elton, 414-30, gives an excellent summary of the work of Pollard (*EHR*, 38, 1923) and Adair (ibid) and his own equally sound re-

search into the origins of the Privy Council

3 Nicolas, *Proceedings of the Privy Council*, 7, p3

4 *L&P*, 16, 107 (3)

5 Elton, p385

6 E. R. Adair, 'Rough Copies of the PC Register', *EHR*, 38 (1923), p417; D. Gladish, *Tudor Privy Council*, Retford (1915), p136; PRO, PC2/f1

7 BM, Cotton MS, Titus, B, i, f191

8 H. Nicolas, *Proceedings of the Privy Council*, 7, pp22, 34, 87, 121

9 J. Dasent (ed), *Acts of the Privy Council*, 2, p240 (cited hereafter as *APC*)

10 BM, Stowe MS, 571, f21

11 BM, Cotton MS, Vespasian, C, xvi, ff104, 106. The reference to his wife as Lady Paget in folio 106 renders its date during Paget's clerkship slightly suspect

12 PRO, SP1/165/ff73-4

13 PRO, SP1/166/ff73-4

14 *L&P*, 16, 1056(64); BM, Stowe MS, 571, f21

15 BM, Cotton MS, Tiberius, D, i, f2. Cf J. E. Neale, *Elizabethan House of Commons* (1949), pp331-48, for an excellent summary of the duties of the two clerks of Parliament a generation later

16 *Lords' Journals*, I, p164

17 Nicolas, *Proceedings of the Privy Council*, 7, p247

18 *L&P*, 16, 1195-7, 1253; *Spanish Calendar*, 6 (1), p199. The reason given Lord William for his recall was that he was too important a man for the post!

19 *State Papers of Henry VIII*, 8, p611; Caius College MS, 597. This MS is the letter book of Paget's clerk and contains copies of all his official correspondence while he was ambassador in France, beginning with his initial instructions. All of the items are reproduced in *L&P*

20 *L&P*, 17, 402, 435; *L&P*, 17, 727, 817; BM, Cotton MS, Caligula, E, iv, f147

21 *L&P*, 17, 435

22 *L&P*, 17, 589

23 *L&P*, 17, 838

24 *L&P*, 16, 1335, 1440, 1444, 1447-8; Nicolas, *Proceedings of the Privy Council*, 7, p282; BM, Cotton MS, Caligula, E, iv, f115

25 BM, Stowe MS, 554, f14b. In June he was allowed £31 for extra couriers and two months later, in August 1542, a grant of £53 was made

26 *L&P*, 18 (1), 358

27 PRO, SP1/167/ff109-10; *L&P*, 16, 1303

28 *L&P*, 16, 1335

29 *L&P*, 16, 1334, 1363; BM, Cotton MS, Caligula, E, iv, f115

30 *L&P*, 17, 128, 232, 935

31 *L&P*, 17, 418, 839
32 J. Ponet, *Treatise of Politique Power*, p136, reproduced in W. S. Hudson, *John Ponet, Advocate of Limited Monarchy*, Chicago (1942)
33 *L&P*, 17, 95, 400, 418, 755, 838
34 *L&P*, 17, 328, 383, 9
35 *L&P*, 18 (1), 29, 62
36 *L&P*, 18 (1), 106
37 *L&P*, 17, 263, 755; 18 (1), 71, 107
38 Strype, *Ecclesiastical Memorials*, I, i, pp562-4
39 *L&P*, 17, 479, 495, 935, 1203
40 *L&P*, 17, 212; BM, Cotton MS, Caligula, E, iv, f138
41 *L&P*, 18 (1), 125, 163
42 *L&P*, 17, 128, 143, 145
43 *L&P*, 17, 166, 167(2), 182
44 *L&P*, 17, 185
45 *L&P*, 17, 200, 206, 232
46 *L&P*, 17, 246, 248
47 *L&P*, 17, 263, 269
48 *L&P*, 17, 286, 297-8. Undoubtedly the French were guilty of deliberately deceiving their own ambassador in ascribing the idea to Paget (cf *State Papers of Henry VIII*, 8, p719, in which the admiral refers to the idea of the joint war as 'of mine own devise'). It is impossible to doubt from the genuine indignation of Marillac at Paget that he was taken in by the deception
49 *L&P*, 17, 328
50 *L&P*, 17, 254
51 *L&P*, 17, Appendix B, 22
52 *L&P*, 17, 838
53 BM, Cotton MS, Caligula, E, iv, f95
54 *L&P*, 17, 1204; 18 (1), 91, 113
55 *L&P*, 18 (1), 44
56 *L&P*, 17, 485, 494, 554
57 *L&P*, 17, 328, 371, 418
58 *L&P*, 17, Appendix B, 22
59 *L&P*, 17, 461, 479, 495, 500, 603
60 *L&P*, 17, 485, 554
61 *L&P*, 17, 500, 655, Appendix B, 22
62 *L&P*, 17, 656, 659
63 *L&P*, 17, 755, 838
64 *L&P*, 17, 1204
65 *L&P*, 17, 1235
66 *L&P*, 18 (1), 62, 71, 106
67 *L&P*, 18 (1), 62
68 *L&P*, 18 (1), 92, 125, 134, 163
69 *L&P*, 18 (1), 217, 353

70 *L&P*, 17, 1156
71 The absence of any references to or salutations from his wife in his official correspondence for the embassy makes this a strong probability
72 *L&P*, 18 (1), 217, 250, 252
73 *L&P*, 18 (1), 298, 310, 361
74 *L&P*, 18 (1), 322, 339, 389
75 *L&P*, 18 (1), 340, 403, 422
76 *L&P*, 17, 1203; 18 (1), 183, 217
77 *L&P*, 16, 580(87), 780(3); 17, 817
78 BM, Harleian MS, 1507, f193; *Notes and Queries*, series I, 11 (June 1855), p494
79 BM, Stowe MS, 692, f78b. The original of this grant, dated 27 April 1544, is in the manuscripts of the Marquess of Anglesey, Box 50, 1827

CHAPTER FOUR   *PRINCIPAL SECRETARY OF STATE: PART ONE* (pp55-78)

1 *L&P*, 18 (1), 450. Cf M. A. S. Hume (ed), *Chronicle of King Henry VIII*... (1889), p106, for a strange and wonderful—and entirely false—account of Paget's background and appointment
2 F. M. G. Evans, *The Principal Secretary of State*, Manchester (1923), pp10-15
3 G. R. Elton, *Thomas Cromwell, Aspects of his Administrative Work*, unpublished thesis, University of London (1948), Chapter II, pp101-20, is especially valuable for its analysis of Cromwell's developing of the secretaryship
4 Elton, p356, holds this division was Cromwell's own contribution to efficient administration
5 BM, Stowe MS, 193, f170-1, is a copy of the ordinance establishing the dual office
6 Evans, *Principal Secretary*, pp6-9
7 *L&P*, 20 (1), 631
8 BM, Stowe MS, 571, f21; *L&P*, 19 (1), 368, 1036; 20 (1), 557
9 BM, Additional MS, 35818
10 *Collection of Ordinances and Regulations for the Royal Household*, Society of Antiquaries (1795), p210; *L&P*, 21 (1), 969; 20 (2), 982
11 *L&P*, 18 (2), 293, 346, 438
12 *L&P*, 19 (1), 1, 1036
13 *L&P*, 19 (2), 4; 20 (1), 780
14 *L&P*, 19 (1), 282; 21 (1), 1379
15 PRO, SP1/198/f176; SP1/199/f89
16 *L&P*, 20 (2), 864

17 In the summer of 1545 only one item, *L&P*, 20 (1), 1261, a Privy Council letter in draft form with Paget's corrections, is preserved

18 *L&P*, 20 (2), 116; 21 (2), 503

19 *L&P*, 21 (2), 115, 186, 252

20 PRO, PSO2/10; SP11/13/f48; Evans, p170; BM, Lansdowne MS, 156, 28 (f105)

21 *L&P*, 19 (2), 93, 216; 21 (1), 586

22 *L&P*, 20 (1), 1102

23 *A Treatise of th'Office of a Councellor and Principall Secretarie to her Majestie*, in Conyers Read, *Mr Secretary Walsingham and the Policy of Queen Elizabeth*, Cambridge (Mass) (1925), I, p439

24 *L&P*, 18 (2), 280; 19 (1), 903; 20 (2), 26; 21 (1), 81; 21 (2), 410

25 *L&P*, 19 (2), 19; 21 (1), 545, 1257-8

26 *L&P*, 21 (1), 1300; 18 (1), 550

27 *L&P*, 19 (1), 943; 20 (2), 38

28 *L&P*, 21 (1), 92

29 *L&P*, 18 (2), 45; 19 (1), 481; 20 (1), 891; 20 (2), 14, 238

30 PRO, SP1/202/ff152-4; *L&P*, 21 (1), 356

31 *L&P*, 19 (2), 331

32 *L&P*, 18 (2), 516; 19 (1), 1

33 *L&P*, 19 (1), 1024; 21 (2), 27, 238

34 *L&P*, 21 (1), 576 (BM, Harleian MS, 5087, 4); 21 (2), 282

35 BM, Harleian MS, 283, f273

36 *L&P*, 20 (1), 1183; 20 (2), 242; 21 (1), 371

37 *L&P*, 20 (2), 30

38 *L&P*, 20 (2), 412, 427, 496(68), p232; 21 (1), 121

39 *L&P*, 21 (1), 633. In a letter to Petre he denied ever having made a penny out of any suit he made to the king for another's advancement, except in two instances

40 *L&P*, 19 (1), 566, 624

41 *L&P*, 19 (1), 803

42 *L&P*, 19 (1), 188, 230; 20 (1), 1032, 1121, 1222, 1284; 20 (2), 225

43 J. Venn (ed), *Grace Books of Cambridge University*, Delta, Cambridge (1910), p37; *L&P*, 21 (1), 204

44 *APC*, I, pp158-223, 534-62

45 PRO, SP1/166/f73; *L&P*, 21 (2), 54 is a series of questions for the council with marginal notes of the answers in Paget's hand

46 *L&P*, 19 (1), 878; 21 (1), 1358

47 Anglesey MS, Box I, 4, 5. Both these items are dated November 1541 when he was in France, and must have been acquired by him on his return as secretary

48 *L&P*, 20 (2), 30. Lord Deputy St Leger writes that he knows Paget is one of the first to see a letter addressed to the council. *L&P*, Addenda I (2), 1809. In 1550 a paper of Paget's to the council indicated this had been his practice. BM, Egerton MS, 2603, ff33-4

49 PRO, SP1/190/f58. See also *L&P*, 21 (2), 141 for the return to him

by the action of the council in London of letters he had sent for its information

50 *APC*, I, pp200-4; *L&P*, 20 (1), 1015

51 *L&P*, 19 (I), 89, 323. Wriothesley and Gardiner in these examples. *L&P*, 18 (1), 559-60 show Paget in the process of learning by this technique. They are both drafts of council letters to an English ambassador, one by Paget and the other by Gardiner. The Paget draft was apparently discarded by the council in favour of the more diplomatic and tactful Gardiner version. The date is May 1543, three weeks after Paget became secretary

52 *L&P*, 21 (1), 122

53 PRO, SP10/1/15(f67)

54 *L&P*, 20 (1), 426 (PRO, SP1/199/f89)

55 *L&P*, 21 (2), 14

56 PRO, SP10/1/f67. See *L&P*, 21 (2), 156 for a typical example of a conciliar discussion of several Irish reforms with the king's decision on each point noted by Paget in the margin. *L&P*, 21 (2), 54 is a similar document about Boulogne

57 *L&P*, 19 (1), 318

58 *L&P*, 21 (2), 547

59 *L&P*, 21 (1), 1342. This was the beginning of a Paget–Arundel political alliance which lasted until the accession of Queen Elizabeth

60 *L&P*, 21 (2), 734

61 PRO, SP1/204/f187; *L&P*, 21 (2), 212 is an interesting example of a letter which began as a personal letter from Paget, but was changed to the plural and sent by the council with the king

62 *L&P*, 21 (2), 52, 167, 203

63 *L&P*, 21 (2), 27-8, 58-60, 83, 115, 124, 134, 141

64 Evans, pp250-1. See also Paget's remark to Petre that the king's secretary was always 'fellow to a baron' in PRO, SP1/199/f89

65 Evans, p251

66 *L&P*, 20 (2), 1045

67 Evans, p8

68 *L&P*, 19 (I), 946

69 *L&P*, 20 (2), 709; Addenda I (2), 1774

70 *L&P*, 21 (1), 1181; *Wriothesley's Chronicle of England*, Camden Society, new series, 11, part i, pp167-9; Henry Christmas (ed), *Select Works of John Bale*, Parker Society (1849), pp203-5

71 Hume (ed), *Spanish Chronicle*, p112

72 *L&P*, 21 (2), 554-5, 697

73 *L&P*, 21 (1), 197, 399; 20 (1), 892, 1099

74 *L&P*, 20 (2), 212, 213, 222, 231, 268, 272, 302, 358, 425, 453, 472-3, 697, 709, 713, 729, 746, 752, 769; 21 (2), 172

75 *L&P*, 20 (1), 1194, 1214. In this instance the letter to Paget was written three days before that to Wriothesley

76 F. C. Dietz, *English Government Finance, 1485-1558*, University of

Illinois Studies in the Social Sciences, **9** (1920), pp152-8; *L&P*, **19** (1), 272

77 *L&P*, 19 (2), 212, 751

78 Dietz, pp152-8

79 *L&P*, 19 (1), 278(4); 20 (1), 125(12)

80 *L&P*, 20 (1), 75, 358; 20 (2), 453

81 *L&P*, 20 (1), 1300. Wriothesley took the lead in this activity to judge from this letter, which was directed to Paget only because of the chancellor's absence

82 *L&P*, 20 (1), *passim*

83 *L&P*, 19 (2), 159; 20 (1), 996; 20 (2), 492; 21 (1), 200

84 *L&P*, 21 (1), 241, 264

85 *L&P*, 20 (2), 217; 21 (1), 106, 291, 1374

86 *L&P*, 20 (1), 646, 978, 1221; 20 (2), 143, 281; Anglesey MS, Box 1, 9

87 *L&P*, 20 (1), 1079, 1139; 20 (2), 234

88 *L&P*, 20 (2), 616

89 *L&P*, 20 (2), 334; *APC*, I, p318

90 *L&P*, 19 (2), 31; 20 (1), 666, 676

91 *L&P*, 19 (1), 902; 21 (1), 504, 527, 597

92 The mathematics is Paget's!

93 S. Haynes (ed), *Calendar of State Papers ... by William Cecil ..* (1740), I, p54; *L&P*, 20 (1), 623

94 Dietz, pp152-8; *L&P*, 20 (1), 1194, 1316; 20 (2), 36, 729

95 *L&P*, 20 (1), 1143, 1239, 1265

96 *L&P*, 20 (1), 16, 1145

97 *L&P*, 20 (2), 212, 453

98 *L&P*, 20 (2), 746, 752

99 Dietz, pp152-8; *L&P*, 21 (2), 336

100 *L&P*, 21 (1), 1066, 1421, 1448, 1477

CHAPTER FIVE   PRINCIPAL SECRETARY OF STATE: PART TWO (pp79-108)

1 Evans, p305; *L&P*, 20 (1), 749; 21 (1), 1153, 1384; Hume (ed), *Spanish Chronicle*, pp109-11

2 *L&P*, 19 (1), 557, 716; 19 (2), 787; 20 (1), 877; 20 (2), 234; 21 (1), 483, 496

3 *L&P*, 19 (1), 568; 20 (1), 1156

4 *L&P*, 20 (2), 784, 910(27)

5 BM, Lansdowne MS, 156, 28; Stowe MS, 571, f21; *L&P*, 19 (1), 105 refers to the promotion of a former Paget servant to courier

6 *L&P*, 21 (1), 643 (ff64-5); *APC*, I, p527

7 *L&P*, 21 (2), 11, 370; 20 (1), 1210

8 *L&P*, 19 (2), 392; 20 (1), 905, 958; 20 (2), 604; 21 (1), 1177; 21 (2), 78, 248, 370, 582

9 *L&P*, 19 (2), 144; 21 (1), 254, 975; 21 (2), 289

10 *L&P*, 18 (2), 304-5; 19 (1), 287; 20 (2), 845

11 *L&P*, 19 (1), 150, 161, 454, 952; 20 (1), 1199; 20 (2), 788

12 *L&P*, 20 (2), 194; 21 (2), ppxxi-xvii, 23; P. de M. G. Egerton (ed), *Services of Lord Grey of Wilton*, Camden Society (1847), p4

13 *L&P*, 19 (2), 194

14 *L&P*, 19 (1), 230, 556, 994; 20 (1), 1022; 20 (2), 159. Many ambassadors, however, were on friendly and even teasing terms with Paget. See *L&P*, 20 (2), 776, for an amusing letter from Bishop Thirlby

15 *L&P*, 18 (2), 458; 19 (1), 128, 972

16 *L&P*, 19 (1), 572; 19 (2), 220, 308, 700; 20 (1), 794; 20 (2), 111

17 *L&P*, 19 (2), 643; 20 (1), 213; 20 (2), 217

18 *L&P*, 19 (1), 1013; 21 (1), 1310; 21 (2), 638

19 *L&P*, 19 (1), 767; 19 (2), 658; 20 (1), 590, 634; 20 (2), 217, 1004ii; 21 (2), 638, 673; PRO SP68/1/f86

20 *L&P*, 20 (1), 1087; 20 (2), 178; 21 (1), 1207, 1398; 21 (2), 36, 239, 373, 713

21 *Venetian Calendar*, 6 (3), appendix, 115

22 *L&P*, 20 (1), 1315; 21 (2), 517

23 *L&P*, 20 (2), 511, 659; 21 (2), 14

24 *L&P*, 19 (1), 472ii; 20 (2), 560; 21 (1), 1398; 21 (2), 276, 380

25 *L&P*, 20 (2), 560, 649, 1061; 21 (1), 181; 21 (2), 11

26 *L&P*, 19 (1), 147, 530; 19 (2), 304; 20 (2), 399, 586; 21 (2), 458, 469, 1398ii, 1463; 21 (2), 158, 315

27 *L&P*, 20 (1), 1087

28 *L&P*, 20 (1), 1293; 21 (1), 1463; 21 (2), 276

29 *L&P*, 21 (1), 1227; 21 (2), 84

30 *L&P*, 21 (1), 469; 21 (2), 547

31 *L&P*, 21 (1), 1464; 21 (2), 239; *Spanish Calendar*, 9, pp2, 19, 30-1, 88-9, 109-11

32 And on occasion reproved rash officers for neglecting to use the ciphers which he supplied. *L&P*, 19 (2), 500

33 *L&P*, 20 (1), 1134; 20 (2), 928; 21 (1), 553, 1095; 21 (2), 358

34 *L&P*, 20 (1), 1147; 21 (1), 373, 553; *L&P*, Addenda, I(2), 1754

35 *L&P*, 18 (2), 330; 20 (2), 967, 976

36 BM, Cotton MS, Vitellius, B, xxi, ff152-5; *L&P*, 19 (2), 745; 20 (1), 372, 1223, 1233; 21 (1), 126, 337, 369

37 *L&P*, 20 (1), 858; 20 (2), 515; 21 (2), 695; *APC*, I, p527 records the reward of £50 to the young Lord Grange, one of the moving spirits in the murder of Cardinal Beaton

38 *L&P*, 20 (1), 40, 448, 509, 522, 608, 725. £10 reward to him from the Privy Council is noted in *L&P*, 20 (2), 256

39 *L&P*, 20 (2), 553

40 *L&P*, 20 (1), 428, 452, 1067, 1074, 1125; 20 (2), 171, 442, 487

41 *L&P*, 20 (1), 696, 827, 831; 20 (2), 85

42 *L&P*, 19 (1), 1026; 20 (1), 256; 20 (2), 472, 706(80-81), 922, 934; 21

(1), 650(84), 891
43 *L&P*, 21 (2), 91, 259, 414, 444, 480, 518, 760
44 *Spanish Calendar*, 8, 309 (*L&P*, 21 (1), 1464)
45 *L&P*, 19 (1), 208, 231, 243, 271
46 *L&P*, 19 (1), 520, 529, 530, 603
47 *L&P*, 19 (1), 525, 566, 578, 526-7
48 *L&P*, 19 (1), 572
49 Ibid, 619, 626; PRO, SP1/188/ff178-82
50 *L&P*, 19 (1), 648, 666, 682, 695
51 Ibid, 674, 676, 730, 766. Norfolk (674) dates his return as the tenth, but Chapuys's date, the twelfth (730), seems more probable in view of his departure from Antwerp on the ninth
52 Ibid, 716
53 *L&P*, 19 (1), 779, 812, 878
54 Ibid, 864, 889
55 W. D. Hamilton (ed), *Wriothesley's Chronicle*, Camden Society (1875), I, pp148-9
56 *L&P*, 19 (1), 1013
57 *L&P*, 19 (1), 940, 946
58 *L&P*, 19 (2), 223, 424
59 *L&P*, 19 (2), 524 (f95)
60 *L&P*, 19 (2), 5, 105; PRO, SP1/191/f21
61 *L&P*, 19 (2), 125, 181
62 *L&P*, 19 (2), 175
63 Ibid, 268, 304
64 Ibid, 216, 235, 276
65 *L&P*, 19 (2), 331, 344, 374
66 Ibid, 391-2; PRO, SP1/193/f86
67 *L&P*, 19 (2), 454, 456, 470
68 Ibid, 479, 507, 518; PRO, SP1/194/ff213, 224
69 PRO, SP1/195/f120
70 *L&P*, 19 (2), 582, 596, 746 (PRO, SP1/195/ff41, 69)
71 *L&P*, 20 (1), 29, 80, 212; PRO, SP1/197/ff135-74
72 *L&P*, 19 (2), 784; 20 (1), 30
73 *L&P*, 20 (1), 43, 76; PRO, SP1/197/ff81-97; 1/198/ff3-10
74 PRO, SP1/198/ff98-121
75 PRO, SP1/198/ff161-4
76 PRO, SP1/198/ff183-92, 195-7
77 *L&P*, 20 (1), 302, 305
78 PRO, SP1/198/f213
79 *L&P*, 20 (1), 457; PRO, SP1/199/ff3-7, 43-8
80 PRO, SP1/199/ff49-51, 70, 74-87; *L&P*, 20 (1), 406
81 PRO, SP1/199/ff89-91
82 PRO, SP1/199/f176
83 *L&P*, 20 (1), 494, 542; PRO, SP1/199/f209
84 PRO, SP1/202/f22

85 *L&P*, 20 (2), 26
86 *L&P*, 20 (2), 56, 123
87 *L&P*, 20 (2), 421
88 *L&P*, 20 (2), 455, 738, Appendix 30
89 *L&P*, 20 (2), 604
90 Ibid, 737
91 Ibid, 732, 749
92 Ibid, 810, 876
93 Ibid, 827, 828
94 Ibid, 836, 856
95 PRO, SP1/197/f228; C. Sturge, *Cuthbert Tunstal* (1938), pp249, 261; *L&P*, 20 (2), 880
96 *L&P*, 20 (2), 919, 954
97 *L&P*, 20 (2), 890
98 *L&P*, 20 (2), 969, 984, 1000
99 *L&P*, 20 (2), 1001, 1011, 1057, 1058; 21 (1), 13, 23
100 Ibid, 550
101 *L&P*, 21 (1), 610; Anglesey MSS, Box I, 33
102 *L&P*, 21 (1), 632
103 *L&P*, 21 (1), 637, 639, 670, 685
104 *L&P*, 21 (1), 712, 725, 733, 749
105 Ibid, 691, 763
106 Ibid, 771
107 *L&P*, 21 (1), 831
108 Anglesey MSS, Box I, 8; *L&P*, 21 (1), 806, 816
109 *L&P*, 21 (1), 837, 838, 840, 841, 850
110 *L&P*, 21 (1), 849, 855, 862, 891
111 Ibid, 941, 943
112 *L&P*, 21 (1), 989
113 *L&P*, 21 (1), 994, 1007, 1014, 1024

CHAPTER SIX STRUGGLE FOR POWER (pp109-29)

1 A. F. Pollard, *Political History of England*, 6 (1910), p2
2 *L&P*, 20 (1), 235
3 Ibid, 973; 20 (2), 149, 178; 21 (1), 1406; 21 (2), 392
4 *L&P*, 21 (2), 23 is the *ex post facto* letter of Paget's drafting which legitimised the action. See also the introduction to this volume, pp12-17, and Philip de M. G. Egerton (ed), *Services of Lord Grey of Wilton*, Camden Society (1847), p4, and Herbert of Cherbury, *Life and Raigne of King Henry VIII* (1741), pp607-8
5 *L&P*, 21 (2), 273. One of the clearest evidences of Paget's position is to examine the indices of the last two volumes of this series. Only Henry VIII is mentioned more often than he is, as almost half of the 5,000 documents calendared concern Paget directly
6 *L&P*, 19 (1), 80(27); BM, Additional MS, 6113, f114; Cotton MS,

I

Caius, C, iii, f133b

7 *L&P*, 19 (1), 80(27), 105; Anglesey MS, Box 16 and Box 48, 2170 Paget returned the favour of the house, after the ambassador's death, by taking his younger brother, William Layton, into his favour and securing for him a royal appointment into church position. (*Staffordshire Historical Collections*, 1937, p182; *L&P*, 19 (1), 649)

8 *Staffordshire Historical Collections* (1939), p131; BM, Stowe MS, 692, f78b

9 *L&P*, 20 (1), 566; 20 (2), 910(27); 21 (1), 736, 1538; 21 (2), 331(65)

10 BM, Harleian MS, 806, ff83-4; 1077, f7; *L&P*, 20 (2), 910(31), 955; 20 (1), 302(20)

11 *L&P*, 20 (2), 30. There is a good possibility that Paget was as anxious for the alliance as Sir Thomas Moyle, the would-be father of the bride. See *L&P*, 19 (2), 532. However, the marriage arrangements were never completed

12 *L&P*, 21 (2), 213, 252

13 *L&P*, 20 (1), 131, 282. Kepier was valued at £205 per annum in *Calendar of Patent Rolls*, Edward VI, 4, 360

14 Cox had a dreadfully tender conscience over this lapse and blamed Paget for seducing him. *L&P*, 21 (2), 282

15 Anglesey MS, 1829; *L&P*, 20 (1), 846(31, 91). This licence in May 1545 compares with a simultaneous one to the Duke of Suffolk, the king's brother-in-law and a great magnate, for one hundred liveried retainers

16 *L&P*, 20 (2), 707(52); 21 (1), 149(39); Anglesey MS, 775-6

17 *L&P*, 21 (1), 716(16); Anglesey MSS, Boxes 13, 14

18 Anglesey MSS, Box 13, 804, 805; 1944 is a list of 39 'articles for ordering my lord's things about Burton' prepared by his bailiff, and deals with his timber, fishing rights, iron ore, coal, horses, etc

19 *L&P*, 21 (2), 332(76), 474(7); Anglesey MSS, 1735-6, 1831. Anglesey MS, 1738 indicates the bishop's lands were valued at £150 rent, while the rent of £366 on the Burton lands would have made these properties sell at over £10,320. Paget actually laid out about £6,040

20 *Journals of the House of Lords*, I, pp289-90; Anglesey MS, 1832

21 PRO, SP1/194/ff201-2. This outburst was caused by a slight to one of the English ambassadors for which the Earl of Hertford was equally responsible. Paget, however, blamed Gardiner alone

22 PRO, SP1/195/f68 (*L&P*, 19 (2), 595); *L&P*, 20 (2), 399; 21 (1), 1329

23 *L&P*, 20 (1), 1082; 20 (2), 627, 788, 838; 21 (1), 74, 214

24 *L&P*, 21 (1), 1227; 21 (2), 84

25 *L&P*, 19 (1), 230

26 *L&P*, 19 (1), 293; 20 (I), 837, 859, 939

27 *L&P*, 20 (1), 987, 1145; 20 (2), 118

28 *L&P*, 20 (2), 119; 21 (1), 1075. The latter document contained 'a portraiture of a monster lately taken in ... the seas'

29 *L&P*, 21 (2), 140
30 *L&P*, 20 (2), 412, 427; 21 (1), 121, 1263
31 *L&P*, 20 (1), 1145; 20 (2), 539; 21 (1), 92; 21 (2), 260
32 *L&P*, 21 (1), 557, 1439; 21 (2), 21
33 *L&P*, 20 (2), 416
34 *L&P*, 21 (1), 1227; 21 (2), 84
35 *L&P*, 20 (2), 610; 21 (1), 661
36 *L&P*, 21 (1), Introduction, xlix
37 Ibid, 391, 439
38 Ibid, 289, 346
39 Ibid, 776, 783, 790, 810, 823, 836, 848, 1227; 21 (2), 173
40 *L&P*, 21 (1), 1181
41 S. R. Cattley (ed), *Acts and Monuments of John Foxe* (1838), 5, pp544-60; R. Parsons, *Treatise of Three Conversions of England*, St Omer (1603-4), 2, p493
42 Northampton Record Society, Fitzwilliam MS, Paget letter-book, 31. (Hereafter cited as Ntht, Paget Ltr-book.) *APC*, 2, pp15-22
43 *APC*, I, p493
44 *L&P*, 21 (2), 14
45 *L&P*, 21 (1), 1398; *APC*, I, pp510-11
46 *APC*, I, pp511-25
47 *L&P*, 21 (2), 167, 194
48 Cattley (ed), *Acts and Monuments of John Foxe*, 5, pp563-4
49 *L&P*, 21 (1), 1526
50 Ntht, Paget-Ltr-book, 30; another copy is in BM, Cotton MS, Titus, B, ii, ff91-4, which Strype, *Ecclesiastical Memorials*, 2, i, p87, misdates as August 1547
51 See *Spanish Calendar*, 9, p6, for the attempt at mediation in Germany which Paget had first suggested five months earlier
52 *APC*, I, pp527-34; *L&P*, 21 (2), 14, 44, 58, 82, 122, 129, 134, 139, 172
53 *L&P*, 21 (2), 347. There is no record in the council register of both men being present together until early November, but De Selve dates the episode as over a month earlier. This dispute and blow may have occurred on 20 September when the London councillors met at Lisle's house, though he was then too sick to peruse a letter. (Ibid, 134.) In view of Lisle's fiery nature, he might have surmounted this obstacle, however!
54 *L&P*, 21 (2), 381
55 Ibid, 213, 488, 493
56 Hume (ed), *Spanish Chronicle*, pp142-3
57 *L&P*, 21 (2), Introduction, pxxxvi, 546
58 Ibid, 548, 552-6
59 *L&P*, 21 (2), 554
60 *L&P*, 21 (2), 697; W. D. Hamilton (ed), *Wriothesley's Chronicle of England*, Camden Society, ns, 11, Part I, p177; J. G. Nichols (ed), *Chronicle of the Greyfriars of London*, Camden Society (1852),

p53; Hume (ed), *Spanish Chronicle*, pp143-7
61 *APC*, I, pp556-62; *L&P*, 21 (2), 660
62 *L&P*, 21 (2), 713, 725
63 Cattley (ed), *Acts and Monuments of John Foxe*, 5, pp691-2; 6, pp163-74; 7, pp588-91
64 *Correspondence Politique de Odet de Selve* (ed by Germain Lefevre-Pontalis), Paris (1888), p216. (Hereafter cited as *Corr Politique*)
65 *L&P*, 21 (2), 634; *APC*, 2, p326; *Spanish Calendar*, 9, pp30-1
66 Ibid, pp30-1
67 *L&P*, 21 (2), 605, 756; *Spanish Calendar*, 9, p2
68 *APC*, I, p566
69 *L&P*, 21 (2), 710; *APC*, I, p564
70 *L&P*, 21 (2), 760; BM, Cotton MS, Titus, B, ii, f51; PRO, SP10/8/4. This letter from Paget to Somerset exists in another copy in BM, Cotton MS, Titus, F, iii, f274, and is printed in Strype, *Ecclesiastical Memorials*, 2, ii, pp429-37

CHAPTER SEVEN THE PROTECTOR'S CASSANDRA
(pp130-59)

1 PRO, SP10/1/1&2
2 P. F. Tytler, *England Under the Reigns of Edward VI and Mary* (1839), I, p163. (Hereafter cited as *Tytler*)
3 *APC*, 2, pp3-6; *Spanish Calendar*, 9, pp100-104; *Wriothesley's Chronicle*, 1, pp178-80; BM, Cotton MS, Titus, B, ii, f51
4 *APC*, 2, pp5-8; BM, Egerton MS, 3026, f3; PRO, SP68/1/ff6-12
5 *APC*, 2, pp12-14, 33; BM, Cotton MS, Titus, B, ii, f53; Additional MS, 33591, f2
6 *APC*, 2, pp15-22. A copy of this testimony is in the Paget letterbook of the Northampton Record Society's Fitzwilliam Papers, ‖31
7 A. F. Pollard, *England under Protector Somerset* (1900), p29; *Thomas Cranmer*, New York (1904), p185; PRO, SP10/1/11 is a list of the proposed creations on which Paget had indicated the elimination of two earldoms and several baronies
8 *APC*, 2, pp20-22
9 PRO, SP10/19/f1; Anglesey MS, Box 3, 1333
10 Bodleian Library, Ashmolean MS, 1109, f85; J. G. Nichols, *Literary Remains of King Edward VI*, Roxburghe Club (1857), I, pxciv. Paget promptly set to work collecting the arrears of fees due from the other knights! (Bodleian, Ashmolean MS, 1134, f235)
11 *Wriothesley's Chronicle*, I, p182; BM, Egerton MS, 3026, f3; *APC*, 2, p34
12 *Spanish Calendar*, 9, pp46-51; BM, Egerton MS, 3026, f3; Harleian MS, 353, ff3-7
13 *Spanish Calendar*, 9, pp51, 69-71, 90-93; *Corr Politique*, 169; BM,

Harleian MS, 249, ff16-17; 284, f9

14 J. A. Muller (ed), *Letters of Stephen Gardiner*, Cambridge (1933), pp253-4, 268-72; PRO, SP10/1/f26

15 In a conversation with Vanderdelft. *Spanish Calendar*, 9, pp183-8

16 *Calendar of Patent Rolls*, Edward VI, I, p97. (Copy in BM, Additional MS, 35838, ff33-45.) The new patent was recorded in the council book on 21 March

17 *Spanish Calendar*, 9, pp100-4; J. G. Nichols, 'The Second Patent Appointing Somerset Protector', *Archaeologia*, 30 (1844), pp463-89; BM, Additional MS, 35838, ff48-9

18 PRO, SP10/2/f1; 10/5/f17; and 46/1/f296

19 *Corr Politique*, 215, 306, 319, 506; *Spanish Calendar*, 9, pp298-9

20 *Corr Politique*, 119; *Spanish Calendar*, 9, pp83-6, 88-9, 100-4

21 *Corr Politique*, 415; *Spanish Calendar*, 9, pp30, 51, 109-11

22 *Corr Politique*, 122; *Spanish Calendar*, 9, p179; PRO, SP68/3/f7

23 *Corr Politique*, 216; BM, Cotton MS, Titus, F, iii, f273. (Printed in Strype, *Ecclesiastical Memorials*, 2, i, pp34-5)

24 PRO, SP10/1/ff8, 28, 30; C. H. & T. Cooper, *Athenae Cantabrigiensis*, Cambridge (1858), I, pp221-4; J. Venn, *Grace Book Delta*, Cambridge (1910), p54; BM, Sloane MS, 3562, f53

25 *Spanish Calendar*, 9, pp104-6

26 *L&P*, 21 (2), 199; *APC*, 2, pp25, 101; *Spanish Calendar*, 9, p106; Anglesey MS, Box 3, 1828

27 PRO, E101/426/1 is Paget's account book for his first six months. BM, Royal MS, 18A, xlvi, ff1-9; Stowe MS, 571, f29b

28 BM, Lansdowne MS, 825, f104; Stowe MS, 571, ff12-14; Additional MS, 30198, f26; Anglesey MSS, Box 1a

29 *Return of the Name of Every Member . . .*, Parliamentary Papers (1878), lxii, Part I, pp375-7; J. C. Wedgwood, *Staffordshire Parliamentary History*, William Salt Society (1919), I, pp1-1v; *Commons' Journals*, I, pp8-9

30 Particularly concerning conduct of the duke's diplomacy secret from the rest of the council. See the fragment of a secret letter into Scotland in the British Museum, Cotton MS, Caligula, E, iv, f62

31 *Tytler*, I, pp88-90; *Spanish Calendar*, 9, pp145-7; *Corr Politique*, 220-415; PRO, SP15/1/f26; 68/2/f97; BM, Cotton MS, Galba, B, xii, ff28-31; Ntht, Paget Ltr-book, 1; in this letter Paget admits on 30 August 1547 he is still swamped with the work of the secretary's office

32 A. F. Pollard, *England under Protector Somerset*, pp103-15; *Spanish Calendar*, 9, pp109-11, 150-3, 183-8

33 Ntht, Paget Ltr-book, 3

34 *Spanish Calendar*, 9, pp265-6, 282-3, 342-4; Anglesey MS, Box 2, 2; BM, Cotton MS, Titus, F, iii, f273

35 *Corr Politique*, 119, 128; *Spanish Calendar*, 9, pp46-51, 106-7; PRO, SP68/1/ff46, 74

36 *Corr Politique*, 210, 215, 216; Ntht, Paget Ltr-book, 1
37 *Corr Politique*, 220-21, 238, 254, 293; *Spanish Calendar*, 9, pp235-6
38 Ntht, Paget Ltr-book, 3. A list of the nobility and gentry and their
    military obligations in the Public Record Office (SP10/5/fl7) must
    date from shortly after this time
39 *Corr Politique*, 215; *Spanish Calendar*, 9, pp140-4; *APC*, 2, pp115
    ff; T. B. Howell, *State Trials*... (1816), I, pp486, 493; G. Burnett,
    History of the Reformation of the Church of England, Pocock edn,
    Oxford (1865), 2, p115. Paget may have reported the intrigue to the
    protector, for he was certainly writing him secret letters on the
    council's activity at this time. See Ntht, Paget Ltr-book, 1
40 Nichols, 'The Second Patent...', *Archaeologia*, 30 (1844), pp463-
    89; *Calendar of Patent Rolls*, Edward VI, 2, pp96-7; S. Haynes &
    W. Murdin, *Collection of State Papers... by William Cecil* (1740-
    59), I, pp91-3
41 Pollard, *Somerset*, pp207-10
42 Ibid, p217; BM, Lansdowne MSS, 238, ff305, 307, 315-16
43 BM, Lansdowne MSS, 238, ff313, 318b-325
44 Hume (ed), *Spanish Chronicle*, p171; *APC*, 3, pp414-15; Anglesey
    MS, Box 14, 818
45 PRO, SP10/4/33
46 BM, Harleian MS, 6989, ff141-7; PRO, SP68/4/f83
47 BM, Cotton MS, Titus, F, iii, f273
48 This bitter note was doubtlessly caused by Paget's current investi-
    gation of the treasurer of the chamber with a view to small econ-
    omies there. J. P. Collier (ed), *Trevelyan Papers*, Camden Society
    (1863), pp11-12
49 Paget had a wealthy man's dislike for this 'soak the rich' policy.
    The tax, however, did yield less than the subsidy used by Henry
    VIII (F. Dietz, *Finances of Edward VI & Mary*, Smith College
    Studies, 1918, 3, ii, pp84-5. Cited hereafter as *Dietz*)
50 Ntht, Paget Ltr-book, 8
51 *Corr Politique*, 304; J. Haywarde, *Life & Raigne of Edward VI*
    (1636), pp198-9; Haynes, *State Papers*, pp68, 84-7, 107; *Commons'
    Journals*, I, p9; BM, Lansdowne MS, 109, f102; PRO, SP10/6/f14
52 *Spanish Calendar*, 9, pp120-4, 249-54; *Tytler*, I, p75; BM, Cotton
    MS, Titus, F, iii, f273
53 *Spanish Calendar*, 9, pp298-302
54 BM, Lansdowne MS, 2, f85; Harleian MS, 6989, ff141-7
55 *Spanish Calendar*, 9, pp428-32, 444-7
56 Ntht, Paget Ltr-book, 10
57 BM, Cotton MS, Titus, F, iii, f273b (PRO, SP10/7/f5); PRO,
    SP68/3/f146
58 Ntht, Paget Ltr-book, 5
59 Ntht, Paget Ltr-book, 7
60 Anglesey MS, Box 2, 2

61 *Spanish Calendar*, 9, pp444-7; Ntht, Paget Ltr-book, 11, 12
62 *Historical Manuscripts Commission*, 12th Report, Appendix IV, p36; *Spanish Calendar*, 9, pp396-8; PRO, SP10/7/ff37, 40, 44
63 *Spanish Calendar*, 9, pp389-90, 393-5. The princess outbluffed the emissaries by threatening not to write a letter of recommendation for Paget to her cousin, Charles V
64 *Spanish Calendar*, 9, pp373-6; PRO, SP68/3/ff110-16. (BM, Harleian MS, 297, f63; Cotton MS, Galba, B, xii, ff90-91; Additional MS, 5935, f82)
65 PRO, SP68/3/ff130, 135-43, 155-6, 158; *Spanish Calendar*, 9, pp410-18
66 BM, Harleian MS, 284, f38
67 Paget was already aware of the line the duke's enemies took three months later in depriving him of the protectorship
68 PRO, SP10/8/f4 (another copy is in BM, Cotton MS, Titus, F, iii, f274. Strype also prints it with serious omissions in *Ecclesiastical Memorials*, 2, ii, pp429-37)
60 PRO, SP68/4/ff53, 57, 71, 83; BM, Harleian MS, 523, ff70-1
70 *Spanish Calendar*, 9, pp418-20, 423-4; BM, Harleian MS, 523, f119
71 Anglesey MS, Box 2, 3; J. E. Nightingale, 'William Herbert, First Earl of Pembroke', *Wiltshire Magazine*, 18, pp95-6
72 Inner Temple, Petyt MS, 538, xlvi, ff451, 456-7. BM, Harleian MS, 1077, f7, confirms this Robert was indeed the brother of William Lord Paget
73 Inner Temple, Petyt MS, 538, xlvi, f452b; Ntht, Paget Ltr-book, 16; BM, Additional MS, 27457, f28
74 *Spanish Calendar*, 9, pp444-7; Inner Temple, Petyt MS, 538, xlvi, f460

CHAPTER EIGHT PEERAGE AND PRISON (pp166-88)

1 *Spanish Calendar*, 9, pp19, 120-4, 337-42; BM, Lansdowne MS, 238, ff319-25
2 *Spanish Calendar*, 9, pp423-4, 444-8, 452-5, 459-60. Undoubtedly, however, Vanderdelft was ignorant of any Paget understanding with Warwick, as he still thought him in bad odour with them on 14 October
3 Paget had hinted at this suspicion in his letter to Somerset of 7 July 1549, though disclaiming it himself. (BM, Cotton MS, Titus, F, iii, f274)
4 Hume (ed), *Spanish Chronicle*, p185; BM, Harleian MS, 284, ff44, 46. In Cotton MS, Nero, C, x, Edward VI gives in his journal his own account of the events of October 1549. Lord St John left Hampton Court on the fifth, for he signed a letter from there with Somerset on the fourth
5 Inner Temple, Petyt MS, 538, xlvi, f466

6 J. Hayward, *Life and Reigne of Edward VI* (1636), pp206-7; *Spanish Calendar*, 9, pp456-9; Inner Temple, Petyt MS, 538, xlvi, f467; PRO, SP10/9/1-9

7 R. Holinshed, *Chronicles* . . ., 3 (1808), p1014; BM, Harleian MS, 2308, f74

8 Ntht, Paget Ltr-book, 28

9 Ntht, Paget Ltr-book, 29

10 *Spanish Calendar*, 9, p456; Kingsford (ed), *Two London Chronicles*, Camden *Miscellany*, 12 (1912), pp19-21

11 Hayward, *Edward VI*, p220; *Grafton's Chronicle*, 2 (1809), p523; Inner Temple, Petyt MS, 538, xlvi, f469; BM, Cotton MS, Caligula, B, vii, f404

12 BM, Cotton MS, Caligula, B, vii, f392; Harleian MS, 353, f76; PRO, SP10/9/25, 26-7, 39. A copy of the 'Cranmer' letter is in Ntht, Paget Ltr-book, 22, misdated as 9 October

13 PRO, SP10/9/27, 29; Inner Temple, Petyt MS, 538, xlvi, f407b

14 *Spanish Calendar*, 9, pp456-9; Hayward, p308; PRO, SP10/9/27, 29, 31

15 Pollard, *Somerset*, p251, dates this episode as the ninth, but Cranmer and Paget clearly say in their letter of the tenth that it occurred that morning. BM, Cotton MS, Caligula, B, vii, f412

16 BM, Harleian MS, 353, f77

17 BM, Cotton MS, Caligula, B, vii, ff410, 412

18 Ntht, Paget Ltr-book, 27; SP10/9/40-3

19 Kingsford (ed), *Two London Chronicles*, p20; Hayward, p232; *Spanish Calendar*, 9, pp459-60, 461-2

20 J. E. Nightingale, 'William Herbert, First Earl of Pembroke', *Wiltshire Magazine*, 18, pp95-6; BM, Cotton MS, Titus, B, ii, ff104-7. Strype, *Ecclesiastical Memorials*, 2, ii, pp473-6, misdates these commissions carelessly as 1547

21 *APC*, 2, p344; PRO, SP10/9/50

22 *Spanish Calendar*, 9, pp488-90; Anglesey MS, Box 49, 2247

23 *Spanish Calendar*, 9, pp467-70, 476-8; Robinson (ed), *Original Letters*, Parker Society (1846-7), 2, pp660-1. Considerable confusion exists as to the date of his creation as Baron Paget, since no record of it exists. Such experts as Sir Edward Coke and J. H. Round have disagreed as to the necessity of a patent of creation before a writ of summons could be issued, but modern writers have held in the affirmative. Stow, Strype, and the author of *Wriothesley's Chronicle* all state that Paget was created a baron on 19 January 1550, at the same time that Russell and St John received their earldoms. The patent of St John, however, merely reveals Paget's presence among the barons witnessing the ceremony, and it would have been highly irregular for him to have been created a baron immediately *before* the ceremony of elevating a baron to an earldom. The most conclusive evidence to the date of the cere-

mony, if one were held, is King Edward's comment in his journal, unfortunately undated: 'Mr Paget, surrendering his controllership, was made L. Paget of Beaudesert, and cited into the higher house by a writ of Parliament.' Cokayne and Gibbs, *Complete Peerage*, 9, Appendix B, p824; Strype, *Ecclesiastical Memorials*, 2, ii, p159; *Lord's Journals*, I, p365; *Wriothesley's Chronicle*, 2, pp31-2; *Calendar of Patent Rolls*, Edward VI, 3, pp4, 162; J. Stow, *Annals* ... (1605), p603; Nichols (ed), *Literary Remains of Edward VI*, 2, p248

24 *Spanish Calendar*, 9, pp488-90; 10, pp5-11, 17-21; Hayward, *Edward VI*, p248; *Wriothesley's Chronicle*, 2, p33; BM, Cotton MSS, Galba, B, xii, f117b; Caligula, E, iv, ff206-7; Royal MS, 18, C, xxiv

25 Kingsford (ed), *Two London Chronicles*, p21; *Wriothesley's Chronicle*, 2, pp31-2; *APC*, 2, p427; BM, Harleian MS, 353, ff78-83; Cotton MS, Caligula, E, iv, f206

26 *Spanish Calendar*, 9, pp467-70, 488-90; 10, pp1-4; BM, Harleian MS, 284, f66; Egerton MS, 2, ff37-48; Cotton MS, Galba, B, xii, ff117-18

27 *Lords' Journals*, I, p365ff; *Wriothesley's Chronicle*, 2, pp31-2; Stow, *Annals*, p603. Several copies of the instructions exist: PRO, SP68/5/ff7-13; BM, Cotton MSS, Caligula, E, iv, ff201-3, 284-6; Additional MS, 4149, ff26-8

28 BM, Cotton MS, Caligula, E, iv, f204b. This volume contains a portion of the letter-book of Paget while at the peace conference, but it is somewhat damaged by fire, and is in places difficult to read

29 BM, Cotton MSS, Caligula, E, iv, ff203-10b

30 BM, Cotton MSS, Caligula, E, iv, ff214-16b; Egerton MS, 3, ff16-19b; Harleian MS, 6069, f18

31 BM, Cotton MSS, Caligula, E, iv, ff232-7, 276-9; Egerton MS, 3, ff16-19b

32 Hayward, *Edward VI*, p271; BM, Cotton MS, Caligula, E, iv, ff282-4; Egerton MS, 3, ff8-10b; PRO, Transcripts 3/20/ff367-9

33 Anglesey MS, Box 2, 4

34 BM, Cotton MS, Caligula, E, iv, f204b; Harleian MS, 204, f75; *Spanish Calendar*, 10, pp54-5

35 *Spanish Calendar*, 10, pp60-4; BM, Egerton MS, 2603, ff33-4; Cotton MS, Nero, C, x, entry of 3 June 1552

36 *APC*, 3, pp28, 30, 64, 71-2, 79; *Spanish Calendar*, 10, pp108-10; PRO, SP10/10/9

37 *Spanish Calendar*, 10, pp60-4, 80-6; *APC*, 3, pp79, 81, 186, PRO, SP68/6/ff65-7

38 Pollard, *Somerset*, pp271-4; *APC*, 3, pp4, 34-8, 81, 225, 293, 340; *Spanish Calendar*, 10, pp108-10; BM, Cotton MS, Nero, C, x, entry of 20 December 1550

39 *APC*, 3, pp28, 236; *Spanish Calendar*, 10, pp65-72, 77-8, 140-4; BM, Royal MS, 18, C, xxiv, entry of 4 May 1551; Harleian MS,

5008, f7

40 *APC*, 3, pp31-134

41 *Calendar of Patent Rolls*, Edward VI, I, p295; 3, pp298-9; 6, p33; *Staffordshire Historical Collections* (1939), pp83, 111, 124; D. Lysons, ... *Parishes in the County of Middlesex* (1800), p38; PRO, SP10/10/36; 10/19/9; Anglesey MSS, Box 2, 1; Box 16, 866; Box 50, 2272

42 *Spanish Calendar*, 10, pp167-70

43 Cattley (ed), *Acts and Monuments of John Foxe*, 6, pp131-3, 162-4, 170-4, 259; S. R. Maitland, *The Reformation in England* (1906), pp253-65; Muller, *Gardiner*, pp198-200

44 PRO, Transcripts 3/20/f381b; SP10/13/f7

45 *APC*, 3, pp4, 8, 23, 24, 52; *Spanish Calendar*, 10, pp140-4

46 *APC*, 2, p433; 3, pp35, 117, 248-51, 328; *Calendar of Patent Rolls*, Edward VI, 5, pp407-8

47 *Spanish Calendar*, 10, pp167-70, 185-7; *APC*, 3, p142

48 *Spanish Calendar*, 10, pp225-30, 261-6, 278-83, 285-6; *APC*, 3, p217; *Tytler*, 2, p17; PRO, SP68/6/ff213-14; BM, Cotton MSS, Titus, B, ii, f48; Nero, C, x, entry of 16 February 1551; R. R. Reid, 'The North Parts under the Tudors', *Tudor Studies*, ed by R. W. Seton-Watson (1924), pp208-30

49 *Spanish Calendar*, 10, pp290-3

50 *APC*, 3, pp328, 347; Anglesey MSS, Box 2, 9-11

51 Nichols (ed), *Literary Remains of Edward VI*, 2, p337; *Spanish Calendar*, 10, pp388-90, 392-4, 405-8, 493; BM, Cotton MS, Nero, C, x, entries of 19 and 26 October 1551; PRO, SP10/13/67

52 *APC*, 3, p379; BM, Cotton MS, Nero, C, x, entry of 11 October 1551; Royal MS, 18, C, xxiv, entries of 9, 10, 12, and 31 October 1551

53 *Spanish Calendar*, 10, pp388-90; Hume (ed), *Spanish Chronicle*, pp219-20. PRO, SP68/9/f22. This letter of 16 October stated officially he had been confined for the past fourteen days

54 *Spanish Calendar*, 10, pp380-81; BM, Cotton MS, Nero, C, x, entries of 7 and 19 October. Palmer added the detail about the muster day plan on the 19th to embellish his original story, forgetting that it had only been decreed by the council on 7 October. (See Royal MS, 18, C, xxiv, entry of that date)

55 BM, Cotton MS, Nero, C, x, entries for 14 and 17 October; PRO, SP46/6/ff124-5; *Spanish Calendar*, 10, pp388-90; J. G. Nichols (ed), *Diary of Henry Machyn*, Camden Society (1848), pp10-12; H. Ellis (ed), *Original Letters* (1827), second series, 2, p214

56 *Spanish Calendar*, 10, pp392-4, 405-8; PRO, SP10/13/67; BM, Cotton MS, Nero, C, x, entry of 1 December 1551

57 BM, Harleian MS, 284, ff96-9, the accounts of the lieutenant of the tower contain no record of expenses of this sort for either Paget or Arundel

58 *APC*, 3, pp414-15, 419, 426; BM, Royal MS, 18, C, xxiv, entries for 18 November 1551 and 11 March 1552; PRO, SP10/5/24; 10/13/79; 10/14/7-9, 26

59 BM, Harleian MS, 249, f40; *Spanish Calendar*, 10, pp468-9; *APC*, 3, 490, 503; 4, pp27-8. Her permit was not so inclusive as Lady Thynne's who was allowed to 'visit her husband and to lie with him when she will'

60 *Wriothesley's Chronicle*, 2, p69 and BM, Stowe MS, 595, f41 erroneously name Northumberland's heir as Paget's successor, but Harleian MS, 5177, f128 and King Edward's *Journal* (Cotton MS, Nero, C, x) shows Sir Andrew as the Dudley involved. BM, Harleian MS, 6074, ff9-10

61 PRO, SP10/14/33-4; *APC*, 4, pp65, 72; BM, Cotton MS, Nero, C, x, entry of 6 June 1552; Anglesey MS, 1838

62 PRO, DL28/7/12; 8/5; BM, Additional MS, 30198, f49; Dietz, p124

63 *APC*, 4, pp65, 93, 131; BM, Lansdowne MS, 2, 78; Cotton MS, Nero, C, x, entries of 16 and 30 June 1551; *Spanish Calendar*, 10, pp536-7; E. Lodge (ed), *Illustrations of British History* (1838), I, pp170-5; PRO, SP10/14/53

64 *APC*, 4, pp162, 176, 187; PRO, SP10/15/58, 59; Anglesey MSS, Box i, 1835-6; Box 2, 14-15; BM, Royal MS, 18, C, xxiv, entry of 6 December 1552

65 *Calendar of Patent Rolls*, Edward VI, 4, pp438, 439; *Spanish Calendar*, 10, pp593-4; *APC*, 4, p203; PRO, SP10/15/72; 18/16; Anglesey MS, Box 31. Paget's enormous debts of £1,094 to his four wards, £380 to Robert Cox's wife, £204 to Thomas Chamberlain of the Merchants Adventurers, and £900 to 'Ralf' indicate where some of the money came from. (Anglesey MS, Box 1, 1835)

66 *Spanish Calendar*, 11, pp12-14, 35-6, 37-8; PRO, C1/1312/5; *Lord's Journals*, I, 1-30 March 1553; BM, Lansdowne MS, 3, f46

67 *Spanish Calendar*, 11, pp40-1, 45-7, 51, 53; BM, Royal MS, 18, C, xxiv, 17 April - 3 July 1553; PRO, SP10/19/*passim*

68 *Spanish Calendar*, 11, pp54-5; *Montagu of Beaulieu MSS*, Historical Manuscripts Commission (1900), pp4-6; Inner Temple, Petyt MS, 538, xlvii, f316; BM, Harleian MS, 35, f364; R. A. de Vertot (ed), *Ambassades en Angleterre*, Leyden (1763), 2, pp39-42 (this published collection of the Noailles dispatches will be cited hereafter as Noailles); PRO, Transcripts 3/20, Noailles letter of 28 June 1553

69 J. G. Nichols (ed), *Chronicle of Queen Jane and Queen Mary...*, Camden Society (1850), p2n; A. de Guaras, *The Accession of Queen Mary*, R. Garnett (ed) (1892), pp89-90

70 *APC*, 4, p293; Nichols (ed), *Chronicle of Queen Jane*, pp8-12; PRO, Transcripts 3/20, Noailles letter of 18 July 1553

71 *Spanish Calendar*, 11, p108; BM, Lansdowne MS, 104, ff1-2; 3, f50; PRO, Transcripts 3/20, Noailles letter of 18 July 1553

72 BM, Royal MS, 17, A, ix, ff1-37; Cotton MS, Titus, B, ii, ff370-4; *Spanish Calendar*, 11, pp94-7; *Wriothesley's Chronicle*, 2, pp88-9; Stow, *Annals*, p611; J. G. Nichols (ed), *Greyfriar's Chronicle*, Camden Society, liii (1852), p80

73 *Spanish Calendar*, 11, p108; *Wriothesley's Chronicle*, 2, pp88-9; *Greyfriar's Chronicle*, p80; BM, Harleian MS, 353, ff139-44

74 BM, Lansdowne MS, 3, f52; Kingsford (ed), *Two London Chronicles*, p27; *Wriothesley's Chronicle*, 2, p89; PRO, Transcripts 3/20, Noailles letter of 20 July 1553

CHAPTER NINE   POLITIQUE VERSUS CATHOLIC (pp189-213)

1 *APC*, 4, Appendix I, p418; *Spanish Calendar*, 11, pp119-21; PRO, Transcripts 3/20, Noailles to the Constable, 3 August 1553

2 Anglesey MS, Box 50, 2272(10); Father Person (*Memoirs*, Catholic Record Society, *Miscellanea*, 2, pp52-4) in 1599 flatly ascribed such a plan to Paget and Arundel. This hindsight view is not improbable given Paget's strong feelings on the subject of the nobility's right to govern

3 Nichols (ed), *Chronicle of Queen Jane and Queen Mary*, p15; *APC*, 4, Appendix I, pp419, 425; *Spanish Calendar*, 11, pp123-5; BM, Harleian MS, 353, ff139-44

4 *Noailles*, 3, pp305-7; *APC*, 4, Appendix I, p419; J. G. Nichols (ed), *Narratives of the Days of the Reformation*, Camden Society (1859), p139; BM, Harleian MSS, 353, ff139-44; 523, ff45b-46

5 *Spanish Calendar*, 11, pp119-21, 172, 192; PRO, Transcripts 3/20, Noailles et al to the king, 23 August 1553; SP11/1/9

6 PRO, *Spanish Calendar* proofs, 12, pp30-5, 219-20; 13, pp87-92; E. Charrière, *Negociations de la France dans le Levant*, Paris (1850), 2, p299

7 *Spanish Calendar*, 11, pp393-7

8 *Spanish Calendar*, 11, pp153-4, 164-5, 189, 227-9; *APC*, 4, p329

9 *Spanish Calendar*, 11, pp212-14, 238-42, 265-72

10 *Spanish Calendar*, 11, pp265-72, 282-5

11 PRO, Transcripts 3/20, Noailles to Henri II, 7 and 22 September and 7 October 1553, and a report of his negotiations since 6 September; *Venetian Calendar*, 5, 560

12 *Spanish Calendar*, 11, pp288-300, 319-24, 327-30

13 *Spanish Calendar*, 11, pp332-6, 454-7

14 *Spanish Calendar*, 11, pp332-45, 347-51, 363-6, 372

15 *Spanish Calendar*, 11, pp332-6, 381-3, 387-92, 414-19; PRO, Transcripts 3/21, Noailles to Henri II, 14 December 1553

16 *Spanish Calendar*, 11, pp393-7, 439-46, 466-75

17 *Spanish Calendar*, 11, pp399-401, 408-13; PRO, Transcripts 3/21, Noailles to Henri II, 9 November and 6 December 1553; Henri II to Noailles, 14 December 1553; Memoir of La Marque's Instruc-

tions *circa* 9 November 1553

18 PRO, SP11/1/20; 69/3/125; Kingsford (ed), *Two London Chronicles*, p31; PRO, *Spanish Calendar* proofs, 12, pp2-4

19 Strype, *Ecclesiastical Memorials*, 3, i, pp52-4; Anglesey MS, Box 50, 2272; Nichols (ed), *Chronicle of Queen Jane*, pp27-30; PRO, SP11/1/15; Edgar Powell (ed), 'Travels of Sir Thomas Hoby', *Camden Miscellany*, 10 (1902), p96; F. Madden, *Privy Purse Expenses of Princess Mary* (1831), p177; *Spanish Calendar*, 11, pp447-8

20 *Spanish Calendar*, 11, pp431-2, 443-6, 446-7; Noailles, 3, pp19-21

21 *Spanish Calendar*, 11, pp439-42, 466-75; PRO, Transcripts 3/21, Noailles to Henri II, 18, 23 December 1553; Noailles to D'Oysel, 22 January 1554; Noailles, 3, pp31-2; PRO, *Spanish Calendar* proofs, 12, pp15-17, 30-5, 63-6. Paget's agent Francesco Bernardi was getting information from the Venetian ambassador at about this time and may have unmasked Carew

22 Nichols (ed), *Chronicle of Queen Jane*, p36; Anglesey MS, Box 50, 2272(12); Noailles, 3, pp43-6; PRO, Transcripts 3/21, Noailles to the Constable, 21 January 1554; SP11/2/20; *Spanish Calendar* proofs, 12, pp53-7, 63-6, 77-82

23 Anglesey MS, Box 50, 2272(12, 13); Noailles, 3, pp43-6; PRO, *Spanish Calendar* proofs, 12, pp53-7, 63-6, 68-9, 77-82; SP69/3/155 (1); Transcripts 3/21, Noailles to Henri II, 1 and 3 February 1554

24 BM, Additional MSS, 15215, f5; 33923, ff184-7; Kingsford (ed), *Two London Chronicles*, pp32-4; Bodleian, Rawlinson MS, B, 102, ff83-5, quoted in *English Historical Review*, 38 (1923), p255

25 PRO, SP11/3/36; *Spanish Calendar* proofs, 12, pp94-7, 111-19

26 Kingsford (ed), *Two London Chronicles*, p34; PRO, *Spanish Calendar* proofs, 12, pp94-7, 124-7, 137-45, 164-70, 197-206; SP11/3/34; Transcripts 3/21, Noailles to Henri II, 30 March 1554; Foxe, *Acts and Monuments*, 8, p618 erroneously blames Elizabeth's imprisonment on Paget

27 PRO, *Spanish Calendar* proofs, 12, pp106-9, 155-8, 164-70, 175-7

28 PRO, *Spanish Calendar* proofs, 12, pp164-70, 175-7, 197-206

29 *Lords' Journals*, I, 1 April to 5 May 1554; PRO, *Spanish Calendar* proofs, 12, pp197-206, 215-17, 219-20, 229-30; Noailles, 3, pp151-4, 166-70

30 PRO, *Spanish Calendar* proofs, 12, pp220-5, 227-9; *APC*, 5, pp9-16; *Lords' Journals*, I, pp450-63

31 PRO, *Spanish Calendar* proofs, 12, pp230-4, 238-43

32 Quoted in F. J. C. Hearnshaw, 'Bodin's Doctrine of Sovereignty', *Tudor Studies* (1924), p119

33 PRO, SP10/8/4

34 PRO, *Spanish Calendar* proofs, 12, pp197-206

35 PRO, *Spanish Calendar* proofs, 12, pp164-70, 197-206, 258-63; 13, pp87-92; R. Persons, *Memoirs*, Catholic Record Society, *Miscellanea* (1906), 2, pp52-8; *Venetian Calendar*, 5, p559; Ponet, *Treatise of Politique Power*, in Hudson, *John Ponet*, pp134-42; Foxe, *Acts*

and Monuments, 8, p618

36 Sir John Harington, *Nugae Antiquae* (1804), I, pp47-9, 53-6; PRO, *Spanish Calendar* proofs, 13, p22; SP69/4/236, 240, 247, 284; Transcripts of E. Harris Harbison from the Archives du ministère des affaires étrangères, Paris, 9, ff160-1, 165 (hereafter cited as Harbison, Aff Etr)

37 PRO, *Spanish Calendar* proofs, 12, pp238-43, 250-4; Noailles, 3, pp195-203, 211, 212-16, 218-22

38 Noailles, 3, pp218-22, 245-7; *APC*, 5, pp25-9; PRO, *Spanish Calendar* proofs, 12, pp258-63, 266-8, 275-6, 278-80

39 PRO, *Spanish Calendar* proofs, 12, pp280-3, 289-91, 319-22; 13, pp1-6; Noailles, 3, p284; BM, Additional MS, 6297, pp28-32; Anglesey MSS, Box 50, 2272(15, 16)

40 *Spanish Calendar*, 11, pp393-7; PRO, *Spanish Calendar* proofs, 12, pp29-30, 38-42, 111-17, 137-45, 158, 315-16; 13, pp373-4; Transcripts 3/21, Noailles to Henri II, 9 March 1554; E. H. Harbison, *Rival Ambassadors at the Court of Queen Mary*, Princeton (1940), Appendix II, pp340-42, is most illuminating on the subject of imperial pensions

41 PRO, *Spanish Calendar* proofs, 12, pp295-6; 13, pp22, 26-8, 45-7, 49-51; Noailles, 3, p284

42 *APC*, 5, pp7-8; PRO, *Spanish Calendar* proofs, 13, pp64-70, 74-5

43 Historical Manuscripts Commission, *Third Report*, Appendix, p37; Noailles, 3, pp355-8; PRO, SP69/5/285-7, 290; *Spanish Calendar* proofs, 13, pp77-8; *Venetian Calendar*, 5, pp590-2

44 PRO, SP69/5/293

45 PRO, *Spanish Calendar* proofs, 13, pp87-92

46 PRO, SP69/5/293; *Spanish Calendar* proofs, 13, pp104, 107-9; Nichols (ed), *Machyn's Diary*, p75; BM, Harleian MS, 4992, f7, quoted in H. N. Birt, *The Elizabethan Religious Settlement* (1907), pp510-11

CHAPTER TEN LORD PRIVY SEAL (pp214-43)

1 PRO, *Spanish Calendar* proofs, 13, pp124-6, 128-33; *Noailles*, 4, pp98-113; Anglesey MS, Box 1, 'Certain Acts and Articles of Acts and Statutes to be Repealed'; *Lords' Journals*, I, 12 November 1554 to 16 January 1555

2 PRO, *Spanish Calendar* proofs, 13, pp128-31, 139-40

3 *APC*, 5, pp101-48; *Noailles*, 4, pp133-7, 146-50, 192-7, 203-8; PRO, *Spanish Calendar* proofs, 13, pp101-3, 147-9

4 *Spanish Calendar*, 11, pp214-21; Nichols (ed), *Narratives of the Days of the Reformation*, p139; *APC*, 5, pp61-3; PRO, *Spanish Calendar* proofs, 12, pp197-206; 13, pp64-70, 87-92

5 Strype, *Ecclesiastical Memorials*, 3, i, p330; Foxe, *Acts and Monuments*, 6, pp593-4; *Noailles*, 4, pp172-4; PRO, *Spanish Calendar*

proofs, 13, pp137-8; BM, Cotton MS, Titus, C, vii, Queen Mary to the Privy Council

6 In the spring of 1555 he threw his own support and that of his nobles' party behind the Deputy of Calais, his friend Wentworth, whose efforts to stamp out heresy in the fortress town were something less than zealous. When Paget and Gardiner were in Calais on diplomatic business the bishop had sought to proceed against one of Wentworth's gentlemen, only to become involved in such a heated dispute with the deputy that he narrowly escaped violence at the indignant commander's hands. Gardiner on his return to the safety of the Privy Council retaliated by sponsoring a conciliar reprimand of Wentworth, which both Paget and Arundel refused to sign. Father Persons, *Memoirs*, p56; Harbison, Aff Etr, 10, ff512-13; *Venetian Calendar*, 6(1), 127; *Spanish Calendar* proofs, 13, pp227-8

7 *Venetian Calendar*, 6(1), 460; *Noailles*, 5, pp369-71; Harbison, Aff Etr, 11, ff320-2

8 *Spanish Calendar*, 11, pp451-3; PRO, Transcripts 3/21, Noailles to Henri II, 1, 23, 26 December 1553; *Spanish Calendar* proofs, 12, pp30-5

9 *Noailles*, 3, pp72-6, 319-20, 355-8; 4, pp23-8, 54-63, 72-5; PRO, *Spanish Calendar* proofs, 13, pp83-5

10 *Noailles*, 4, pp120-4, 133-41, 179-82, 230-5, 285-7; Harbison, Aff Etr, 10, ff521-2; 11, ff24-5; PRO, *Spanish Calendar* proofs, 13, pp162-3

11 *Noailles*, 4, pp294-8; Harbison, Aff Etr, 11, ff39-42; *Historical Manuscripts Commission, Seventh Report*, Appendix, p612; *Venetian Calendar*, 6(1), 75, 80-1, 92. The principal sources of the following account are the journals of Paget's secretary (BM, Cotton MS, Caligula, E, v, ff21-9), the imperialists' dispatches (PRO, *Spanish Calendar* proofs, 13, pp173-222), *Noailles*, 4, pp303-60, and Marillac's account of the Mediation at Marcque (PRO, Transcripts 3/22). Among the secondary sources, Harbison, *Rival Ambassadors* is outstanding on the Hapsburg–Valois manoeuvring that accompanied the mediation

12 PRO, *Spanish Calendar* proofs, 13, pp173-80; *Noailles*, 4, pp318-23; BM, Cotton MS, Caligula, E, iv, ff21-3

13 PRO, *Spanish Calendar* proofs, 13, pp188-93, 198-212, 215-22; BM, Cotton MS, Caligula, E, v, ff24-7

14 PRO, *Spanish Calendar* proofs, 13, pp215-22; *Noailles*, 4, pp329-33

15 *Venetian Calendar*, 6(1), 121, 127

16 BM, Cotton MS, Caligula, E, v, f29

17 PRO, *Spanish Calendar* proofs, 13, pp224-5, 227-30; *Venetian Calendar*, 6(1), 161; *Noailles*, 5, pp25-34, 54-8, 78-83, 101-7

18 *APC*, 5, p52; *Venetian Calendar*, 6(1), 193; PRO, *Spanish Calendar* proofs, 13, 45-7; Harbison, Aff Etr, 11, ff39-42

19 PRO, *Spanish Calendar* proofs, 13, pp150-3, 239-40; *APC*, 5, pp146-80

20 BM, Cotton MS, Titus, B, ii, f176; PRO, *Spanish Calendar* proofs, 13, pp247-8

21 PRO, *Spanish Calendar* proofs, 13, p244; SP11/6/5, 62; *Venetian Calendar*, 6(1), 209; *Noailles*, 5, pp115-22, 166-73, 194-5, 204-5; *APC*, 5, pp180-4; Anglesey MS, Box 1, 25

22 *Noailles*, 5, pp194-5, 204-7

23 *APC*, 5, pp190-97; *Venetian Calendar*, 6(1), 287, 297; Peck, *Desiderata Curiosa*, I, p9; *Noailles*, 5, pp186-91, 206-7, 223-7, 234-8, 242, 252-7; Harbison, Aff Etr, 10, ff218-20; 11, ff226-7

24 *Lords' Journals*, I, 21 October to 9 December 1555; *APC*, 5, pp200-15; *Venetian Calendar*, 6(1), 288-9, 297, 332; Harbison, Aff Etr, 10, ff218-20

25 *Noailles*, 5, pp273-6; Nichols (ed), *Wriothesley's Chronicle*, 2, p132; Strype, *Ecclesiastical Memorials*, 3, i, p469; *Calendar of Patent Rolls*, Philip and Mary, 3, p194; BM, Cotton MS, Vespasian, F, xiii (2), f287; Stowe MS, 571, f17b; Lansdowne MS, 2, f38; Additional MS, 15903, f1; PRO, SP11/7/4; 46/8/f14; 15/4/29; 11/11/45-8; Elton, *Thomas Cromwell*, unpublished thesis, London University Library, pp138-40, 316-32

26 *Noailles*, 5, pp284-7; PRO, SP68/8/492; *APC*, 5, pp232-74

27 *Noailles*, 5, pp49-54, 134-7

28 *Noailles*, 5, pp234-8, 257, 261-4, 298-303; Harbison, Aff Etr, 11, f353. Harbison, *Rival Ambassadors*, pp279-96, gives an excellent account of the conspiracy

29 *Noailles*, 5, pp304-7, 318-21; PRO, SP11/7/10; 8/34; 9/1, 22; Harbison, Aff Etr, 9, f583

30 *Venetian Calendar*, 6(1), 434, 448, 450; Anglesey MS, Box 50, 2272 (20, 21); *Noailles*, 5, pp325-30, 362; PRO, *Spanish Calendar* proofs, 13, pp259-60

31 *Venetian Calendar*, 6(1), 448, 460; BM, Stowe MS, 147, f178

32 *Venetian Calendar*, 6(1), 460, 464, 481; *Noailles*, 5, pp351-2, 361-3; BM, Stowe MS, 147, f178; PRO, Transcripts 3/22, G. de Noailles to the constable, 11 June 1556

33 Anglesey MS, Box 2, 22; *Noailles*, 5, pp364-5; PRO, SP11/9/22; *Venetian Calendar*, 6(1), 482; C. H. Garrett, *The Marian Exiles*, Cambridge (1938), p107

34 *Venetian Calendar*, 6(1), 460, 482; *Noailles*, 5, pp351-8, 361-3; PRO, SP11/7/40; Transcripts 3/22, G. de Noailles to the constable, 11 June 1556; Harbison, Aff Etr, 11, ff298, 320-2, 325-6

35 Cf Paget's statement of expenses in BM, Cotton MS, Galba, B, xi, f29

36 *Venetian Calendar*, 6(1), 464, 479, 481; PRO, SP69/8/503; Harbison, Aff Etr, 11, f298

37 Garrett, *Marian Exiles*, pp107, 114; Ponet, *Treatise of Politique*

Power, pp140-1 (MS fragment in PRO, SP46/124/ff215-16)

38 *Venetian Calendar*, 6(1), 486, 489, 505; J. Strype, *Life of...Sir John Cheke*, Oxford (1821), pp105-6; Vowell, alias John Hooker, *The Discourse and Discovery of the Life of Sir Peter Carew*, J. Maclean (ed) (1857), pp63-4

39 *Venetian Calendar*, 6(1), 486, 489, 505; Ponet, *Treatise of Politique Power*, pp140-1; Harbison, Aff Etr, 11, ff325-6

40 Although Paget with several others of his party fits the Venetian ambassador's 'one of the chief members of the Privy Council' and 'this same lord', surely Michiel would have referred to Paget by name in his cipher, since the Privy Seal was well known to the Seignory. Nor can one rely too heavily on a continental's casual reference to a 'lord' of the council actually indicating a peer

41 PRO, Transcripts 3/22, G. de Noailles Advis to the Constable, 18 June and 5 October 1556; *Spanish Calendar* proofs, 13, pp271, 276; *APC*, 5, pp299-338; *Venetian Calendar*, 6(1), 723

42 PRO, Transcripts 3/22, G. de Noailles Advis to the Constable, 18 June 1556; *Noailles*, 5, pp352-8; Harbison, Aff Etr, 11, ff320-2

43 Anglesey MSS, Box 2, 23-6

44 *Calendar of Patent Rolls*, Philip & Mary, I, pp194, 301; Anglesey MSS, Box 2, 24; Box 49, 1845; *APC*, 4, pp387, 396; 6, p359; PRO, SP69/2/98; *Spanish Calendar* proofs, 12, pp197-206; 13, pp87-92, 247-8; *Venetian Calendar*, 6(1), 481

45 *Calendar of Patent Rolls*, Philip and Mary, 3, pp54, 81-2, 554; PRO, SP69/7/442; Anglesey MS, Box 1, 'My Lord Treasurer's book touching the Queen's debt'; Box 2, 20, 21, 29

46 Anglesey MS, Box 2, 25, 28; Nichols (ed), *Machyn's Diary*, pp168-9; BM, Cotton MS, Titus, B, iv, f122; *Venetian Calendar*, 6(1), 594; PRO, Transcripts 3/22, Advis, 19 July and 16 August 1556; F. de Noailles to Henri II, 15 December 1556; SP11/11/45-8; *Spanish Calendar* proofs, 13, pp366-9, 576

47 Anglesey MS, Box 2, 25; BM, Lansdowne MS, 1453, f129; *Calendar of Patent Rolls*, Philip & Mary, 3, p317; PRO, *Spanish Calendar* proofs, 13, p385; Dietz, pp110-11

48 Anglesey MS, Box 48, 2168; *Calendar of Patent Rolls*, Philip & Mary, 2, pp189-90; 3, p86; PRO, SP12/196/ff62-82; 15/7/39; Req 2/20/137; Transcripts 3/23, Instructions for Sieur de Cassaigne, 10 April 1557

49 *Venetian Calendar*, 6(2), 723; PRO, Transcripts 3/22 & 3/23, F. de Noailles' letters to Henry II, the Constable, M. Bourdin, and his advises of 19, 24 November, 15, 25 December 1556, and 8 & 22 January 1557; Anglesey MS, Box 2, 25; copies of the council's opinion exist in BM, Cotton MS, Caligula, E, v, ff36-9, and in the Inner Temple, Petyt MS, 536, xlix, ff77-80

50 PRO, *Spanish Calendar* proofs, 13, pp285-7, 373-4; Transcripts 3/23, F. de Noailles' letters and advises of 3, 22, 27 February, 8, 20,

21 March, and 28 April 1557; Anglesey MSS, Box 2, 30-32
51 PRO, Transcripts 3/23, F. de Noailles' letters and advises of 22 February, 8, 20, 26 March, and 5 April 1557
52 PRO, *Spanish Calendar* proofs, 13, pp290-91, Transcripts 3/23, Letters and advises of F. de Noailles of 10, 28, 29 April, and 1 May 1557; Harbison, Aff Etr, 19, ff282-6
53 *APC*, 6, p132; Historical Manuscripts Commission, *Calendar of Salisbury MSS*, I, p142; PRO, *Spanish Calendar* proofs, 13, p298; SP69/10/579, 635; Transcripts 3/23, Instructions for Sieur de Cassaigne, 10 April; Advises of F. de Noailles of 6, 8, 31 May 1557
54 *APC*, 6, p177; Anglesey MSS, Box 2, 29; Box 50, 2272(50); PRO, *Spanish Calendar* proofs, 13, pp302, 307; SP11/11/30, 31; 15/8/14; 69/13/790; Harbison, Aff Etr, 13, ff230-31
55 PRO, *Spanish Calendar* proofs, 13, pp321-40, 349-50, 355-7; SP11/12/7; BM, Cotton MS, Titus, B, ii, f74
56 BM, Harleian MS, 6949, ff29-41
57 Anglesey MSS, Box 2, 29, 33; PRO, SP11/12/50; *Spanish Calendar* proofs, 13, pp361-2, 366-9, 376; Nichols (ed), *Machyn's Diary*, pp168-9
58 PRO, *Spanish Calendar* proofs, 13, pp378-80, 385-7, 394-6, 399-400, 402-3
59 PRO, SP69/13/827-8; *APC*, 6, pp409, 412, 422
60 *Venetian Calendar*, 6(3), 1285; *Lords' Journals*, I, 7-17 November 1558; Nichols (ed), *Machyn's Diary*, p178; PRO, *Spanish Calendar* proofs, 13, pp437-8

CHAPTER ELEVEN ELDER STATESMAN (pp244-52)

1 Corpus Christi College, Cambridge, MS 543, ff31b-35b, printed in *English Historical Review*, 65 (1950), pp93-8; BM, Cotton MS, Vespasian, F, xiii, f287; *Spanish Calendar*, Elizabeth, I, pp2, 4-6; *Venetian Calendar*, 7, 1
2 *Spanish Calendar*, Elizabeth I, pp7-13; *Venetian Calendar*, 7, 1
3 Haynes, *State Papers* . . ., pp208-9; *Lord's Journals*, I, 23 January to 8 May 1559; Anglesey MS, Box 50, 2272(27); *Spanish Calendar*, Elizabeth, I, pp37-40; J. E. Neale, 'The Elizabethan Acts of Supremacy and Uniformity', *English Historical Review*, 65 (1950), pp304-32
4 PRO, *Spanish Calendar* proofs, 13, pp452-4; SP12/3/11, 34; BM, Lansdowne MS, 4, f213; Anglesey MS, Box 50, 2272(28); *Spanish Calendar*, Elizabeth, I, pp48-52, 55-9, 85-6, 228-9
5 Anglesey MSS, Box 1, 'Touching Wynes'; Box 2, 39; *APC*, 6, p400; 7, p25; Haynes, *State Papers* . . ., p210; BM, Lansdowne MS, 81, f64; *Calendar of Patent Rolls*, Philip and Mary, 4, pp402-3
6 Anglesey MSS, Box 2, 36, 37; J. Bain (ed), *Calendar of Scottish Papers*, I, 602; *Spanish Calender*, Elizabeth, I, pp111-15, 122; *Cal-*

endar of State Papers Foreign, 1559-60, pp186-7, 213-14, 267-8

7 Nichols (ed), *Machyn's Diary*, p248; *Spanish Calendar*, Elizabeth, I, pp126-7, 135; PRO, SP12/12/1

8 PRO, SP70/20/ff14-15; 21/ff63-4; 2/f227

9 *Spanish Calendar*, Elizabeth, I, pp180-84, 186-95, 199-203; *Calendar of State Papers, Foreign* (1560-61), pp586-7

10 *Calendar of State Papers, Foreign* (1558-9), pp185, 315; (1562), p580; (1563), pp257, 520, 553-4; BM, Harleian MSS, 158, f142b; 2185, f30; Cotton MS, Caligula, B, v, f152; Bodleian, Ashmolean MS, 1110, f60b; Anglesey MS, Box 50, 2272(29); *Spanish Calendar*, Elizabeth, I, pp228-9; Nichols (ed), *Machyn's Diary*, p258

11 Anglesey MSS, Box 1, 'Whole Lands of the Late Lord Paget', Box 2, 36, 37; Box 40, 1708, 1951; Box 49, 2249; Historical Manuscripts Commission, *Middleton MSS*, p496; PRO, SP12/15/35; *Calendar of Patent Rolls*, Elizabeth, I, p326; BM, Lansdowne MSS, 62, ff110-15; 82, f165; 84, f173; Cotton MS, Titus, B, iv, f132-3

12 PRO, SP70/62/ff99-100; Nichols (ed), *Machyn's Diary*, p309; Shaw, *Staffordshire*, I, plate 16; Anglesey MS, Box 50, 1859

13 Somerset House, PCC, Chayre, 27

14 PRO, C142/137/47 Inquisition post-mortem; BM, Harleian MSS, 806, ff83-4; 1077, f7; 1393, f13b. If the present Marquess of Anglesey were to die without male heirs, his young daughter would revive under a new Queen Elizabeth the title of Baroness Paget

15 *Gentleman's Magazine* (1818), p119

BIBLIOGRAPHY

Only principal references cited in the text are listed

I MANUSCRIPTS

British Museum. Lansdowne, Stowe, Cotton, Harleian, Arundel, Additional, Royal, Egerton, and Sloane Collections

Plas Newydd, Anglesey. Paget Manuscripts of the Marquess of Anglesey

Public Record Office. State papers for the reigns of Henry VIII, Edward VI, Mary I, and Elizabeth I; Court of Requests (Req 2); Duchy of Lancaster Accounts (DL); Early Chancery Proceedings (C 1); Exchequer Accounts (E 101); Inquisitions post-mortem (C 142); Privy Seal Office papers (PSO 2); Transcripts from the Bibliothèque Nationale Archives du ministère des affaires étrangères, by A. Baschet (Transcripts 3/20-23)

Northampton Record Society. Fitzwilliam Manuscripts

Somerset House, London. Prerogative Court of Canterbury Wills

II PRINTED SOURCES

The Accession of Queen Mary, ed by R. Garnett (1892)

Acts of the Privy Council, ed by J. Dasent, 32 vols (1890-1907)

Ambassades en Angleterre de MM de Noailles, ed by R. A. de Vertot, 5 vols (Leyden, 1763)

Calendar of Patent Rolls, Edward VI, Mary, Elizabeth, ed by R. H. Brodie et al (1924)

Calendar of Salisbury Manuscripts, Historical Manuscripts Commission, vol I

Calendar of State Papers, Domestic, ed by R. Lemon, vol I (1856)

Calendar of State Papers, Foreign, Edward VI & Mary, ed by W. B. Turnbull, 2 vols (1861)

Calendar of State Papers, Foreign, Elizabeth, ed by J. Stephenson, vols 1-5

Calendar of State Papers, Spanish, ed by G. A. Bergenroth, M. A. S. Hume, R. Tyler, 13 vols (1862). Page proofs of vols 12 and 13 in the Public Record Office

Calendar of State Papers, Spanish, Elizabeth, ed by M. A. S. Hume, 4 vols (1892-9)

Calendar of State Papers, Venetian, ed by R. Brown et al, 9 vols (1864-98)

Chronicle of the Greyfriars of London, ed by J. G. Nichols, Camden Society (1852)

Chronicle of Queen Jane and Queen Mary, ed by J. G. Nichols, Camden Society (1850)

Collection of Ordinances and Regulations for the Royal Household, Society of Antiquaries (1795)

'Commonplace Book of Lord Paget', *Gentleman's Magazine,* vol I (1818), p119

Correspondance Politique de Odet de Selve, ed by Germaine Lefèvre-Pontalis (Paris, 1888)

Diary of Henry Machyn, ed by J. G. Nichols, Camden Society (1848)

Foxe, John. *Acts and Monuments,* ed by S. R. Cattley and G. Townsend, 8 vols (1837-41)

Grafton, R. *A Chronicle at Large...,* ed by H. Ellis (1809)

Hooker, J. (alias Vowell). *The Discourse and Discovery of the Life of Sir Peter Carew,* ed by J. Maclean (1857)

Illustrations of British History, ed by E. Lodge, 3 vols (1838)

Journals of the House of Commons, vol I (1803)

Journals of the House of Lords, vol I, *sl, sa*

Leland, John. *Collectanea*, ed by W. Hearne (Oxford, 1715)

Letters and Papers, Foreign and Domestic, of the Reign of Henry VIII, ed by J. S. Brewer, J. Gairdner, and R. H. Brodie, 21 vols (1862-1932)

Letters of Stephen Gardiner, ed by J. A. Muller (Cambridge, 1933)

Literary Remains of King Edward VI, ed by J. G. Nichols, 2 vols, Roxburghe Club (1857)

Narratives of the Days of the Reformation, ed by J. G. Nichols, Camden Society (1859)

Original Letters Illustrative of English History, ed by H. Ellis, 2nd series, 4 vols (1827)

Original Letters Relative to the English Reformation, ed by H. Robinson, 2 vols, Parker Society (1846-7)

Persons, R. *Memoirs*, in Catholic Record Society, *Miscellanea*, vol 2 (1906)

A Treatise of Three Conversions of England, 3 vols (St Omer, 1603-4)

Ponet, John. 'Treatise of Politique Power', in W. S. Hudson, *John Ponet, Advocate of Limited Monarchy* (Chicago, 1942)

Proceedings and Ordinances of the Privy Council, ed by H. Nicolas, 7 vols (1834-7)

Services of Lord Grey of Wilton, ed by P. de M. G. Egerton, Camden Society (1847)

Spanish Chronicle of King Henry VIII, ed by M. A. S. Hume (1889)

State Papers of Henry VIII, 11 vols (1830-52)

Stow, J. *The Annals of England* ... (1605)

'Travels of Sir Thomas Hoby', ed by E. Powell in Camden Society *Miscellany*, vol 10 (1902)

Trevelyan Papers, ed by J. P. Collier, 2 vols, Camden Society (1863)

Two London Chronicles, ed by C. L. Kingsford, Camden Society *Miscellany*, 12 (1912)

Tytler, P. F. *England under the Reigns of Edward VI and*

Mary, 2 vols (1839)
Wriothesley's Chronicle of England, ed by W. D. Hamilton, 2 vols, Camden Society, ns, 11

III SECONDARY WORKS

Aylmer, G. E. *The King's Servants* (New York, 1961)
Burnett, G. *History of the Reformation of the Church of England*, Pocock edition (Oxford, 1865)
A Complete Collection of State Trials, ed by W. Cobbett and T. B. Howells, vol I (1816)
Dietz, F. C. *English Government Finance, 1485-1558*, University of Illinois Studies in the Social Sciences (1920)
Finances of Edward VI and Mary, Smith College Studies, vol 3, no 2 (1918)
Elton, G. R. *Thomas Cromwell, Aspects of his Administrative Work*, unpublished thesis, University of London Library (1948)
Emmison, F. E. *Tudor Secretary* (Cambridge, Mass, 1961)
Evans, F. M. G. *The Principal Secretary of State* (Manchester, 1923)
Friedmann, P. *Anne Boleyn*, 2 vols (1884)
Garrett, C. H. *The Marian Exiles* (Cambridge, 1938)
Gladish, D. M. *The Tudor Privy Council* (Retford, 1915)
Harbison, E. H. *Rival Ambassadors at the Court of Queen Mary* (Princeton, NJ, 1940)
Haywarde, J. *Life and Raigne of King Edward VI* (1636)
Herbert of Cherbourg. *Life and Raign of King Henry VIII* (1672, 1741)
Loades, D. M. *Two Tudor Conspiracies* (Cambridge, 1965)
Lysons, D. . . . . *Parishes in the County of Middlesex* (1800)
Maitland, S. R. *The Reformation in England* (1906)
Muller, J. A. *Stephen Gardiner and the Tudor Reaction* (New York, 1926)
Neale, J. E. 'The Elizabethan Acts of Supremacy and Uniformity', *English Historical Review*, 65 (1950), pp304-32

The Elizabethan House of Commons (1949)

Nichols, J. G. 'The Second Patent Appointing Somerset Protector', *Archaeologia*, 30 (1844), pp463-89

'The Paget Coat of Arms', *Notes and Queries*, series I, 11 (June 1855), p95

Pollard, A. F. 'The Lords' Journals', *English Historical Review*, 30 (1915), pp304ff

England under Protector Somerset (1900)

Thomas Cranmer (1904, 1927)

Read, C. *Mr Secretary Walsingham and the Policy of Queen Elizabeth*, 3 vols (Oxford, 1925)

Reid, R. R. 'The North Parts under the Tudors', in *Tudor Studies*, ed by R. W. Seton-Watson (1924)

Shaw, S. *History and Antiquities of Staffordshire*, 2 vols (1748)

Slavin, A. J. *Politics and Profit: A Study of Sir Ralph Sadleir, 1507-47* (Cambridge, 1966)

Strype, John. *Ecclesiastical Memorials*, 3 vols (Oxford, 1820-40)

Life of ... Sir John Cheke (Oxford, 1821)

Sturge, C. *Cuthbert Tunstal* (1938)

Wedgwood, J. C. *Staffordshire Parliamentary History*, William Salt Society, 2 vols (1919)

Zeeveld, W. G. *Foundations of Tudor Policy* (Cambridge, Mass, 1948)

INDEX